The American Assembly, *Columbia University*

THE STATES AND
THE URBAN CRISIS

Prentice-Hall, Inc., *Englewood Cliffs, N. J.*

Printed in the United States of America.

Current printing (last number):
10   9   8   7   6   5   4   3

PRENTICE-HALL INTERNATIONAL, INC. (*London*)
PRENTICE-HALL OF AUSTRALIA, PTY. LTD. (*Sydney*)
PRENTICE-HALL OF CANADA, LTD. (*Toronto*)
PRENTICE-HALL OF INDIA PRIVATE LIMITED (*New Delhi*)
PRENTICE-HALL OF JAPAN, INC. (*Tokyo*)

Preface

"America is in the midst of an urban crisis demonstrating the inadequacy and incompetence of basic public policies, programs and institutions and presenting a crisis of confidence." So concluded the participants in the Thirty-sixth American Assembly, which met at Arden House, Harriman, New York, October, 1969, to consider the role of the states in their relationship to the metropolis. Among their recommendations for improvement in state performance were "removal of constitutional restrictions, awakening of political responsiveness, restructuring of state and local government, and changes in the federal-state-local fiscal system." Their report, printed as a pamphlet, may be obtained from The American Assembly.

This volume, edited by Alan K. Campbell of Syracuse University, was prepared as advance background reading for the Arden House Assembly and will be used at regional Assemblies on this subject across the nation. It is also intended for the student and the general reader.

The program on *The States and the Urban Crisis* was made possible by a generous grant from The Ford Foundation and Carnegie Corporation of New York, equally, on the endorsement of The Citizens Conference on State Legislatures, the National Municipal League, Urban America, Inc., the League of Women Voters and The Urban Coalition. None of these organizations is to be associated with the views contained on the pages which follow; and The American Assembly, a non-partisan, educational organization, takes no official stand on the matters it presents for public discussion.

Clifford C. Nelson
President
The American Assembly

iii

Table of Contents

Alan K. Campbell, Editor

Introduction

Condemned, berated and harassed, state government has served as both the whipping boy and the scapegoat of the American governmental system. Long dominated by rural interests, recently forced to reapportion themselves, state legislatures along with the executive branches of state government are now being asked to take more responsibility for their cities.

The metropolitanization of the country—both the rural to city migration and the internal sorting out between city and suburbs of people and industry—has forced new demands on the states.

In this volume scholars, journalists and practitioners examine how the states have responded to this new environment, why their response has not been more relevant and extensive, and the likelihood of the response improving. In order to analyze these questions this volume begins with a description of the urban problems needing attention; then examines the obstacles, real and imagined, to state governments finding and adopting solutions; and the political potential states possess for more vigorous action.

The obstacles to state action are divided into constitutional, organizational, fiscal and political categories. Frank Grad analyzes those state constitutional provisions which have "inhibited the solution of urban problems in most states." He points to limitations on the power of local governments to tax and borrow, to zoning practices and other protective measures used by suburbs to "insulate themselves" against central city problems, to home rule provisions which inhibit state action. He contends that any constitutional

1

provision that weakens the power of state government "is likely to weaken its capacity to deal with urban problems."

Daniel Grant in his analysis of local government reorganization argues that governmental fragmentation "still constitutes one of the most serious obstacles to a national attack on urban problems." He states, "To develop a sensible structure is to remove one important obstacle on the road to urban progress."

The fiscal dilemma of urban areas and states is described by Roy Bahl as another obstacle to effective attacks on urban problems. He argues that state fiscal policy and governmental fragmentation has produced substantial disparities between rich and poor areas. Bahl suggests ways in which states could aid their urban areas—assumption of functions and adoption of a more progressive state tax system—and the potential contribution of 1969 federal proposals for revenue sharing. Under the present system he contends that suburbs exploit their cities and that state government does little to offset this exploitation.

John Kolesar in describing what some states have been doing in the fields of urban planning and development does find a few states beginning to apply their resources to urban problems. Despite these efforts he concludes that unless the basic ground rules are changed "to reduce the overwhelming forces that work against both direct action and planned development" there will be little chance that states can make a basic contribution to solving urban problems.

John DeGrove brings the federal government into the picture by describing its programs and activities and concludes that present federal programs should be replaced "with a combination of incentives and restrictive measures that will allow the pursuit of broad national urban policies."

The likelihood of state action depends in the last analysis on whether states possess the political will to act. James Reichley examines this possibility and finds that reapportionment based on one man-one vote increases the political power of suburbs more than cities. Added to other political influences in state houses across the country the resulting balance does little to aid cities. Some hope for state action is found in the growing numbers of labor union members in the suburbs, and the growth of liberal sentiment in middle- and higher-income suburban areas. Despite these small omens of hope Reichley argues that "to achieve any genuine reconstruction of the cities, it will be necessary . . . to include the needs of the cities in some *total program* for the reconstruction of our entire society. In this way, the interest as well as the moral sympathy of the suburban and outstate majority could be touched."

In the final chapter, the possibility of such a program being developed and its political strength is discussed. Although this examination of current political forces in American society does not lead to any very optimistic prognosis, it is concluded that the tools of the social scientist are not sufficiently precise to determine with certainty the potential for such a program.

Therefore, ". . . since there are 50 states, certainly one, two or three of them might begin moving in these new directions. One of the advantages always claimed for the American federal system is that the states provide laboratories for experimentation. There have been brief periods in history when some states, most notably Wisconsin and New York, have played that role. Perhaps now is another time for the employment of that kind of state power."

Alan K. Campbell and Donna E. Shalala

1

Problems Unsolved, Solutions Untried: The Urban Crisis

Everybody talks about the urban crisis, deplores it, insists something be done about it, but few define or explain it. Definition is difficult—difficult because the impact of the crisis varies from person to person and group to group.

For the Negro youngster in the central city ghetto, it is overcrowded schools, inadequate facilities and insensitive, ill-trained teachers.

ALAN K. CAMPBELL *is Professor of Political Science and Dean of the Maxwell Graduate School of Citizenship and Public Affairs at Syracuse University. He was director of the school's Metropolitan Studies Program from 1961–1968. Previously he was Deputy Comptroller for Administration for New York State and, prior to that, chairman of the political science department at Hofstra College. In 1967 Dr. Campbell was delegate-at-large and chairman of the Committee on Local Government and Home Rule of the New York State Constitutional Convention. In 1968 and 1969 he served on the Secretary's Advisory Committee on Urban Development of the federal Department of Housing and Urban Development. Dean Campbell has written numerous articles for political science, scholarly and business journals and is the author of* Metropolitan America *(with Seymour Sacks).*

DONNA E. SHALALA *is Assistant Professor of Social Science and Assistant to the Dean of the Maxwell Graduate School, Syracuse University. Her areas of specialization are metropolitan politics and state and local government.*

For the welfare mother it is feeding and housing a family, with increasingly inadequate resources as costs continue to soar.

For the aged person it is old neighborhoods breaking up and deteriorating, growing property taxes and skyrocketing food costs—all to be provided from a fixed income.

For the big city mayor it is not-to-be-denied demands from municipal employees for higher pay combined with equally insistent demands from the general public for better quality services, all to be met from a deteriorating tax base and lagging state aid.

For the suburban commuter it is traffic jams and insufficient parking facilities, and a suburban environment which every day resembles more the city environment supposedly escaped.

For the unskilled in search of work, it is nonexistent jobs or jobs located many miles from place of residence, or jobs denied because of employer and union discrimination added to limited and often irrelevant training opportunities.

For many urban scholars it is a system of local government characterized by overlapping, fragmented jurisdictions with tax bases unrelated to public service needs, and with public power, particularly zoning, used for anti-social purposes.

For militant black and disillusioned youth it is demonstration of America's refusal to allocate its resources to humane and social purposes, instead of to destructive ends.

For many other Americans, the urban crisis is racial strife, crime in the streets, polluted air and water, and a generally deteriorating environment.

The urban crisis is all of these things and many more. For the average citizen the crisis is defined by how it affects him personally. It is the direct personal impact which he feels and understands.

Substance vs. Resources, Organization, and Politics

In contrast, for the public official and the student of urban affairs the crisis is a whole set of interrelated substantive problems. Further, these problems must be analyzed and attacked with available resources; with a governmental system designed for other problems of another age; and, perhaps most difficult of all, with a political constituency unready to permit the application of the resources or the organizational skills obviously necessary.

It is the substantive problems which everyone wants solved. Not everyone, however, is aware of the resources such solutions would necessitate, nor the changes in governmental organization the solutions imply, nor the sharp and sometimes bitter divisions within the political constituency over what should be done and how it should be done.

These interrelationships between substance, resources, the organizational system, and political attitudes make it difficult to fully comprehend the nature of the urban crisis. In analyzing the crisis, these various aspects are often pulled apart and unless great care is exerted, the "pulling apart" results in a misleading portrayal of what needs to be done.

Perhaps this misrepresentation most often occurs in discussions of the inadequacy of the present governmental structure. So much emphasis has been placed by scholars of urban affairs on the fragmented, overlapping character of local government that this characteristic has become, in the minds of many, the urban crisis. In fact, the Council of State Governments has argued, "The basis of the problem is the absence of general local government organizations broad enough to cope with metropolitan matters."

State Government: Fallen Arch?

Despite the dangers inherent in taking apart for analytical purposes the various aspects of the urban crisis, it is essential that this be done if the analysis is to be manageable. The purpose of this volume, to examine various aspects of state governments' response to the urban crisis, is appropriate in veiw of the central role which many argue that states ought to play in the domestic governmental system.

State governments have been described as "the keystones of the American governmental arch." [1] They sit midway between the local governments on the one hand, which are their creatures, and the federal government on the other, which constitutionally possesses only delegated powers. By virtue of their position, state governments possess the power, and theoretically the responsibility, for attacking practically all those problems which in sum equal the urban crisis.

Despite this central position of state governments, there is no part of the system which has been more criticized. It may be argued, as Martin Meyerson and Edward Banfield have in the case of Massachusetts, "It is hard to see how the Commonwealth can fail to become

[1] Daniel J. Elazar, "The States and the Nation," in Herbert Jacob and Kenneth N. Vines (eds.), *Politics in the American States* (Boston: Little, Brown and Company, 1965), p. 449.

the equivalent for all practical purposes of eight or more metropolitan governments" (*Boston: The Job Ahead*). Although this remark is specifically directed to Massachusetts, it is relevant to all states. States do have responsibilities for their local governmental systems. They have the power to assume functions which are now performed locally. They could adapt their aid systems to the facts of urbanism, and they could adjust boundaries of local governments to fit current urban reality.

The issue here is what, in fact, states have done, why they have done what they have, and why they have not done more. In order to set the stage for this overall analysis, it is necessary that the substantive problems which face urban areas be understood. It is to these problems that states must address themselves if they are to make any contribution to meeting the challenge of the urban crisis. To discuss resources, power, governmental organization, and politics, without reference to the substantive problems, is to ignore the central purpose of power, organization, and resources.

Interdependence vs. Independence

Two interrelated phenomena are most often selected as defining the fundamental forces of American urbanism, or, better said, metropolitanism. One is the "sorting out" of both population and economic activities as between city and suburb, and the other is the multiplicity and fragmentation of the local governmental system which overlies each metropolitan area.

Most of the substantive problems flow, at least in part, from these two facts of metropolitanism. The "sorting out" has left many central cities and some suburbs with segments of the population most in need of expensive public services, and the redistribution of economic activities has reduced the relative ability of these areas to support such services.

Similarly, the redistribution has spread the problems of adequate transportation, air and water pollution control, land-use control, and other physical needs over a wider and wider area while there is no local government jurisdiction coterminous with the expanding area of settlement. Thus, the economic and social life of each metropolitan area is characterized by interdependence while the individual governmental units within the area struggle for independence.

While small-unit government has long been tenaciously supported by suburbanites, a move for more local control has been gaining ground in city neighborhoods. Called "community control" by its advocates, it is most avidly sought in some of the nation's ghettos and is most frequently centered on the schools.

Whether called home rule or community control, it is usually held to be consistent with demands for an increased role for state and federal governments. Advocates of both often demand more state and federal aid, stricter state and federal standards, and more state and federal involvement.

Perhaps all this ferment points to the need for a reallocation of power and responsibility—a "creative" or a "new" federalism. Perhaps not, but it is clear, as Wallace Sayre has said, that "the formal, outmoded doctrines of limitations, separation and competition stand in the way of both explanation and understanding of the actual, developing relationships between the state government and the local governments." [2]

Structural issues, however, do not stand alone. They are raised in response to substantive problems which need solution. New structures are advocated and old structures defended in response to what people believe government "ought" to do.

What government "ought" to do is, in part at least, determined by the problems. It is these problems—education, jobs, housing, transportation, pollution, and many more—which form the context in which structure and policies must be judged.

Social Characteristics and Problems

The "sorting out" process has caused a concentration of interrelated social problems in central cities and, increasingly, in some low-income suburbs. Whether the heart of the problem is jobs, education, housing, or low income no one knows, although each characteristic is claimed by one or another social analyst as being the key determinant of the total social malaise.

EDUCATION

Whichever one may be the key, quality education for the young must be available if long-term change is to be achieved. That such education is not now available in many city school districts and in some suburban districts is clear. Study after study has confirmed it. Recent research has also suggested that increased resources alone are

---

[2] Wallace Sayre, "Constructive Steps for the Betterment of State-City Governmental Relations," *A Report to the Governor of the State of New York and the Mayor of the City of New York* (New York: New York State-New York City Fiscal Relations Committee, November 1956), p. 57.

not sufficient to guarantee quality education. For example, economist Jesse Burkhead's study[3] found that the single best indicator for predicting a child's success in school is his family income. This finding confirms the interrelationships among the problems of housing, jobs and the other aspects of poverty. Whether the cause is inadequate resources, or family income, or the social environment, the ghetto child starts out behind his middle-income counterpart and each year falls further behind. In large cities, the proportion of disadvantaged youngsters in schools is higher, and more often than not they are non-white.

The nonwhite child is represented in larger proportion in the schools than in the total population of cities. This difference in population and enrollment proportions is a result of age distribution, family composition, and the greater tendency of white parents to send their children to private and parochial schools.

Table I compares, for 1960 and 1965, the proportion of the total population of the largest cities which was non-white to the proportion of non-white public school enrollment.

Not only is the non-white child likely to be overrepresented in the total school system, he also attends a school that is predominantly non-white. In its study, "Racial Isolation in the Public Schools," the U.S. Commission on Civil Rights found in 75 of the major central cities surveyed that: (1) 75 percent of all Negro students in elementary grades attended schools that were 90 percent or more Negro; (2) almost 90 percent of all Negro students attend schools which have a majority of Negro students; (3) in the same cities, 83 percent of all white students in those grades attend schools with 90 to 100 percent white enrollments.

The Commission also found that segregation in central city schools was growing. Surveying 15 large northern cities, the Commission revealed that from 1950 to 1965, as Negro enrollments grew, 84 percent were absorbed by schools more than 90 percent Negro and 97 percent by schools already over 50 percent Negro.

Not only are central city schools becoming increasingly segregated, but, simultaneously, the resource gap between city and suburban schools is increasing. Both the stagnant tax base of cities and their increasing need for non-educational services—police, fire, welfare, sanitation—have put a severe strain on their ability to support education out of their own resources.

Potentially available for redressing the balance are state and

[3] Jesse Burkhead, *Input and Output in Large City High Schools* (Syracuse: Syracuse University Press, 1967).

TABLE I. *Nonwhite Population Contrasted with Nonwhite School Enrollment for Fifteen Largest Cities: 1960–1965*

City	Percent Nonwhite of Total Population		Percent Nonwhite of School Population	
	1960	1965*	1960	1965
New York	15%	18%	22%	28%
Chicago	24	28	40	52
Los Angeles	17	21	21	21
Philadelphia	27	31	47	55
Detroit	29	34	43	56
Baltimore	35	38	50	61
Houston	23	23	30	34
Cleveland	29	34	46	49
Washington	55	66	78	88
St. Louis	29	36	49	60
Milwaukee	9	11	16	21
San Francisco	18	20	31	43
Boston	10	13	16	26
Dallas	19	21	26	27
New Orleans	37	41	55	63

Source: U.S. Department of Health, Education and Welfare, Office of Education, National Center for Educational Statistics, Division of Statistical Analysis, Reference, Estimates and Projections Branch; and Seymour Sacks, *Educational Finance in Large Cities*, forthcoming (Education in Large Cities Series), Syracuse University Press, 1970. U.S. Bureau of the Census: *Statistical Abstract of the United States, 1968*, 89th ed. (Washington, D.C., 1968).

* Non-white figures based on 1960 ratio of Negroes to total non-white population applied to 1965 Negro population.

federal aid, but neither has moved far in that direction. Federal aid has done more than state aid. Of the 36 largest cities, only six in 1967 (latest year for which data are available) received more aid per student than their suburbs and only two more aid per capita. On the average, these 36 cities received 81 percent less aid than their suburbs—$20.72 per capita, compared to $37.66.

On a per student basis the New York situation is illustrative. For the year 1966–67 the central cities in the state's six metropolitan areas received, on the average, over $100 less per student than the school districts in the counties in which these cities are located. The following table gives the figures for each city and county or counties.

TABLE II. *Total State Aid Per Pupil in Selected Cities of New York State: 1966–67*

City	City Aid	Aid in Rest of County
Albany	$307	$493 (Albany)
Binghamton	393	571 (Broome)
Buffalo	351	425 (Erie)
Rochester	297	453 (Monroe)
Syracuse	356	531 (Onondaga)
New York City	319	453 (Nassau, Rockland, Suffolk and Westchester)

Source: New York State Constitutional Convention, Committee on Local Government and Home Rule, 1967.

The problem, however, is more than simply insufficient resources. Teacher attitudes about student potential for educational accomplishment cause ghetto pupils to be viewed and taught differently than pupils in other areas. Such expectations are perfectly obvious to children, and thereby influence their willingness to learn. In addition, teachers normally prefer not to teach in ghetto schools and, since seniority in most school systems brings with it greater rights of school selection, the teachers in ghetto schools tend to be the least experienced ones.

Out of this mix of segregation, inadequate financing and classroom environment comes a student unprepared to participate in the mainstream of American life. Whether the failure lies in the environment outside or inside the school is debatable. There are research findings to support both positions; the reality is a massive educational failure.

SCHOOLS AND COMMUNITY

While central city schools have been failing, most suburban schools have become the heart of their communities.

These suburban schools are both the products and symbols of the postwar search of millions of Americans for a better life. The white, middle-income family exodus to the suburbs has been well-documented and may well be gaining momentum.

The decline in the white population in central cities between 1960 and 1966 averaged about 150,000 per year; between 1966 and 1968, the per year decline was 500,000. Throughout the 1960s, white population gains in the suburban areas surrounding central cities averaged well over one million per year; these gains were about 1.7 million per year from 1960 to 1966 and 1.3 million per year from 1966 to 1968.

These new residents, and those who went before them, of the new outside central city housing tracts, without any other public centers, except for shopping plazas, have made the schools and their children the center of their lives. There is almost universal agreement that a good school system makes a good community. Only rarely does a suburban locality spend less than 50 percent of its local tax revenues on education, in contrast to about 30 percent in cities. This willingness to devote a large proportion of public resources to education is another reason why educational facilities as well as opportunities are superior in these areas to those in central cities. In fact, the quality of schooling available has now itself become a magnet, drawing increasing numbers of people to suburbia.

There are, of course, other factors which have contributed to the push and pull from the nation's central cities: (1) quantitatively and qualitatively inadequate central city housing during a period of rapid population increase; (2) a popular desire to live in a quasi-rural setting; (3) federal government home building subsidies; (4) the spatial decentralization of industry; and (5) racial prejudice.

During the nineteenth century, metropolitan areas were relatively compact with socially and industrially diverse cities at their core and essentially middle class, residential areas at their fringe. Their full flowering is a twentieth-century phenomenon—a post-world War II event.

Near mid-century, the men and women who had been a part of the "baby boom" of the 1920s began to form families and to have children at an exceedingly rapid rate. For the most part, housing on sites preferred by these young families simply was not available within the central city. Where available, it was too expensive.

These mostly young families began to move at an unprecedented rate from cities to inexpensive suburban housing sites, usually no smaller than one-quarter acre. Builders like Levitt, using mass production techniques, transformed cheap potato fields and cabbage patches into boom towns filled with the now famous houses selling for $7,999 and up. The mass migration to these new, as well as older, outside central city residences, however, involved more than a search for decent housing. For many, this movement also represented a search for community.

Throughout the nineteenth century, ethnicity or nationality was the basis of community in the nation's large cities. After 1860, city residential areas began to form a mosaic of rather tightly organized immigrant neighborhoods. Yet, gradually, these small communities within the cities began to disintegrate because of internal social discord and, more importantly, the availability of increased alternatives for places of residence as incomes grew.

Although the melting pot analogy gives a false impression of what occurred, an increasing proportion of second and third generation Americans did reject ethnicity as the only criterion for community. As a result, the suburban neighborhoods to which many of them moved were less characterized by ethnicity, except that they were white, than by life-style and income. Clustering, on the basis of these criteria, was made easier after the Second World War as the nation's builders constructed large tracts of housing, clearly differentiated not only by lot size and number of bedrooms, but by price, too.

HOUSING IN SUBURB AND CITY

The greatest exodus of population from central city to outside central city would have been substantially slowed had it not been for federal government subsidies to middle-income home buyers. Since the 1940s, the federal government has actively encouraged middle-income home ownership with two key subsidy programs. First, it has underwritten mortgages both through the Federal Housing Authority and Veterans Administration programs. Second, it has permitted income tax deductions for mortgage interest charges and real estate taxes. These deductions exceed by a considerable amount the combined costs each year of all federal housing programs for the poor—that is, programs whose impact is almost exclusively inside the central city. One writer has observed that the per capita housing subsidy received by the wealthiest 20 percent of the population is twice that received by the poorest 20 percent. Alvin Schorr, writing in *The Social Service Review,* explains that this country has never spent for housing of the poor a sum of money that begins to offset the disadvantage they suffer:

> In 1962, the federal government spent an estimated $820 million to subsidize housing for poor people. (The sum includes public housing, public assistance, and savings because of income tax deductions.) In the same year, the federal government spent an estimated $2.9 billion to subsidize housing for those with middle incomes or more. (The sum includes only savings from income tax deductions.) That is, the federal government spent three and one-half times as much for those who were not poor as for those who were.

Closer examination shows that the subsidy is heaviest for the largest incomes. Therefore, a second, rather more refined pair of figures may be helpful. In 1962, the federal government spent $820 million to subsidize housing for poor people—roughly 20 percent of the population. For the uppermost 20 percent (with incomes over $9,000) the federal subsidy was $1.7 billion. A family in the uppermost fifth got about twice as much, on the average, as a poor family.[4]

The enormous commitment of the federal government to suburban housing accentuated the plight of those remaining in central cities. First, the loss of many middle- and higher-income taxpayers left the city with fewer resources to support its public services. Second, recent research findings indicate that the presence of middle-income children in the schools would have improved the quality of education for all children.

The result of the first failure—to keep middle- and upper-income homeowners in the city—caused a deterioration in the cities' housing supply. It is estimated that there are some eight million sub-standard housing units in the United States. Housing inadequacy hits hardest low-income city residents and particularly low-income Negroes. The proportion of all non-white housing classified as deteriorating, dilapidated or lacking full plumbing in the nation's 14 largest cities is given in Table III.

Since overcrowding exists in many of these units the problem goes far beyond simple physical inadequacy. Health deficiencies, family disruption, physical squalor, and an increasing rodent population are all products of such housing conditions.

Low-rent public housing is potentially an important source of housing for low-income families but in metropolitan areas it has been confined to central cities almost without exception. The U.S. Commission on Civil Rights reported that of the quarter of a million public housing units that have been built by city housing authorities in the 24 largest metropolitan areas, in only one—Cincinnati—has the city housing authority been permitted to build outside the central city. In that city, the housing authority built 76 low-rent units in its suburbs. Thus, the public housing program, inadequate as it is even in the cities, has served to intensify the concentrations of the poor and the non-white in the central city.

The estimates of what can be done and what is needed vary, but the President's Commission on Civil Disorders called for the provision of 600,000 low- and moderate-income housing units over the

---

[4] Alvin Schorr, "National Community and Housing Policy," *The Social Service Review*, Vol. 39, No. 4 (December 1965), pp. 434–435.

TABLE III

City	Percentage of Nonwhite Occupied Housing Units Classified Deteriorating or Dilapidated, 1960	Percentage of Nonwhite Occupied Housing Units Classified Deteriorating, Dilapidated or Sound, but Without Full Plumbing, 1960
New York	33.8%	42.4%
Chicago	32.1	42.8
Los Angeles	14.7	18.1
Philadelphia	28.6	32.0
Detroit	27.9	30.1
Baltimore	30.5	31.7
Houston	30.1	36.7
Cleveland	29.9	33.9
Washington, D.C.	15.2	20.8
St. Louis	40.3	51.6
San Francisco	21.3	34.0
Dallas	41.3	45.9
New Orleans	44.3	56.9
Pittsburgh	49.1	58.9

Source: U.S. Department of Commerce, Bureau of the Census.

next year and 6,000,000 over the next five years. This demand is in sharp contrast with the new program of the Department of Housing and Urban Development which calls for 1,650,000 public-assisted housing starts over the next five years. Even this program is mammoth when contrasted with what has been done over the past few years. In 1968 there were 113,000 public-assisted housing starts; in 1967, 51,000; in 1966, 49,000. In other words, the need for public-assisted housing has not nearly been met over the past five years and, although there is now a call for a substantial increase over what has been done in the past few years, that increase itself is vastly short of the need.

JOBS AND PLACE OF RESIDENCE

While federal housing subsidies made large-scale population growth in the outside central city economically feasible for the middle class, the decentralization of industry opened up job opportunities for those who moved. Had it not been for industrial decentralization, workers who wanted to live in the suburbs would have had to commute far greater distances to their place of employment —something few probably would have done. For, as location theory literature amply demonstrates, even in the automobile age, workers show a marked reluctance to separate their place of residence very widely from their place of employment. The forces which influenced the mid-century movement of industry from the central city to the outside central city include: (1) the search for space; (2) the spread of external economies; (3) taxes; and (4) the decentralization of consumers.

Perhaps the most important cause of postwar industrial decentralization was the search for space. As Edgar H. Hoover and Raymond Vernon, in *Anatomy of a Metropolis*, have observed—"There is scarcely a survey of industrial migration in metropolitan areas which has not placed this factor high on the list of migration causes." Underlying this search for space was the increased use of continuous-flow production processes which required sprawling sites not generally available in the central city because of the nature of its grid-pattern street system.

While large plants were pushed to the outside central city by space requirements, some small plants were pulled there by the outward spread of external economies. Traditionally, small scale plants which were marginally competitive had to cluster at close proximity in congested areas of the central city in order to take advantage of external economies—savings accruing from many plants sharing labor and capital which cannot be employed efficiently by individual plants. Yet, as rentable manufacturing space became available in suburban industrial parks, and as the quality and quantity of outside central city public services improved, many small plants began to break away from their congested city locations.

Relatively low taxes, like the spread of external economies, have tended to pull some firms from the central city to the outside central city. Generally speaking, however, central city/outside central city tax differentials have been greatly overrated as a determinant of industrial location within metropolitan areas. There are, to be sure, some firms of the low productivity "footloose" type which have been highly sensitive to slight potential competitive advantages. For the most part, however, industrialists tend to agree that taxes are at most a secondary consideration in location choice.

In the late 1940s and early 1950s, retail trade, like some other industries, was not pushed but pulled from the central city. As Hoover and Vernon indicate, "Whether retail buyers have traveled on foot, by horsecar, or by auto, one element in their choice of an outlet has been the desire to conserve the time and cost of transportation." Aware of this desire for nearby shopping facilities, retail trade, with a few important exceptions, followed, and in some cases anticipated, the flight of the central city population to the outside central city. Though the central city continued to monopolize retail trade activities requiring extensive comparative shopping, it has increasingly lost department stores and smaller shops selling standard goods to suburban shopping centers which expanded at a rapid rate, even in those metropolitan areas where vast sums were spent to revitalize the downtown business district.

The flight has continued into the sixties, as Dorothy K. Newman demonstrates in a recent article. From 1960 to 1965, at least 62 percent of the valuation permits for new industrial buildings and 52 percent for stores and other mercantile buildings were issued for construction in the suburbs of metropolitan areas.

TABLE IV. *Percent of New Private Nonresidential Building Outside the Central Cities of Standard Metropolitan Statistical Areas (SMSAs), by Region, 1960–65*

Type of New Nonresidential Building	Percent of Valuation of Permits Authorized for New Nonresidential Building				
	United States	North-east	North central	South	West
All types	47	53	49	34	53
Business	47	54	47	33	52
Industrial	62	71	59	46	69
Stores and other mercantile buildings	52	68	57	34	56
Office buildings	27	26	30	22	32
Gasoline and service stations	51	61	52	39	57
Community	45	47	47	33	53
Educational	45	47	46	34	50
Hospital and institutional	35	35	36	20	48
Religious	55	66	57	42	60
Amusement	47	41	60	46	45

Source: Dorothy K. Newman, "The Decentralization of Jobs," *Monthly Labor Review*, May 1967, p. 8.

EMPLOYMENT

This shift in economic activities has caused suburbs to gain in jobs while cities are the losers. According to a 1967 report of the

U.S. Chamber of Commerce, *The Metropolitan Enigma,* cities have been losing employment in the manufacturing, wholesale and retail sector of the economy at a rate of about half of one percent per year, while suburban areas have been gaining at a rate of two and a half percent. Of particular relevance has been the loss of manufacturing jobs. Such jobs declined in cities from 1958 to 1963 by six percent, while suburban manufacturing employment increased by 15.6 percent.

Forced to live in central cities, low-income job seekers, looking for employment near their place of residence, are confronted not only with an absolutely declining number of jobs, but also with jobs which tend to require occupational skills greater than they possess. The result is higher and higher rates of unemployment and underemployment in these areas.

The Riot Commission reported that there were about two million unemployed in the country in 1968 and even a larger group—ten million—underemployed. Six and one-half million of the latter group work full-time and earn less than the annual poverty wage. Five hundred thousand hard-core unemployed live within central cities, lack basic education, work sporadically, and are unable to cope with problems of performing and holding a job. A substantial part of this group, according to the commission, is Negro, male, and between the ages of 18 and 25.

In an effort to find jobs, a small but growing number of central city residents, in large part non-white, have begun to commute to places of employment in the outside central city. This "reverse commuting," however, is not an answer to the overall problem of such unemployment, if for no other reason than that it is expensive and time-consuming.

Central city residents using public transportation must spend more time and money to reach jobs in suburbs than those commuting to the city. According to estimates, a worker from Harlem pays $40 a month to commute to a job (by public transportation) in an aircraft plant in Farmingdale, Long Island, a parts plant in Yonkers or Portchester (Westchester) or a shipyard on Staten Island. The cost to a resident of Bedford-Stuyvesant is $50 a month to commute to the same jobs. In addition, rush-hour schedules are usually not arranged for commuters from city to suburb—rather the opposite.

INCOME AND WELFARE

This pattern of job location added to education, housing and discrimination has produced an income and poverty distribution which accentuates the disparities between city and suburb. In general, the gap between median family income in the suburb and city is increasing. Average median family income in the central cities in 1960 was $5,940 compared to $6,707 in the suburbs. In 1964 it was $6,697 for central cities and $7,772 for suburbs. Estimates for 1967 are $7,813 for the central city family while for the suburban family it has increased to $9,367. Thus, the gap has increased since 1960 from a suburban advantage of $767 to a 1967 advantage of $1,446 —a doubling.

The lower median income figures in the city actually hide the amount of poverty which exists in these cities. Anthony Downs, in a recent study for the Committee for Economic Development, found poverty twice as prevalent in the cities as in the suburbs—16.2 compared to 8.6 percent.

Although not everyone living in poverty is on welfare, the increasing poverty in central cities has added substantially to their welfare expenditures. Welfare cases are concentrated in central cities in every state. For example, 44.2 percent of New York State's population lives in New York City, while 70.2 percent of the state's welfare load is located there. In Philadelphia the proportions are 17.8 and 29.6; Boston, 13.6 and 32.0; and in St. Louis, 15.5 and 25.5.

Thus, welfare expenditures, which are increasing rapidly, have seriously strained the tax bases of many of the nation's largest cities. Although aided by federal and state governments, welfare is still in many states a heavy local charge. This local burden has caused demands that welfare be moved from the local fiscal base to the state and, by some, to the federal. The justifying argument is that welfare problems are not caused by local governments but rather are the product of national phenomena—the move from countryside to city, the legacy of slavery and technological change.

What the present welfare system, with all its inadequacies, has done in human terms can only be estimated. Large numbers of children are now growing up in dependency. The stories of human waste and loss of dignity have enormous implications for a nation founded on the principle of equality and opportunity. What is also not known is whether the 1969 presidential proposals will reverse present patterns. It is clear, however, that if Congress accepts the program as recommended, the amount of funding is wholly inadequate, and the work requirement could in some parts of the country become repressive.

HEALTH

Insufficient welfare funding, low income, and poor health go hand in hand as both cause and effect. Higher infant mortality rates, lower life expectancy, higher incidence of disease, and poor diets characterize those who live in poverty. In addition, efforts in the last few years by local governments, states, and most notably the federal government to improve and increase the availability of health care have created a situation of crisis proportions. According to a recent presidential report,

> Expansion of private and public financing for health services has created a demand for services far in excess of the capacity of our health system to respond. The result is a crippling inflation in medical costs causing vast increases in government health expenditures for little return, raising private health insurance premiums and reducing the purchasing power of the health dollar of our citizens.[5]

Low-income groups suffer most from lack of health services. Recent studies confirm the effects of poor health on school attendance and employment stability. There is little question that a hungry youngster finds being attentive in a classroom difficult. Or that years of inadequate diet affect the strength and stamina of a worker.

Poor families also spend less on health care—this is particularly true of nonwhites who are represented in larger proportion in that group. This can be seen by looking at total health expenses per person per year for families with income under $2,000. In 1962 whites spent $130 while nonwhites only $63.[6]

A relatively new health threat—drug addiction—has become a daily torment in the ghetto. The cost of this health problem must be measured not only in the effects on the addicts themselves but also in its impact on other residents and on the community environment. A New York State Narcotics Commission study showed that the average daily cost of drugs for addicts was $30.53. Governor Rockefeller in releasing the report said, "It is commonly held that five dollars worth of property must be stolen to realize one dollar in cash. Thus, addicts must steal $150 per day to pay for drugs."

Theft rates then are demonstrably related to drug addiction in large cities.

[5] "President Warns of 'Massive Crisis' in Health Care," *New York Times*, July 13, 1969.

[6] *Report of National Advisory Commission on Civil Disorders* (New York: Bantam Books, 1968), p. 271.

CRIME

The other causes of crime are complex and by no means fully understood. That it is related to the social characteristics of urban ghettos is generally accepted; that it is an outgrowth, in part, of those sharp contrasts between the affluence shown every day on television and the reality of poverty is debatable but probably true.

Although the social and economic causes of crime in urban areas are vaguely known to the average citizen, his chief concern appears to be, if recent election returns are a fair measure, what has become known as crime-in-the-streets. Crime rates, however carefully those rates must be judged, are increasing. That crime rates are higher in cities than suburbs is not debatable, although the rate of increase is not that different.

Distinct from the crime problem but related to it in the minds of many is the tension between black neighborhoods and the police. As the President's National Advisory Commission on Civil Disorders said, "Negroes firmly believe that police brutality and harassment occur repeatedly in Negro neighborhoods. This belief is unquestionably one of the major reasons for intense Negro resentment against the police."

The widespread belief in the Negro community that police brutality exists has been fully documented. Simultaneous with this belief in police brutality is a demand in ghetto areas for better police protection. In other words, the black belief that the police perform their functions with unnecessary brutality does not mean that there is no desire in the ghettos for police protection.

Although these social problems—education, housing, jobs, crime, and health—have their greatest impact in cities, they are not unknown to the suburbs and are increasingly being found there. As more and more people move to suburbia, the population becomes more heterogeneous. Just as there has been a "sorting-out" process taking place between city and suburb, a similar process is occurring within suburbia. The result is communities with homogeneous populations but increasing heterogeneity between communities.

As this process works itself out more and more suburban communities have city-like characteristics and all the problems associated with those characteristics. Only focused and relevant government action can overcome the social maladies which this process will produce in suburbia as it already has in cities.

Hardware Problems

Although the most crucial problems facing metropolitan America are those social ones just described, the new spread pattern of settlement and technological change has produced another set of difficulties which might be termed the *hardware problems*. These are problems of transportation, water supply, sewerage disposal, and land-use control.

The movement of people and goods is central to the functioning of every metropolitan area. In fact improvements, if that is what they are, brought through limited access highways have been responsible, in part, for the new settlement patterns. The widespread use of motor transport has permitted an increasing number of commercial and industrial firms, once tied to the central city because of its transportation facilities, to migrate to suburban areas where congestion costs are lower. Delays have been only partly alleviated by one-way streets, reversible lanes and other new traffic control techniques. Until ways are found to eliminate streets serving as parking lots, pedestrian crosswalks and truck delivery docks, and public transit facilities improved to the point where the metropolitan population is willing to abandon its overwhelming reliance on the automobile, traffic jams will remain the daily experience of travelers.

The private automobile, although the cheapest and fastest mode of transport, is inefficient, particularly in the largest central cities. Current public transportation facilities unfortunately do not offer a viable alternative. Equipment is often old and poorly maintained, while schedules are more often ignored than followed.

The present organization for the performance of the transportation function makes it extremely difficult to coordinate different modes of transportation and to relate the transportation system to non-transportation activities. The already cited problem of relating a transportation system to the location of jobs relative to where potential workers live is but one example.

SEWERAGE, AIR, AND WATER POLLUTION

An urban society is a society with concentrated wastes—wastes which unless disposed of in a sanitary fashion will pollute the whole environment—the water drunk, the air breathed, and the scene observed. Solid wastes contaminate the entire environment; liquid wastes the nation's streams, rivers, lakes, and surrounding oceans;

and auto exhausts, factory smoke-stacks, and home incinerators pollute the air once thought to be free. Neither suburban nor urban, these problems are metropolitan. They touch the lives of every metropolitan citizen, yet he has no local government with sufficient jurisdiction, imagination or resources to respond.

Each American generates five pounds of rubbish every day. The traditional techniques of collecting, transporting, and disposing of solid wastes are simply inadequate. Trucking refuse more than twenty miles is hopelessly uneconomical for city governments. Dumps take up valuable land; open burning is increasingly unfeasible because of smog; and incineration leaves considerable residue and generally produces fumes. The 1969 survey by the federal Solid Wastes Program indicates that 94 percent of existing dump operations are insufficient to the point of being "a national disgrace." The solutions are expensive but necessary. The new incinerators, while costly, are effective; sanitary landfill techniques are useful but if improperly located may pollute underground water resources. The most recent method which Chicago and a number of industries have tried is compaction or compression—using machinery that crushes scrap into manageable solid bales.

There is probably no area of urban problems which lends itself better to potential technological breakthrough than pollution control. If but a few of the dollars now used for space research could be applied to major research and development effort in this area, significant improvements could be made.

LAND-USE CONTROL

Fundamental to all these problems—social and physical—is land-use control. Such control determines locations of residences and jobs; transportation routes; sewerage and water system placement; and community population mix. Currently such decisions are made by local officials, highway engineers, and powerful real estate groups, all influenced by state and federal actions.

This has produced the present spread pattern of population settlement and the distribution of economic activities. In fact, the system itself made the present spread pattern inevitable. The issue is not that the present pattern is wrong, but that the decision system does not allow for the consideration of alternatives by providing a method for area-wide decision-making.

Another result is the tremendous expense in providing government services, particularly capital plant, for this residential pattern. Sewerage systems, water systems, and highway systems must follow the population. In 1962 the New York Regional Plan Association calculated for the New York metropolitan area that the capital cost of providing these public services for each new home in a suburban community is $16,800 per house. Such cost, of course, might be reduced if a decision were made to promote and encourage compact communities.

The catalog of problems could be continued but there is no need. The existence of urban and metropolitan problems, however, should not be allowed to obscure the potential benefits which a metropolitan society could provide for all its citizens. Such a society could offer new and expanded employment opportunities, a wide range of residential choice—from city apartments to homes in semi-rural areas, neighborhoods which range from close-knit communities to leave-one-alone environments, cosmopolitan theater and music to bowling alleys for leisure-time pursuits, and educational resources with a depth, variety and quantity never before known. It is this potential which the urban crisis stifles for too many people. To solve the problems is to make possible the realization of this vast potential—a potential unavailable at any other time or place.

Conclusion

A discussion of the specific problems which have created the urban crisis and an awareness of their relationship to each other—invariably raises questions about the assignment of governmental responsibilities. Which level of government is responsible for which problems? The answer to this question is: all levels of the governmental system are responsible and all must be involved.

Students of these matters generally agree that of the various parts of the governmental system, states have performed least well. Local governments, particularly city governments, have vigorously strained their tax bases to meet some of the problems of their areas. Suburban jurisdictions, responding to constituency demands, have concentrated on providing quality educational services. The federal government has initiated many new relevant programs and approaches to urban problems, even though the allocation of resources has been wholly inadequate.

Such efforts do not characterize state governments. Some have participated in a few of the federal programs, even when not required to do so. Others have provided permissive legislation permitting local governments to join together to deal with certain problems, while others have established state level administrative departments which have been assigned the responsibility for at least examining the kinds of problems detailed here.

Some governors with moderate success have made strenuous efforts to induce their legislatures to respond to the facts of urbanism. As James Reichley explains in his article in this volume, Governor Rockefeller did force the New York State legislature to establish an Urban Development Corporation. Governor Hughes of New Jersey did present to his legislature the only full-fledged state urban program ever proposed, but other governors and legislators have simply found excuses ranging from the constitutional to the political for inaction.

Despite the failures, states have been making relatively strong fiscal efforts to meet their traditional responsibilities. State taxes have been growing at a rate of 11.5 percent per year since 1950, while federal taxes have increased at the lower rate of 8.9 percent. State and local taxes together have increased even more rapidly at a rate of 12.7 percent per year. However, this fiscal effort requiring in many cases high courage on the part of state political officials has not, in general, resulted in substantial contributions to new urban programs. States have instead continued their normal services and have not responded to the new dimension created by urbanization and metropolitanization.

Many reasons are given for this state failure, and most of them are examined in this volume. They include the constitutional restrictions on state power, which as is often forgotten are self-imposed and may, in fact, reflect state reluctance to take action rather than explaining why the states are unable to move in new directions. Fiscal restraints, both political and constitutional, are also often cited. It is true that state tax structures are not as progressive nor as responsive as the federal one, but many states have not tapped their own most lucrative tax sources, or, when they have imposed new taxes, have not adopted a productive rate schedule.

The inadequacy of the local government system is also often cited as standing in the way of a state response. Yet, this local government system is itself a product of state decisions, albeit sometimes imbedded in constitutions. At the other end of this scale, the federal government is also sometimes cited as moving into the states' sphere, thereby eliminating or reducing the potential of the states. Yet it is often claimed, and probably with more justice, that such federal moves have been made in response to the failure of states.

Finally, and perhaps closest to reality, is the claim that the distribution of political power within states stands in the way of state action. This distribution—regional, party, and interest group—forms a combination of political power which, on the whole, tends to be anti-city.

Most of the ways in which states might help their urban areas are clearly within their legal competence. They could induce reorganization of local government. They could improve their aid system to reflect urban needs. They could assume direct responsibility for functions that are now performed locally. They could reallocate their resources. It is this combination of legal ability and lack of action which gives this political explanation its greatest force.

The problems which need state action will not go away. The concentration of poverty in the cities, the growing heterogeneity of the suburbs, the inadequacy of educational services in city and some suburban jurisdictions, and the relationship between jobs and place of residence are all problems which form a part of the urban crisis.

Unless action is taken, societal tensions will increase, racial strife will take more ominous forms, and the disillusionment of the young with "the system" will grow.

Although it is possible that the rest of the governmental system will respond without the states, it seems unlikely. The key, therefore, to an adequate response to these problems is the role which states can and may play.

Frank P. Grad

2

The State's Capacity to Respond to Urban Problems: The State Constitution

In all fifty states, the relationship of the cities and other local jurisdictions to the government of the state is defined by law, and the most permanent and most difficult-to-change rules of that relationship are found in the 50 state constitutions. Not every state constitution deals expressly with the subject of local government, but because the state constitution defines state power generally, it has a direct impact on the state's capacity for the solution of its urban problems, whether or not local government is an express constitutional subject.

It is generally agreed that state constitutional provisions have inhibited the solution of urban problems in most states. The need for housing, social welfare and health services and job training, the vast need for better and more schools, the need for transportation facilities, the growing need for environmental controls in metropolitan regions have been caused by unprecedented immigration from rural areas into the cities since World War II, aggravated by a movement

FRANK P. GRAD *is Professor of Law and Director of the Legislative Drafting Research Fund at Columbia University. He was a consultant to the Rhode Island and Pennsylvania State Constitutional Conventions and has prepared various materials on the drafting of state constitutions, including the sixth edition (1963) of the National Municipal League's* Model State Constitution. *Professor Grad has been active in several other fields including health and housing law.*

from the cities to the suburbs by the middle class. The costs of rendering the necessary services have doubled and tripled in some instances in the years between the early forties and the late sixties, and wide disparities have appeared between the capacities of the central cities and the suburbs to meet them. Each of the 212 Standard Metropolitan Statistical Areas in the United States was served in 1967 by an average of 91 local governments (varying however from less than 10 to over 1100 per area),[1] each of which differed with respect to its powers and functions and its revenue powers and tax base. The capacity of the various local governments to meet costs is usually limited by restrictions on the power to tax or to borrow. In addition, social, economic, racial and other disparities have been exacerbated by restrictive or discriminatory zoning practices and other protective measures by which many suburbs have sought to insulate themselves against the problems of the inner cities.

The brief catalogue of urban problems makes evident the extent of state constitutional involvement, for rising costs face constitutional restrictions on state and local tax and borrowing powers, and the substantive problems encounter limitations on the structure and powers of local government. The multiplicity of governments in metropolitan areas requires leadership and planning on a broad scale, both of which are likely to be inhibited by constitutional limitations on the state's capacity to assert effective control over its localities so as to face up to the social and economic disparities within the urban area.

Emphasis on constitutional limitations in this chapter should not be taken to mean that their removal will of itself release the states' energies. While constitutional limitations inhibit the states' capacity to deal with urban problems, these limitations may themselves be regarded as a symptom of the problem itself. The continued presence of constitutional restrictions on the states' powers to act may itself be a clue to their readiness to do so.

Impact of State Constitutions on State Powers

To appreciate the limiting and "freezing" effect of state constitutional restrictions, a brief consideration of the nature of state constitutions and their standing in the hierarchy of laws may be useful, particularly because it is relevant to the state's role as the source of

[1] National Commission on Urban Problems, *Building the American City* (1968), pp. 324-325.

delegated power upward to the federal government, and downward to the local governments.

THE NATURE OF THE STATE CONSTITUTION

State constitutions differ from the federal constitution in scope and in effect. The federal constitution is a document of grant and delegation, for in spite of its enormous powers, the federal government must trace all its powers to one of several constitutional grants made to it by the original states. The states have plenary powers simply by virtue of their original sovereignty; they retain all the powers it is possible for government to have except insofar as these powers have either been delegated to the federal government, or have been limited by the state constitution.

State constitutions are instruments of limitation. The state does not *derive* power from its constitution, but rather, the state constitution limits the exercise of the state's power either absolutely—as in the bill of rights—or qualifiedly, as for instance by assigning certain powers to certain specific branches of government, or by conditioning the exercise of powers in prescribed ways. One consequence of state constitutions as documents of limitation is that they limit powers even when they purport to grant them, for the express grant of powers in a document of limitation is usually interpreted to mean that the power must be exercised in the precise way in which it has been granted. It may mean, by negative implication, moreover, that the specific powers granted by enumeration are *all* of the powers that may be exercised, because the enumeration of some may be taken to prohibit the exercise of those not enumerated. Since the state has plenary powers without constitutional grant, one way to give meaning to a purported grant is to draw a negative implication as to powers not included.

State constitutions differ from the law regularly passed by the legislature in a number of ways. They are far more difficult to amend, and they carry with them a very powerful sanction, in that all laws inconsistent with them suffer the risk of invalidation. Thus, state constitutions at their best are designed to give a specially protected status to that part of the state's law that exemplifies some of the lasting, most highly protected values of the polity, such as a sound frame of government and the protection of individual liberties. At their worst—and indeed this reflects the conditions in many states—the state constitutions, because of their higher position in the hierarchy of laws and their greater difficulty of amendment, are the repository of the values—and fears—of the past, by virtue of their relative rigidity providing a special sanctuary for the positions of special interest groups, and for positions that, though possibly responsive to the problems of the past, fail to confront the issues of the present or the future. The renewed interest in state constitutional revision in the sixties demonstrates that many state constitutions fail to meet the needs of contemporary government.

The price that must be paid for the specially protected status of state constitutional provisions is rigidity and inability to respond to changed needs. When the constitution incorporates matters not truly reflective of present values, then it is likely to be less a frame of government and more of a geologic accretion of protections against the fears of the past. So, for instance, early post-revolutionary constitutions reflected a fear of the unlimited powers of the executive and thus contained many restrictions on executive powers. The disclosure of widespread irregularities during the late nineteenth century was followed by a fear of untrammeled legislative power, and later, specifically, by fear of fiscal irresponsibility and legislative give-aways to major corporate and particularly railroad interests. The early twentieth century brought a fear of representative democracy generally, and increased reliance on direct democracy, initiative, referendum and recall. The fear of the rising immigrant city population brought with it greater restriction on voting rights reflected in longer residency requirements. The majority of state constitutions reflect these successive layers of fear, severely limiting the state government's freedom of action.

An impotent state government can no more deal with urban problems than it can with any others, and since the problems of the cities are the foremost problems of government today, the general inadequacy of state constitutions—and of state government—is particularly disabling in this area. The removal of state constitutional limitations and the strengthening of state government generally will strengthen its capacity to deal with urban problems.

THE CHANGED TASKS OF GOVERNMENT

It is common to refer to a state constitution as an instrument of government. An instrument is a tool whose suitability and adaptability can only be gauged in the relationship to its set task. The urban problem is the major problem of our age for all levels of government. Hence the state's capacity to deal with problems presented by the metropolitan areas in them provides a proper measure for the capacity of states to govern generally. Not all of the states are fully urbanized as yet, but in 1969 there were only three states left in the union (Alaska, Idaho and Wyoming) which did not include at least one "Standard Metropolitan Statistical Area," and thus the solution of urban problems is truly the major business of the states today.

When discussing the changing role of the states within the federal system, some commentators point to the relative loss of state power against the encroachment of the strong central authority of the federal government. Other commentators, however, have pointed out that there may well not be any loss of state powers to the federal government, but rather that there is simply more government around. Indeed, the states, whether on their own or stimulated by programs that are federally inspired, carry out many more governmental functions than they have ever done in the past, and many of the new state functions are indeed carried out by local government.

First and foremost, the powers of government have been enhanced not only by broader areas of policing and control, but by the many new service functions that governments on all levels have begun to assume. Vast new areas of governmental concern have been added to the statute books in the last few decennia. Such areas include public health, legislation dealing with matters of environmental pollution such as air pollution and water pollution, environmental controls such as food and drug legislation, housing legislation, and regulation of radiation hazards; social welfare and social insurance legislation including medical assistance for the aged or medically indigent; labor legislation including fair labor standards and labor relations legislation as well as provisions for manpower training and utilization; and vast areas of legislation to provide technical services to businesses, to education, to medical and other scientific research, to mention but a few. The vast expansion of governmental interests is indicative of a mature industrial and primarily urban society which requires not the mere policing activities that government was called upon to render during the nineteenth century, but the rendition of services which such an industrial and urban society demands.

The growth of governmental interests is also reflected by the very size of the governmental establishment. In 1969, one out of every 5.5 persons gainfully employed in the United States worked for a government. This is almost a doubling of the number of persons so employed at the beginning of the 1930s. Moreover, since the end of World War II the number of persons employed by state and local governments has been increasing at a considerably greater rate than the number of persons employed by the federal government. As Alan K. Campbell has put it, "The most dynamic part of the American

economy today is the state-local government sector of the economy.
. . . The rate of growth in expenditures, revenues and employment
by state and local governments [is greater than] the growth rate of
all other parts of the economy, public or private." [2] The enormous
increase in the number of functions that all parts of the governmental establishments have to carry is reflected in a growing recognition of the interdependence of the different levels of government.

At one time, as long as regulatory power was the main tool of government, it was possible to conceive of three separate layers of government, each with its separate functions. The top layer consisted of
regulatory powers of the federal government delegated to it by the
states but nevertheless supreme by virtue of the supremacy clause of
the federal constitution. The second layer, state government, was
considered sovereign in every respect except insofar as powers had
been delegated to the federal government. The third layer, of local
government, was treated as the lowest in every respect because
wholly dependent on delegation by the state for its existence; for as
everyone knows local government is a creature of the state and
exists only by grace of state delegation. As this author has had occasion to say in another context,

> . . . it is questionable whether this layer cake diagram was ever a wholly
> adequate description of government in the United States. It certainly is
> so no more. For although it may be possible to structure regulatory func-
> tions in this hierarchical fashion, it has proved to be impossible to struc-
> ture service functions in this manner. . . . In a sense when the business
> of government consists more in the rendition of services than in the
> enforcement of regulations, the question of whose power is being exer-
> cised, whether the federal government's or the state's or the municipal-
> ity's, may become largely irrelevant so long as the service is being ren-
> dered effectively.[3]

The trouble with state constitutional arrangements in most of the
50 states is that constitutions have interfered with rather than advanced the rendition of services and the execution of governmental
functions demanded by an urban society.

SPECIFIC LIMITATIONS ON STATE POWERS

The point has already been made that any constitutional provision that weakens the power of state government is likely to weaken

---

[2] Alan K. Campbell, "The Most Dynamic Sector," *National Civic Review*, LIII
(1964), p. 74.

[3] Frank P. Grad, "The State Constitution: Its Function and Form for Our
Time," *Virginia Law Review*, LIV, No. 5 (1968), pp. 928, 938.

its capacity to deal with urban problems. There are, however, a number of state constitutional provisions that may have particularly adverse effects. These include limitations on the executive power, limitations on the assumption of local functions by the state, limitations on the state's capacity to affect local government structures and boundaries, and limitations on the state's fiscal power that disable it from providing the needed means for assistance.

Restrictions on Executive Leadership—The alliance of suburban and rural interests in the state legislatures, following their reapportionment, provides little hope for the immediate future that the impetus for effective urban policy will come from the legislative leadership. The solution of urban problems by the states will clearly require strong executive leadership, yet in many states the governor is given limited powers, cannot succeed himself, and is not truly the master of his own administration. Students of government agree that the most desirable method of accomplishing executive leadership is to have as few elected executive officers as possible, leaving the selection of department heads and of the members of his own cabinet to the governor to the fullest extent possible. Yet in many states numerous department heads, often ten or more, ranging from the commissioner of highways to the commissioner of education, the attorney general, the controller, and the heads of numerous other agencies are elected and have their own constituencies. They are not really responsible to the governor because he cannot remove or replace them. In many instances, their constituencies may be larger than the constituency of the governor because they may have been elected by a greater vote. The development of a state's urban policy is closely related to aspects of state and regional planning which require the coordination of activities of different state departments, all subject to the primary leadership of the governor himself. When such important departments as the state education department, the highway department, or the department of institutions or other agencies are not subject to gubernatorial control and policy guidance, the planning function and the policy-making function are substantially interfered with and the development of a consistent urban policy greatly inhibited.

Similar consequences flow from commission government. Distrust of executive leadership has in the past led to constitutional requirements calling for commissions to head certain departments in most of the states. Frequently the members of the commission serve for overlapping terms, and in many instances their terms may be longer than that of the governor. Again the result is loss of gubernatorial leadership and loss of control, which far outweighs the purported gain of political independence which at one time was thought to flow from commission government.

The development of sound urban policies may in many instances be a function of the reorganization of state government with a view to its operating more effectively. While additional departments and agencies of government may in all states be created by legislation, all of the states have established from two to as many as two dozen agencies by constitutional provision, thus effectively freezing the possibility of future developments. Whenever particular departments and agencies are constitutionally fixed, sound reorganization of state government to meet changing needs becomes an impossibility unless the constitution is amended. But even when there are no constitutional limitations on the departments and agencies, state governmental reorganization is ultimately a legislative matter in which the governor can provide only a limited amount of leadership. It is for this reason that the National Municipal League's *Model State Constitution*, and a number of states that include Alaska, Hawaii, and Michigan, provide for executive reorganization subject only to legislative veto; the method had been proposed initially for the federal government in the Hoover Commission Report. Under this scheme, the governor is free to reorganize state departments and agencies in any manner he sees fit by submitting his reorganization plan to the legislature, which may not amend it but may veto it within 60 days of submission. Unless vetoed by joint resolution, such a reorganization plan becomes effective as submitted. It is perhaps significant that concern for executive reorganization is reflected in some of the newer state constitutions which recognize the necessity for gubernatorial leadership to deal with emergent problems.

Restrictions on State's Power to Alter Structure or Boundaries of Subdivisions—Many state constitutions prescribe the structure of local governments, create particular local officers and provide for their functions. The list of constitutional officers is particularly heavy on the county side. Most states refer to at least one or two of the following county officers in their constitution: county attorney, auditor, bailiff, clerk, commissioner or supervisor, constable, coroner, elisor, inspector or measurer, jailer, marshal, poor superintendent, president of county court, ranger, register or recorder of deeds, registrar of voters, register of wills, revenue commissioner, road commissioner or superintendent, sergeant, surrogate, surveyor, tax collector, tax receiver, and treasurer. In most instances, the constitution also provides for the officer's qualification, selection, duties and term. One of the most common examples is the constitutional inclusion of the office of the county sheriff, with the result that in many urban counties there is an expensive elected county sheriff of limited functions side by side with a regular modern county police force. Neither the county nor the state has the power to abolish the sheriff's office, useless though it may be, and in many instances the continued existence of such a county office may by implication prevent the very abolition of counties because the constitution provides for a county sheriff and other county officers and there has to be a county for them to serve in.

Generally there are no municipal officers referred to in state constitutions, so that the state would generally be free to change the structure of municipal government but for the constitutional home rule protections which form a separate topic for discussion later on.

It should be noted that the existence of a mass of constitutionally protected local offices not only inhibits structural change, but it has far-reaching political effects. Such offices supply grist for the political mill, and it is a common experience at constitutional conventions that long-term incumbents generally become a special lobby against governmental reorganization.

To the extent that constitutions impose limitations—as they frequently do—on the method of changing county and municipal lines, they create a major problem for rational government in metropolitan areas. With rapid speed of urbanization, jurisdictional lines have become artificial and irrational divisions within the coherent entity of metropolitan areas, although they still have important legal consequences.

When a municipal boundary or county line runs down the middle of a city street, anomalies and discrepancies of regulation and enforcement are sure to occur on either side, and rational administration and economies of scale are likely to be lost. More important, even, is the fact that constitutional protection of local boundary lines perpetuates the social and economic disparities within metropolitan areas. Since two-thirds of the nation's population and an even greater portion of its economic activities are found in metropolitan areas, these areas could meet a far greater proportion of their needs for urban services if their resources could be tapped equitably. Artificial boundary lines, separating areas with stronger and weaker tax bases in the area, and separating localities with different levels of need for service, prevent the equitable and rational application of the resources of the metropolitan area as a whole.

In spite of the desirability of flexible adjustment of local boundaries, a great deal of rigidity has been built into them by state constitutional provisions, particularly with respect to county boundaries. In a number of states (e.g., Iowa, Maryland, Minnesota, North Dakota and Ohio), laws affecting county lines cannot become effective until submitted to a vote of the people in the counties affected; in Louisiana a two-thirds popular vote of approval is necessary, and in Alabama, a two-thirds vote of each house of the legislature. The consolidation of two or more counties, or the division or the abolition of a county—significant because many metropolitan areas include more than one county—is even more restricted, with referenda required to be held separately in each of the counties affected, and special majorities a common requirement in many states. The requirement that a majority of voters within each of the affected jurisdictions must consent invariably leads to political campaigns to protect suburban communities against purported metropolitan encroachments, and has almost invariably stood in the way of rational realignment of county and municipal lines.

Fiscal Restriction on the States—The most significant limitation on the state's capacity for response to urban problems is to be found in the fiscal area. While the proposed solution to the broad variety of urban problems may differ significantly, there is considerable agreement that inroads can only be made upon urban problems by an infusion of vast sums of money. In spite of the possible realization of federal "revenue-sharing" bloc grants, and the expansion of federal programs in the fields of housing, planning, health, social welfare, education and employment, it is nonetheless clear that the states will be called upon to devote ever larger parts of their revenues to deal with the urban problems, be it through their own efforts or be it merely in matching federal grants and in carrying out programs stimulated and supported by the federal government. A state that constitutionally limits its ability to raise revenue, to incur indebtedness, or to make expenditures disables itself from coping with urban issues in any realistic fashion.

We are not at present discussing state constitutional limitations on the fiscal capacity of local governments to resolve urban problems on their own. Rather, the focus is on state fiscal limitations that prevent the state from coming to the assistance of the cities, and thereby leave the major burdens on the governments even less able to carry them, the cities and local governments themselves. There has never been any evidence that constitutional limitations on state fiscal powers make for more responsible financial management. While it has never been shown that the absence of fiscal limitations in a state constitution will by itself lead to more flexible and wiser management of a state's financial affairs, it is indeed clear that the presence of rigid fiscal limitations leads to subterfuges and to covert fiscal devices which both fail to protect the state against financial irresponsibility and hide the real dimensions of the state's obligations behind a number of smoke screens.

State Tax Limits—Although constitutional state tax limits still loom large in many states, there is clear evidence that they are gradually losing their importance. In most states that have a constitutional tax limit, it is expressed as a limit on the real property tax, in terms of a fixed percentage of the assessed valuation of all of the taxable real property in the state. While this limitation is still very real, because in many states the property tax is still relied on to produce a substantial part of the state's revenue, by the beginning of 1968 there were 44 states with general sales taxes, 35 with broadbased income taxes, and 30 with both. In addition, many states rely on a variety of general taxes, such as on tobacco products, gasoline, and on the transfer of real estate and stocks and bonds. The states that have moved into the income tax and sales tax field include most of the major urban states, including California, Massachusetts, Michigan and New York; Illinois has a sales tax, but no personal income tax. For the 50 states as a whole, sales tax receipts of all kinds accounted for more than 58 percent of total state revenue, personal and corporate income taxes for more than 23 percent, and property taxes for only 2.7 percent, with the rest from various other licensing and tax sources.[4] The fifty-state totals, however, hide the fact that in many states taxes on real, personal and intangible property account for a far greater percentage. Other constitutional limitations also affect the picture. So, for instance, the requirement that taxes be both uniform *and* equal has inhibited the adoption of graduated state income taxes. A number of states impose a "flat" percentage income tax and seek to vary its impact by a system of exemptions —this results in an inadequately progressive system. The Michigan constitution makes doubly sure to reach the result of "equal" taxation by expressly prohibiting the imposition of a graduated income tax. Of necessity, a flat income tax rate is not only regressive and socially undesirable, but it also imposes a stringent limit on revenue production. (Dr. Roy Bahl discusses the effectiveness of the state tax structure and its relationship to the fiscal problems of urban areas in Chapter 4.)

[4] Advisory Commission on Intergovernmental Relations, *State and Local Taxes: Significant Features, 1968,* pp. 1, 11.

Restrictions on State Expenditures—Two kinds of constitutional restrictions on state expenditures have an impact on urban problems. The first, a most direct limitation, prohibits the state from expending moneys to political subdivisions, or assuming any of their obligations. Fortunately this direct limitation is to be found in only a few state constitutions, although these do include one or two states with large urban areas. In California, for instance, the legislature may not give public money or anything of value to municipal corporations, except for certain enumerated welfare and highway construction purposes; somewhat similar provisions may be found in Texas. In Delaware, no appropriation of public money may be made in aid of counties or municipalities, and Louisiana and New Mexico prohibit the support of "public corporations," which category includes incorporated local governments.

Normally state constitutions do not designate a particular level of government which is to carry such expenditures as the costs of social welfare or of health care. This is left to ordinary legislation, yet unduly great pressures upon local governments may build up to the point that an attempt is made to reallocate such expenditures constitutionally. So for instance under the enormously burdensome impact of Medicare and Medicaid legislation which swelled the social welfare costs of local governments throughout the state of New York, the 1967 state constitutional convention proposed as a constitutional requirement that the state assume all social welfare costs within the state. It should be noted that such a result could have been achieved—and, now that the proposed new constitution has been defeated—could still be achieved by ordinary legislation. The transfer of welfare costs to the state government was viewed as a major relief measure for the hard-pressed cities and communities in the state—and was one of the two or three major factors in the defeat of the proposed new constitution. (The usefulness of transferring welfare or other functions is also discussed in Chapter 4.)

Another common constitutional limitation which is likely to have a seriously limiting effect on the state government's ability to resolve particular problems, especially in the context of greater emphasis on community action and activities by neighborhood groups and organizations, is the prohibition against expenditures of state funds or the extension of state credit for the benefit of private persons or corporations or nonpublic institutions. A parallel restriction is usually imposed on the expenditure of local or municipal funds. Many community projects and many neighborhood improvement groups are organized as private associations, membership corporations, or even business corporations. In many instances, some governmental functions and services could be effectively rendered, and potentially incendiary situations in slum and ghetto areas resolved, by providing the community and neighborhood groups with the means to work on problems of their own.

It is possible to seek judicial construction to the effect that works undertaken by communities or neighborhood groups are sufficiently imbued with a public purpose so as to make it permissible for government to spend money for such purposes. Some states and localities have in fact gone ahead and made this decision administratively, but it is certain that in the eighteen states that provide the limitation, the effect is one of considerable inhibition. Most of the states that prohibit expenditures for private persons and corporations do, however, exempt assistance to various categories of persons in need of social welfare.

State Debt Limits—Almost all state constitutions deal with the subject of state debt and most impose limitations on the state's power to incur obligations. When a state severely limits its own capacity to borrow, it deprives itself of the ability to assist in the solution of urban problems calling for substantial capital investment which cannot be undertaken by the municipalities alone. This is true particularly with respect to schools and housing; in both of these areas the municipalities' fiscal capacities usually stand in inverse relationship to their needs. The most liberal states limit the incurring of indebtedness to purposes of public nature; the most rigid limit it to a fixed and usually inadequate dollar amount or to a percentage of the assessed value of the real property in the state. Limits on general indebtedness may be as low as $100,000 in Nevada, or one percent of the assessed value of taxable real estate in Virginia. In many states the general debt limit may be exceeded after a popular referendum, usually by a majority of the votes cast on the question, but in some instances by a special majority such as a majority of the total number of votes cast at the election at which the question was submitted.

To be sure, most states have more than a single debt limit. Debts for revenue-producing capital investments are either separately authorized or are not charged against the general debt limit. In addition, separate borrowing authorizations are provided for a wide variety of special purposes such as airport facilities, bridges, tunnels, construction of state university buildings, hospital construction, parks and recreation facilities, port and harbor improvement, public buildings of various kinds, roads, and urban redevelopment. In about half the states, however, the state is forbidden to incur indebtedness on behalf of local government, to assume its local debt or to lend it state credit; in all of these states, state borrowing for a local capital investment would have to be separately authorized by constitutional amendment.

While obviously designed to protect the state against fiscal irresponsibility, referendum requirements on public indebtedness for a special purpose have indeed been among the most stringent limitations on the states' capacity for response to urban problems and particularly urban problems that relate to construction of housing in their inner cities. Normally a referendum on a state bond issue must obtain a majority (or special majority) of the votes cast on the issue by the voters of the state as a whole. When central city issues, such as low-income or middle-income housing, are involved, the rural and the suburban areas, which see no need for such housing and which actively oppose it (frequently on racial grounds) within their own jurisdiction, often gang up on the central city voters and defeat the bond issue. This has been the persistent course of history in the state of New York. On the other hand, bond issues for highway construction have generally managed to win with the same combination of rural and suburban voters coming out in favor, as against the city dweller who would rather build housing.

Rigid fiscal limitations, as has already been pointed out, invariably lead to subterfuge, which in turn damage the possibility for an integrated and rational attack on city problems. When the state approaches the limits of its taxing or housing powers the normal course has been to create special purpose public corporations or authorities with separate taxing powers or separate powers of incurring indebtedness which will not burden the state tax or debt limits. Such special authorities, public corporations or special purpose districts may frequently impose user charges rather than taxes. They may also incur indebtedness which does not pledge the state's full faith and credit, and by the same token, they will avoid the constitutional requirement of a referendum before bonds may be issued. Sometimes they will adversely affect the tax base of the local governments whose jurisdictional lines they may overlap. Invariably, they will hide the real fiscal picture of the state, because, though the state may not have pledged its credit, realistically it must stand behind the authority of special district bonds in order to make them salable. A rather typical example of such a subterfuge agency is the creation, in 1968, of the Urban Development Corporation in New York. Frustrated by the repeated defeat of housing bond issues

—as well as by the slowness and lack of capacity on the part of local governments to make headway with existing housing programs—the legislature, prodded by the governor, created a superagency to undertake, by itself or in partnership with private investors, the redevelopment of "substandard" areas. The new public corporation can set aside local laws, ordinances, zoning codes, charters, and construction regulations, and may substitute compliance with the state's building construction code "when, in discretion of the corporation . . . compliance is not feasible or practicable. . . ." In addition to substantial exemptions from local taxation, the new corporation has the right to issue bonds. While the state has provided initial funding, it does not pledge its full faith and credit—which would affect the debt limit—but rather commits itself, whenever the corporation's reserves are depleted, to appropriate an amount sufficient to make the succeeding year's amortization and interest payments! While granting the need for fulfilment of the functions for which the Urban Development Corporation was created, it must be recognized that such special public corporations or authorities invariably become another level of government which, protective of its own jurisdiction, will interfere not only with the free exercise of the state's powers but also with the powers of the municipalities. Often established to resolve a temporary fiscal problem, such special purpose districts and authorities are likely to create a permanent problem of duplication of functions, overlapping jurisdictions and irrationality of governmental structure. Once established, moreover, such authorities or special purpose districts take on a life and vitality of their own and become permanent governmental institutions that cannot be abolished. Run, generally, by appointed technocrats, they are not responsible to the electorate in any meaningful way. The more successful they are, the more successfully they intrude into the functions of general purpose governments.

Impact of State Constitution on Local Powers

Constitutional restrictions placed on the state governments in facing urban problems disable the local governments as well, because the localities cannot look for help to the state when the state has effectively deprived itself of the capacity to render it. There are, however, many more direct constitutional limitations on the local governments' ability to act; these include constitutional restrictions on permissible structure of local government, on the range of powers, and on the scope of their fiscal powers. The usual discussion of state constitutional limitations on local governments is likely to be restricted to a consideration of these direct limitations, generally by reference to the subject of "home rule." The subject of municipal home rule powers encompasses both the range of permissible structures of local government and the range of allotted municipal powers. Under the impact of emerging urban problems, a considerable shift of attitude has taken place, and the views of the sixties on home rule differ significantly from those of the past.

STRUCTURE AND POWERS OF LOCAL GOVERNMENT—HOME RULE

Local governments are the creatures of the state. Regardless of whether the subject of local government is mentioned in the state constitution, local governments have only the powers granted them by the state; they have no inherent powers. Some local governments began as mere administrative subdivisions of the state; this is true of many counties and townships. Other municipalities obtained a charter from the state legislature, granted either by special legislation or under general provisions of the constitution or law. Such chartered, or incorporated municipalities—including cities and villages—could, by virtue of their charter powers, exercise powers subject to, but independent of, the powers of the state. While incorporated specially chartered municipalities started far back in history, industrialization and urbanization during the late nineteenth century increasingly led to demands for greater municipal autonomy. The demands were to formulate and adopt a charter of the people's own choosing, and to exercise powers of municipal government free from state interference.

Aside from reflecting traditional values of local pride and independence, the demands for home rule were an early response to the malapportionment of the state legislature. Rural interests predominated in the legislatures at the turn of the century, and the legislatures neglected and distrusted the growing cities. This underlies the desire of the cities for independence from legislative domination. The home rule movement succeeded during the first half of this century to embody some home rule protection in the constitutions of about half of the states, and in a substantial number of states, home rule concepts were embodied, not in the constitutions, but in state law.

A distinction is often made between "constitutional" home rule and "legislative" home rule, depending on the source of the home rule powers. As a result, a good deal of definitional confusion has arisen, because many state constitutions do not grant home rule powers to local governments directly, but rather authorize, or instruct, the legislature to go ahead and grant home rule powers. Since there is no way to compel the legislature to legislate, there have been instances where a constitutional mandate to provide for local self-government powers has been wholly ignored. Thus, unless the constitution itself provides a method for the adoption by the municipality of a home rule charter, as well as an express grant of home rule powers, the legislature may be the true source of the municipality's powers, even in instances where the constitution contains general references to home rule.

The traditional form of home rule first provides for a procedure—usually involving a petition, election of a charter commission and submission of the new charter to the vote of the people—for the adoption of home rule charters, and then proceeds to set out the powers of home rule municipalities. These powers are considered to be exclusive—that is, they cannot be divested by state legislation. Within the specially protected sphere of home rule powers, where a state statute conflicts with a local ordinance passed by a home rule municipality, theory has it that within the municipality the local ordinance will control. To bolster home rule powers, there frequently are provisions which prohibit the legislature from passing special legislation relating to local government matters, allowing only for the passage of general laws affecting all municipalities, or all municipalities within a specified class.

Constitutional provisions on home rule differ from state to state in several respects. In some states the grant of home rule is restricted to one or two or only to the very largest cities within the state. In some home rule has been extended to all cities, and some even go so far as to grant home rule powers to villages, and even to counties and towns which previously had not been considered incorporated municipalities.

A major difference between grants of home rule power is found, too, in the manner in which these powers are defined. Some state constitutions leave the definition to the state legislature. Others define the grant of home rule in rather general terms, allowing the local government to act as to all matters relating to its "property, affairs or government" or words of a similar nature. A few state constitutions grant powers very specifically. So, for instance, the Utah constitution grants the power to adopt a charter to provide for all powers relating to municipal affairs; adopt police, sanitary and similar regulations not in conflict with general law (but not including the power to regulate public utilities not municipally owned if regulated by general law); levy and collect taxes and special assessments; borrow money; furnish all local public services; purchase, hire, construct, own, maintain, operate or lease local public utilities and acquire by condemnation or otherwise property necessary for such purposes; grant local utility franchises and regulate exercise thereof; make local improvements and acquire by condemnation or otherwise property for such purposes and protect and preserve improvements; and issue and sell bonds.

The theory of this traditional form of home rule is to grant to home rule municipalities a sphere of activities inviolate from legislative interference by the state. Such phrases as "property, affairs and government" are, however, subject to judicial interpretation, and constitutional home rule protections—as well as legislative home rule protections—have been far less effective than the sweep of the guarantee of powers would indicate. In construing home rule powers, courts have generally adhered to "Dillon's Rule," a construction applicable to municipal powers, formulated about a hundred years ago, practically for all times, that a grant of powers to a municipality must be narrowly construed. The underlying idea of the rule has been that in making a grant of powers to the municipality, the state did not mean to give away any more of its powers than appear on the face of the granting document. This means that powers which might be derived from the grant by necessary implication will be kept to an absolute minimum. In practice, when two interpretations of a grant of power are possible, courts will normally adhere to that interpretation which provides the lesser powers. This traditional mode of interpretation has created a number of difficulties.

It has long been clear that home rule powers are not what they seem. Because home rule powers are generally couched in fairly absolute terms, and because states frequently wish to legislate in areas that affect municipalities, they create a legislative no-man's-land where the municipality is uncertain of its power to act and the state is unwilling to assume the burden. In many instances cities with apparently ample home rule powers will play it safe and seek legislation from the state legislature to accomplish particular municipal purposes rather than to act on their own and subject themselves to the risks of a challenge of their charter powers.

Throughout the country the experience has been that whenever municipal action, whether by ordinance or otherwise, is in conflict with state legislation, the courts will defeat municipal action on one of two theories. The courts may find that the subject of action was not included within "property, affairs and government" of the municipality or within any of its express powers. Alternatively, they will find that even though the subject matter was included within the property, affairs and government of the city, it nonetheless was a matter of "state concern" and that consequently the state legislature had the preeminent right to legislate.

Under the "state concern" theory, a municipal subway system has been held to be outside the effective range of property, affairs and government of a city, as has the matter of regulations of the city's housing and occupancy standards for multiple dwellings! In the litigation of home rule powers, municipalities almost invariably lose when there is a contest between state legislation and municipal ordinance. Municipalities do slightly better when the state has not yet acted and when the challenge is directed merely to some legislative act of the municipality allegedly beyond its home rule powers. Because of the difficulties of delineation of home rule powers, the courts have had an unusually heavy role to play, so that a number of commentators refer to the traditional home rule concept as "judicial home rule" rather than constitutional home rule.

EFFECTS OF TRADITIONAL HOME RULE
ON METROPOLITAN ORGANIZATION

The traditional form of home rule assumes that there are certain powers and functions of government that are properly local and others that are properly the states' and proceeds to assign these functions and powers accordingly. The notion of separate spheres of power is in effect an acceptance of the "layer cake model" of the relationship of federal, state and local governments referred to earlier. But such a structuring of government is no longer possible in the light of the many service functions and the many programs that permeate all levels of government. The experience with traditional forms of home rule over the past 50 years has shown that the assignment of particular functions to particular levels of government is unworkable even when the government's functions are far more limited and far less complex than they are today. The assignment of functions did not work in the early part of the century and it cannot work today. The problem has been described by Wallace Sayre:

> For purposes of this discussion, the governmental functions now carried out in New York City may be described in the following categories:
> (1) Those performed by the national government under its own statutes and through its own agencies.

(2) Those provided in whole or in part by the national government but carried out largely through state or city government agencies.

(3) Those performed by the New York State government through its own agencies.

(4) Those performed by city government agencies under assignment from the state government, almost invariably accompanied by some degree of state supervision, ranging from simple reporting requirements to continuous administrative audit. Some of these are also accompanied by grants-in-aid.

(5) Those performed autonomously by the city government through its own agencies.

The fifth category is, of course, the area of home rule powers. The tantalizing question about the category is: In January 1967 what governmental functions can accurately be placed in it? The fact appears to be that, if it is not wholly unpopulated, the category is at least the one with the fewest functions and the one that is declining rather than growing.[5]

The narrow scope of "pure" municipal powers to which Professor Sayre refers is even more limited than would appear, because home rule powers are still further circumscribed by limitations on local taxation and borrowing usually found in another part of the constitution, which do not partake of the grant of protected municipal powers.

Home rule has even had some wholly unexpected and wholly undesirable consequences. While it provides few powers, its capability as a defensive measure was promptly recognized. It enhances considerably the effectiveness of defensive incorporation of municipalities. These defensive incorporations fall into a number of types. One example is furnished by the expensive residential suburban section in an unincorporated area of the state that incorporates, not because it is anxious to carry out municipal functions, but simply because it is in fear of otherwise being annexed by a neighboring municipality with less high standards and with major school, health and racial problems. If the particular state follows the practice of supporting municipalities in proportion to the state revenue derived from them, an added advantage of a substantial saving of taxes is served.

Another species of defensive incorporation is demonstrated by the overwhelmingly industrial section with a day-time population of several thousand workers, and a night-time population of a few score of watchmen and several stray dogs. The result of defensive

---

[5] Wallace S. Sayre, "New York City and the State," in *Modernizing State Government: The New York Constitutional Convention of 1967, Proceedings of the Academy of Political Science*, XXVIII, No. 3 (January 1967), p. 109.

incorporation by an industrial enclave is to protect itself against the school taxes and other municipal taxes of neighboring municipalities whose inhabitants it employs, but for whose children's education it does not wish to pay. In addition to defense against taxation, incorporation also defends against municipal regulation and control. So, for instance, an incorporated industrial enclave will be free of a neighboring municipality's air pollution control regulations, although it will of course spread the emission from its smoke stacks and industrial processes over the neighboring communities.

An excellent example of this type of defensive incorporation is furnished by the Village of Evandale, which is part of the Cincinnati metropolitan area. Incorporated under rather liberal provisions of law in 1951, the "village" embraces 4.05 square miles which are highly developed industrially. At the time of its incorporation it had 98 registered voters. Its assessed valuation in 1951 was $22,260,690 or $44,521 per inhabitant. The charter of the village limits the tax levy to 2 mills. It took a petition by 30 electors to bring about the incorporation, and 79 votes were cast, of which 78 were favorable to bringing the incorporated village into existence. Evandale is bordered by the all-Negro city of Lincoln Heights which, at the time of Evandale's incorporation, had 5,531 inhabitants and an assessed valuation of $590 per capita. Evandale does not contribute to the maintenance of schools and services in Lincoln Heights. In 1957 Cincinnati offered the services of its Air Pollution Control Bureau to other communities in Hamilton County and seven municipalities joined the program. Evandale refused to pay the nominal fee required for participation.

While traditional home rule powers have not added significantly to the efficiency or effectiveness of local governments, they have added some distinctively new problems to the solution of urban problems. There is considerable agreement that one of the major problems in the better organization of metropolitan areas is the existence of too many governments, each of which has limited powers and limited territorial jurisdiction. A rational solution to metropolitan problems with rational allocation of functions, resources and services demands fewer units, with planning and coordination at a higher level of government that has adequate powers and sufficiently wide territorial jurisdiction. None of this can be accomplished when there are scores of independent municipal governments within the metropolitan area, each of which claims exclusive home rule jurisdiction and each of which, by virtue of its home rule charter, is placed beyond the reach of a general governmental reorganization.

Thus, while municipal home rule has not furnished any protection to the cities against sometimes hostile state legislation, it nonetheless stands in the way of rational reorganization of the scheme of government within entire metropolitan areas. Ineffective to protect the municipalities against the legislature, home rule has become all too effective in preventing the breakdown of artificial, archaic and irrational boundaries. It is perhaps a subject for wry amusement that the home rule movement was still in full sway when all the evidence pointed to the need for larger units and few artificial divisions in the early and middle fifties. Many political scientists well remember the frequent conferences on problems of the city in which home rule and metropolitan government would form competing subjects in adjoining conference rooms.

THE SEARCH FOR NEW PATTERNS OF INTERRELATION

Experience with traditional patterns of home rule and clear indications that these patterns gave control over municipal-state relationships to the courts, rather than allowing them to be resolved by the political process, resulted in a search for new patterns. The credit for a truly new and creative approach must go to Jefferson Fordham, who in 1953 developed his "Model Constitutional Provisions for Municipal Home Rule" for the American Municipal Association. Essentially Fordham's approach, subsequently adopted in a slightly different form by the National Municipal League in the sixth edition of the *Model State Constitution*, recognizes the realities of the political process in working out city-state relationships.

Under the 1963 National Municipal League variant of the Fordham approach, the powers of counties and cities are provided for as follows:

> A county or city may exercise any legislative power or perform any function which is not denied to it by its charter, is not denied to counties or cities generally, or to counties or cities of its class, and is within such limitations as the legislature may establish by general law.

In fact, this approach gives up the attempt to define what is a city power and what is a state power. It accepts the reality—driven home again and again by judicial opinions—that in the event of real conflict the state law will control. On the other hand, it removes the no-man's-land of uncertainty between what is a city power and what is a state power, because the municipality is free to act as long as the state has not previously acted in an inconsistent fashion. Moreover, the provision allows municipalities to take the initiative, because they are free to act until the state acts inconsistently by general law. Rather than leave the determination of what is a municipal function and what is a state function to the judiciary, it recognizes that this is primarily a political issue to be worked out between the state legislature and the state's municipalities. Proponents of the Fordham-NML approach have generally stressed the fact that it grants municipalities greater home rule powers than they had before, because it allows the municipalities to take the initiative in legislative action. Proponents have pointed out that once a municipality has acted, the state legislature is less likely to act negatively, merely to defeat the city's power. Proponents have had to concede, of course, that this so-called home rule approach does not give the municipalities any exclusive areas of protection, because under the proposal the state has full power to act inconsistently and to override municipal action by general legislation in any area at all.

The Fordham approach is generally regarded as a new-style home rule model, and it was initially intended to be just that. It would be better to concede that it has little to do with home rule at all. It is true that some municipalities may gain broader powers under the proposal, but this is merely incidental. It does not really provide home rule; it provides something far more important than home rule. It provides a means to resolve and adjust the conflicting claims of the states and the municipalities in the solution of urban problems, and it deprives each group of the alibi that only the other has power to act. Unlike the traditional home rule approach, it does not preserve artificial boundaries between small home rule jurisdictions within the same metropolitan region, but recognizes the power of the state to make order out of chaos—if it really wants to do so—by putting together viable combinations for metropolitan government, overriding if necessary the parochial claims of some local jurisdictions.

The Fordham-NML plan, viewed not as a home rule plan but rather as a plan of shared powers for the adjustment of intergovernmental problems, would afford an opportunity to the states and to the municipalities to achieve a better ordering of urban government. There is, of course, no assurance that they will find it politically expedient to seize this opportunity. The original home rule movement was a response to legislative malapportionment which resulted in rurally dominated legislatures that gave short shrift to urban areas. The decisions of the Supreme Court which established the principle of "one man-one vote," and which have since resulted in the wholesale reapportionment of state legislatures, were expected to bring about a shift from rural domination to city eminence in state legislatures. In the meantime, as discussed in Chapter 7, the suburbs had achieved the balance of power and in consequence, reapportionment has not fulfilled the hopes of cities. The suburbs have formed an alliance with the rural areas, and the cities are in as poor a political position as before. The suburbs, which live off the city and share in its benefits, are loath to share the city's housing, welfare, employment and school integration problems. The last thing the suburbs seek is a scheme of government which would compel them to throw in their lot with that of the central city, with all of the problems that the suburbanite hoped to avoid by moving away from it. Nonetheless, it is clear that traditional approaches to home rule have not worked, and that the only hope for rational organization of urban governments lies in constitutional provisions that will ultimately allow state leadership to move toward a more rational ordering.

The Fordham-NML plan provides the legal and political rules of the game that will make it possible to achieve such leadership without loss of municipal freedoms in the interim. The fact that the Fordham-NML approach has been adopted in five states (Alaska, Massachusetts, Pennsylvania, South Dakota, and by judicial construction, Texas), and has also been proposed in a number of recent constitutional conventions whose proposals failed to pass, provides at least some hope that some states and some municipalities are ready to move in a direction in which a more rational ordering of metropolitan government eventually may be accomplished.

CONSTITUTIONAL RESTRICTIONS ON LOCAL FISCAL POWERS

In discussing constitutional restrictions on local government ability to deal with urban problems, we may well hypothesize a situation in which local government has full power to establish its own structure, and full power to do absolutely anything it wants, and yet be totally incapable of accomplishing anything at all, because it has been deprived of the financial resources by denial of the power to tax or to borrow.

Indeed, while not all state constitutions impose limitations on the *state's* power to tax or borrow, almost all of them impose some restraints on the fiscal powers of local government.

Local Tax Limits—Normally, local governments are constitutionally restricted with respect to the kinds of taxes they may impose, either by express constitutional provision or by leaving the matter to the ultimate determination of the state legislature. Commonly they are restricted, too, with respect to the maximum rate of taxes they may levy. Since the real estate tax is still the main revenue source of local governments, the limitation on the locality's taxing power is usually expressed in terms of a maximum percentage of assessed valuation of the real property within the locality which forms the tax base. In several constitutions, different rates of taxes are fixed for different local governments with one tax limit being set for school districts, another for city government of a particular class, a third for counties and so forth. These rate differentials may be discriminatory.

The overwhelming bulk of constitutional limitations run against the oldest and most often used revenue source, the real property tax. Although in more than a third of the states, local governments, and particularly cities, have been authorized, usually by legislation, to levy a variety of other taxes—such as sales taxes and nonprogressive income taxes—and although the movement in the direction of local diversification of the tax base appears to be spreading, the stringent limitation on local governments with respect to the real property tax has considerably greater impact than similar limitation on the state's taxing powers, because the property tax has become a progressively less important revenue source at the state level. In its report, published in December 1968, the National Commission on Urban Problems noted that locally raised taxes provide about half of the funds to finance urban public services, and that of all tax revenues of urban governments, about five-sixths came from property taxation, with the proportion considerably larger in most metropolitan areas, since other taxes—such as sales and income taxes, which are highly productive—are used only in a very few cases. Difficult questions of social disutility have been raised about real property taxation, such as regressiveness and adverse effects on city housing. Such questions aside, the heavy reliance on property taxation, coupled with rigid constitutional limitation, and constitutionally caused and protected fragmentation of local governments in metropolitan areas, is the cause of the fiscal disparities that underlie much of the crisis of urban financing. The local governments with the lowest real property values will have the least revenues—yet they are the ones most likely to require a variety of expensive urban services. In the light of constitutional limitations, it has been difficult to devise remedies to even the load and apportion the benefits. Statewide financing of certain services and a variety of shared-tax devices have been proposed.

The result of limitations on municipal revenues is to make the municipality more dependent on borrowing for expenditures for which it can do so, and also to make it more dependent on the largess of the state which can directly affect the performance of local government functions by either supporting them or denying them support. Thus, in many parts of the country, local school taxes are wholly inadequate to run the school system and the only way in which the system can function is with state subsidies. So, too, essential welfare and health services in many states can be run by the cities only with state assistance. The annual pilgrimage of mayors to the state capitol to obtain the assistance of the governor and of the legislature to meet the city's needs is a veritable constitutional requirement and has become an accepted part of our governmental system. It undoubtedly does not improve the mayors' mood to realize that an overwhelming amount of the state's revenue comes from the very cities which have been denied revenue sources of their own.

The year 1969 marked the advent of a real movement by the federal government in the direction of bloc grants to help the cities. Whether these grants of funds, not earmarked for any specific purpose, made on a so-called revenue-sharing basis, will provide the cities with substantial additional revenue remains to be seen. The distribution of these funds was to be left to the states, and the manner in which the states perform this function may well be an eleventh hour test of their readiness to deal with urban problems.

Local Expenditures—In addition to restrictions on the power to collect revenue, a number of state constitutions also impose limitations on the local government's power to spend the revenue collected. Restrictions on municipal spending are generally similar to the restrictions on state spending previously referred to. In particular, municipalities may not spend monies or lend their credit for private or nonpublic purposes, and may not support private institutions or organizations.

In the case of the municipalities, this restriction is likely to work considerable hardship when there is great emphasis on community and neighborhood activities, frequently operated through privately incorporated organizations and institutions. Local governments may contract with a private organization for services, and many local governments do contract with private social service agencies, hospitals and voluntary organizations for the rendition of such specific services as social counseling, clinical and other health care, and shelter care of various kinds. Under a contractual arrangement, however, the municipality remains in control and judges the adequacy of the ultimate performance. When dealing with neighborhood and community groups, whose very aim is to accomplish purposes of their own, and who wish to remain fully in control of their activities, the usual contractual arrangements between local governments and private or voluntary agencies are not appropriate. What is needed to avoid spending public money for clearly nonpublic purposes, while at the same time providing funds for recognizable though difficult-to-define public purposes, is either a careful constitutional redefinition of a public purpose, or the complete elimination of the subject from the constitutional sphere, leaving it to the more flexible instrumentalities of legislation to draw the necessary lines.

Local Debt Limits—Limitations on the powers of local governments to borrow money are generally stringent. Normally, municipalities are authorized to borrow on short-term revenue notes in anticipation of revenue to be collected and such short-term borrowings are generally unrestricted as to purpose. When it comes to long-term bonded indebtedness, restrictions on the powers of local government are often detailed and elaborate. In more than two-thirds of the states, there is a constitutional limit on at least some local government debt expressed in terms of a percentage of the assessed value of taxable real estate. A number of states also impose a limit on the property tax rates that can be levied for debt service requirements. Usually municipalities must submit bonded indebtedness to a referendum. A number of state constitutions provide separately for bonded indebtedness which may be incurred by municipalities for revenue-producing capital projects. These special purpose borrowing provisions have the advantage of putting certain objects outside the general debt limit. In many instances, the state constitution imposes different requirements on bond issues of different types of local governments and for different purposes.

Local debt limits have not demonstrably contributed to the fiscal responsibility of local governments. Because local debt limits are based on the real property tax, they create somewhat similar disabilities and disparities as the limitations on local taxing powers. Constitutional limits on local debt have not been unduly burdensome, however, because they are easily avoided by emphasizing borrowing on revenue bonds which are not charged against the debt limit, or by resort to the creation of special purpose districts with borrowing powers of their own. As in the case of limits on state indebtedness, the ultimate result is to becloud the real extent of local obligations and to diffuse responsibility.

Mechanics and Prospects for the Removal
of Constitutional Limitations

At the very outset, the point was made that it is necessary to strengthen state government in order to help it cope with the problem of the cities, because urban problems have become the major problems of the states. The question is no longer whether the states have a role to play in the solution of urban problems. The states are obviously central, and their constitutions impose serious restrictions on their own, as well as on the local governments' capacity to deal with urban issues. The question is, therefore, whether or not the states will play a constructive role or will play a destructive role simply by doing nothing at all.

DEVICES FOR METROPOLITAN REORGANIZATION

In its report, "Alternative Approaches to Governmental Reorganization in Metropolitan Areas," in 1962, the Advisory Commission on Intergovernmental Relations analyzes some ten devices to avoid some of the problems of governmental fragmentation, and of disparities in resources and need for services. The more important devices suggested include the following:

1. Use of extraterritorial powers, to authorize a municipality to exercise planning, zoning and subdivision regulation powers beyond its corporate limits.
2. Intergovernmental agreements, to permit local governments to perform services cooperatively, or on a contractual basis.
3. Voluntary metropolitan councils, to function as coordinating bodies, giving an opportunity to delegates from all of the governments in the metropolitan area to get together and settle differences and counsel together.
4. The urban county, to take over all or a significant part of municipal services and functions, thus, in effect, acting as a metropolitan government in designated areas.
5. The transfer of functions to the state government, to relieve municipalities of heavy burdens particularly in those areas where burdens impinge differently on different governments within the metropolitan areas.
6. Metropolitan special districts, limited or multi-purpose, to operate as a separate level of government, and to allocate costs and services more rationally for the metropolitan area as a whole, for designated purposes.
7. Annexation and consolidation, to reduce the number of governments, and to create larger and more efficient units of government.

8. City-county separation, to divorce urban units of government from rural county government with a different orientation.

9. City-county consolidation, to broaden the rendition of city services and to extend the rendition of city services to the county as a whole, with concomitant resolution of disparities within the metropolitan county. Such consolidation may be a complete merger of governments into one, or a mere unification of some, but not all, of the functions of both governments.

10. Federation, or borough plan, to form a federal system of metropolitan government, with some functions assigned to the area-wide "metropolitan" government, and others remaining in the constituent parts of the federation.

Without a detailed discussion of the strengths and weaknesses of these devices, it is clear that (with the exception of voluntary metropolitan councils) all of them require constitutional amendments for their effectuation, at least in some states. All of the devices referred to have been attempted in some—usually very few—places; for most of them, therefore, experience is limited. None of the devices, moreover, achieve a fully integrated form of metropolitan government; in a sense, they are palliatives and generally recognized as such. Significantly, the most widely used device is the voluntary metropolitan council, probably because it is the least effective, and the least threatening. It does not require constitutional amendment; none of the participating local governments gives up any of its powers; none of its resolutions has any binding effect—and none of its activities appears to make much of a difference to the way local governments in metropolitan areas operate.

In discussing these, and a number of other devices, the 1968 National Commission on Urban Problems comments:

> Understandably, in view of the complex problems involved, none of these ameliorative devices has provided a dramatically effective solution to the difficulties encountered with governmental laycring and diffusion within metropolitan areas. Most of them involve some limitations or drawbacks, along with potential advantages. . . .[6]

Unfortunately, most of the efforts to reorganize metropolitan government have encountered public apathy. Since the turn of the century, fewer than half a dozen city-county consolidations have been successful, but several times that many were defeated at the polls.

> The likelihood of widespread major changes in local government arrangements within metropolitan areas appears dim indeed if one takes account only of the scanty records of past accomplishment on this score.[7]

---

[6] National Commission on Urban Problems, *Building the American City*, p. 333.
[7] National Commission on Urban Problems, *Building the American City*, p. 338.

CONSTITUTIONAL REVISION IN AID OF
METROPOLITAN REORGANIZATION

A small beginning in the right direction may, perhaps, be discerned in recent state constitutional developments. Most of the constitutional revision activities since the mid-forties have been in the direction of some lessening of state constitutional restrictions, both with respect to local powers and fiscal management. The 1947 New Jersey convention produced a document that has relatively few and rather broad fiscal limitations and that, by its silence on the subject, leaves local government entirely to be governed by the legislature—except that special bills to interfere with the internal affairs of local government are prohibited.

Alaska's 1959 constitution follows the Fordham-NML plan of shared powers and is entirely free from tax and debt limits, except for a referendum requirement for state and local debt. Hawaii, under its 1959 constitution, imposes a state debt limit, but leaves the matter of local government and local tax and borrowing powers to the legislature, with virtually no restrictions.

The Michigan constitution, which became effective in 1964, still retains restrictive fiscal provisions (including the prohibition of a graduated income tax), but it does provide for rather broad constitutional home rule powers for all local governments. Moreover, it provides that "notwithstanding any other provision" of the constitution, the legislature may provide for additional forms of government in metropolitan areas, preferably designed to perform multipurpose functions.

The 1967 New York convention, whose work failed to pass, contained a somewhat modified Fordham-NML shared power approach, providing the shared powers formula, as well as a number of enumerated powers, and reservation of powers to be retained by the legislature in a statute of restrictions. It also authorized the creation of a "regional governmental agency" by local law for New York City and one or two of its neighboring counties. But it also retained some of the old county office descriptions as well as a number of rigid fiscal limitations. In all, it offered a rather mixed bag.

The unsuccessful Rhode Island convention which ended in 1968 proposed a Fordham-NML shared power plan for local government, which was apparently not a factor in its defeat.

Particularly significant are the unsuccessful 1967–68 Maryland convention and the successful limited convention about the same time in Pennsylvania.

Perhaps the most forward looking of all of the proposals in the constitutional history of the 1960s was the document prepared by the Maryland convention. The proposal adopted the Fordham-NML shared power approach to local government powers, and made the county the main unit of government, giving it control of the creation of new, and the consolidation of old, local governments within its limits. The city of Baltimore is treated as a county. The establishment of multi-county governmental units and "popularly elected representative regional governments" was provided for, with the legislature having the power to determine by law whether to subject the creation of such regional governments to popular referendum. Fiscal limitations were left to the legislature. These provisions for local government arrangements were years ahead of any other existing state constitution; they were, in fact, one of the main reasons why the proposed Maryland constitution was defeated at the polls. The very possibility that the constitutional provisions might be used as a basis for governmental combinations that pulled the suburbs and the inner city more closely together was enough to defeat the constitution.

The Pennsylvania local government proposal, though considerably ahead of many other state constitutions with respect to permissible local government arrangements, was accepted and voted on affirmatively, on the other hand, precisely because on their face the new authorizations for local government presented no immediate threat. Adapting the Fordham-NML shared powers approach for home rule municipalities, the Pennsylvania constitution now also contains authorization for "area government"—to consist of two or more municipalities or parts thereof—to exercise municipal powers.

One aspect of the Pennsylvania proposal which deserves comment is the fact that although optional charter legislation is authorized, all existing county government arrangements are required to be included in any optional county government law as one of the available options—so that the political establishment was able to propose a forward moving model for the future while retaining reasonable assurances that counties that wanted to would be able to hold on to the patterns of the past.

Conclusion

Even if all the constitutional limitations were to fall tomorrow, it is unlikely that there would be any immediate change in the states' attitude toward the solution of urban problems. Constitutional change must be viewed as a prerequisite of effective state action, but it must be recognized that the establishment of a more favorable constitutional or legal climate would not in and of itself bring about needed change. Even if a state were to adopt the provisions of the Maryland constitution, there is, unfortunately, no reason to believe that the state legislature would make use of its new powers or that the suburbs would immediately join the inner city in a common effort. The evidence is to the contrary. Present constitutional limitations on the whole appear to reflect what the legislators in the state capitols and the people in the suburbs actually want. Proposals that authorize more effective state and local action seem to inspire fear, and the mere authorization of such action is viewed as dangerous. The constitutional restrictions seem at present to suit the mood of the states and of the localities, and, for the time being at least, we appear to have the state constitutions that we deserve.

Daniel R. Grant

3

Urban Needs and State Response: Local Government Reorganization

In groping for a rational response to the urban crisis it is only natural to turn first to the concept of urban reorganization. It seems to be inevitable that when we believe something is *basically* wrong, we begin to think in terms of "wrong" structures, "right" structures, and restructuring or reorganizing. When this happens, all roads lead to state government.

Reorganization roads have traditionally led to the state capitol because "the state giveth and the state taketh away" with respect to the structure of cities. It is no accident that American history is filled with accounts of human activity revolving around the doctrine of states' rights, but with very little corresponding activity concerning a doctrine of cities' rights. Under the federal Constitution, cities simply have no rights as cities, and their legal status is basically determined by the states. In spite of a growing network of direct and indirect communication lines between city governments and federal agencies, the city legally continues to be solely a creature of state

---

DANIEL R. GRANT, *Professor of Political Science and Director of the Urban Regional Development Center at Vanderbilt University, is president-designate of Ouachita Baptist University. He has been a consultant to various planning commissions and metropolitan area surveys and to the United States Advisory Commission on Intergovernmental Relations. He is author or co-author of several works including* Metropolitan Surveys, Political Dynamics of Environmental Control, *and* The States and the Metropolis.

government. Because the state may create or destroy cities, which are simply "municipal corporations," the state is all-powerful in matters of organization and reorganization. This is true, of course, of both urban and rural local governments.

Thus the governmental structure of cities is basically what the states have made it. Less obvious, but no less true, is the proposition that the government of metropolitan areas is what the states have made it or, perhaps more accurately, what the states have permitted it to become. It is important, however, to make a distinction between state-*city* relations and state-*metropolitan* relations since a city and a metropolitan area are not one and the same. As Professor Grad explains in the previous chapter, the city is a municipal corporation created by the state, possessing a charter spelling out its powers and responsibilities. On the other hand the metropolitan area is an economic-social-cultural community frequently three or more times the size of the core city and continuing to grow. The United States Bureau of the Census reports the existence of more than 230 of these "Standard Metropolitan Statistical Areas." Although they constitute the heart of American life, with two-thirds of the population living there, the metropolis is not a governmental entity. It is a happening still awaiting recognition by the state.

The distinction between state-city relations and state-metropolitan relations is therefore more than insignificant hair-splitting, even though popular journalistic treatment tends to use the terms synonymously. The distinction is basic, however, to the discussion which follows on the roles of the states in reorganizing local government.[1]

Relevance of Local Government Structure to Urban Problems

Before examining the role of the state in urban governmental reorganization it is important to consider first whether governmental structure is really relevant to significant urban problems. There was a time when its relevance was almost universally accepted by both political scientists and civic reformers. The only questions were which type of reorganization is "best" and how can it be sold to the voters. In more recent years serious questions have been raised con-

---

[1] At several points in this discussion the writer has followed closely his material in two other publications: Daniel R. Grant and H. C. Nixon, *State and Local Government in America*, Second Edition (Boston: Allyn and Bacon, Inc., 1968), and Lee S. Greene, Malcolm E. Jewell, and Daniel R. Grant, *The States and the Metropolis* (University, Alabama: University of Alabama Press, 1968). The writer is also indebted to William A. Moffitt and Lee Sigelman for research assistance in the preparation of this chapter.

cerning the fundamental importance or relevance of efforts to re-organize local government in metropolitan areas. In view of these questioning voices it might be well to summarize both the affirmative and negative cases.

THE AFFIRMATIVE CASE

The *fact* of metropolitan fragmentation is not in dispute. The 230-plus metropolitan areas are governed by more than 20,000 units of local government. Not every area is fragmented as badly as are the top ten in the United States which average close to 500 separate governments for each. But no metropolitan area is governed by only a single unit of government, and the average for all metropolitan areas is close to 90 separate governments.

Students of local government have contended for many years that governmental fragmentation in metropolitan areas is significantly related to a common set of problems. More than a decade ago 112 metropolitan surveys that had been conducted during a 30-year period were analyzed. Although they varied widely in sponsorship, purpose, methodology, and final recommendations, the surveys showed unusual agreement in setting forth a common set of problems which they attributed to the governmental patchwork quilt in the metropolis. These were not just *urban* problems, such as traffic congestion, crime, or slums; they were uniquely *metropolitan* problems said to be related to governmental fragmentation in the metropolitan area.

The common set of problems identified by the 112 metropolitan surveys includes: (1) the unequal distribution of financial resources and financial burdens between core city and suburbs, and between wealthier suburbs and poorer suburbs; (2) unequal service levels in different parts of the metropolitan area; (3) the absence of area-wide authority to cope with essentially area-wide problems; (4) wasteful duplication and inefficiency through the overlap and fractionalization of units of government within a single area; (5) the inability of citizens to fix responsibility and hold officials accountable for local government action or inaction; and (6) the political segregation of able suburban leaders from involvement in the most serious core-city problems. Although this latter problem did not show up in bold type in most of the 112 metropolitan surveys studied, it should be included as an emerging problem dramatized by both the accelerated war on poverty and the intensified racial tensions of recent years.

Voices continue to be strong in asserting the relevance of governmental fragmentation to the urban crisis. One spokesman for this point of view, Don Hummel, has contended that "if the United States fails to solve the problems of its cities, it will be due in large measure to the failure to modernize local government." He asserted that "nearly all local political jurisdictions lack the authority or the tax resources which will permit them to cope with area-wide problems." Another spokesman for the affirmative case has described the relevance of governmental structure as follows:

> Most of the major metropolitan areas in the United States will more than double their population before the next two decades are over. In the face of this onslaught, . . . the basic governmental structure extant in our metropolitan regions is organized in a most ancient and chaotic fashion. It is as if we had consciously determined to see that the whole thing cannot possibly, under any circumstance, work at all. The tragic thing, of course, is that we have not consciously faced up to this situation and sought to provide fundamental solutions. We have . . . sought to patch up, fix up and prop up a sagging and sorry system of government with quick remedy, ad hoc, special-purpose solutions to overwhelming problems and then only at a late date when these problems become so completely evident that they gain political attention by the sheer size and weight of their impending disruptiveness.[2]

Nelson Rockefeller has been on record for more than a decade as believing that "the metropolitan problem results from the collision of the irresistible forces of the second half of our century with the immovable forms and structures of the first half." Daniel P. Moynihan lent his support to the relevance of local government reorganization to urban problems when he stated in a 1969 address at Syracuse University, "At least part of the relative ineffectiveness of the efforts of urban government to respond to urban problems derives from the fragmented and obsolescent structure of urban government itself." The report of the National Commission on Urban Problems was highly critical of state abdication of zoning and code regulations to the many small units of government and asserted that these constitute "springboards for urban ills."

THE NEGATIVE CASE

Since political scientists have conducted most of the metropolitan surveys which provide the incriminating evidence against local government fragmentation, it is sometimes assumed that the "affirmative case" described above constitutes a kind of "party line" of political

[2] Harold F. Wise, "More Than Planning," *National Civic Review*, 55 (May 1966), p. 241.

scientists. Even if this assumption was once true—and it probably was not—it certainly has run into strong countervailing winds in recent years. Ostrom, Tiebout, and Warren have accused the metropolitan surveyors of arbitrarily jumping to the conclusion that many units of government are automatically bad and that a symmetrical organizational chart is automatically good. These writers question the assumption that "the multiplicity of political units in a metropolitan area is essentially a pathological phenomenon." [3]

Charles Adrian, in *Public Administration Review*, has mounted a strong attack on the assumptions of metropolitan reform advocates, primarily on grounds that such complaints as lack of efficiency and economy are of relatively little concern to the average voter and are rated as serious problems only by the reformers themselves. Adrian accuses metropolitan reformers of "almost total lack of concern with the political process and the probable ignorance . . . of the fact that a democratic public is a 'satisficing' public and not one concerned with optimum economy." He also attacks such assumptions as "the core city of a metropolitan area must 'expand or die' " and "a metropolitan area is a monolithic interest—a single community."

Martin Meyerson and Edward C. Banfield have expressed sharp disagreement with what they call the "crisis view" of the American metropolis. In their book, *Boston: The Job Ahead,* they deny any impending catastrophe for the metropolis and contend that the crisis view leads to "foolish and futile policy prescriptions."

James M. Banovetz, also in *Public Administration Review,* has dissented from the common charge that the core city subsidizes the suburbs because of fragmentation, and has expressed doubts that serious problems of subsidies even exist.

A much more recent argument against the relevance of metropolitan reorganization relates to the growing pressures for decentralization of government and community control, especially with respect to racial minorities. It is said that metropolitan reorganizers are running counter to the trends of this era, and that proposals for area-wide metropolitan government are basically in conflict with the needs and demands for neighborhood and community identification, involvement, and participation. Black power leaders, therefore, tend to feel little attraction to a proposed merger of a predominantly black core city with its predominantly white suburbs, not tending to see "metro" as a solution to the problems of the ghetto.

[3] Vincent Ostrom et al., "The Organization of Government in Metropolitan Areas: A Theoretical Inquiry," *American Political Science Review,* 55 (December 1961), p. 831.

CONTINUING RELEVANCE OF LOCAL GOVERNMENT STRUCTURE

Although the critics of metropolitan government reorganization proposals are persuasive in many respects, this writer believes that governmental fragmentation still constitutes one of the more serious obstacles to a rational attack on urban problems. It is scarcely conceivable that one could read the six or eight most recent major books on urban transportation without concluding that this is a *real* metropolitan problem and that it is clearly related to the fragmentation of local government. There is an ever-increasing outpouring of literature on such subjects as air pollution, water shortage, stream pollution, traffic and parking congestion, mass transit dilemmas and the host of problems related to racial and economic ghettos. History has not been kind to Meyerson and Banfield, whose book denouncing the "crisis view" of the American metropolis was published shortly before the urban riots in Watts, Detroit, Newark, Washington, and elsewhere.

The effects of governmental fragmentation upon urban renewal have been described very well by Scott Greer and David W. Minar:

> Urban renewal is limited by the dichotomy of public and private control, tension between federal and municipal agencies, division of power between different federal agencies, and fragmentation of power at the local community level. . . . At the metropolitan level, the multitude of jurisdictions—cities, towns, suburbs, special districts, counties, and even states—makes any over-all planning of the city a farce. . . . The central city-suburb schisms turn urban renewal into a holy war to recapture the suburban, white, middle class—a war the central city is doomed to lose—and distract attention from the major clientele of the central city: the working class, the ethnics, the disprivileged.[4]

While it is undoubtedly true that many and perhaps most Negro political leaders will oppose proposals for area-wide metropolitan government as schemes for diluting black political power, this constitutes no proof that reorganization is irrelevant to the problems of the ghetto. Indeed, what can be more relevant than the role of governmental fragmentation in creating artificial political walls between "black power" core city governments and "white power" suburban city governments at a time when ghetto problems cry out for joint efforts toward joint solutions? In *Metropolitan America,* a recent study of the fiscal aspects of metropolitanism, Alan Camp-

---

[4] Scott Greer and David W. Minar, "The Political Side of Urban Development and Redevelopment," *Annals of the American Academy of Political and Social Science,* 352 (March 1964), pp. 62, 67.

bell and Seymour Sacks contend that metropolitan fragmentation has serious consequences for the core city's education problem. They conclude:

> The need is for the concentration of educational resources in the central cities. It is in these cities that the educational function is most difficult to perform adequately. Yet the present system distributes resources in exactly the opposite direction, less where the problems are most severe and more where the problems are relatively easy to cope with.

The persistent distress signals from the cities are related too consistently to the fragmented condition of local government to dismiss fragmentation as an imaginary problem in the minds of "purist" academicians. This conclusion was thrust home by the almost pathetic testimony of Mayor Yorty of Los Angeles before a United States Senate subcommittee which was inquiring into the level of services provided in the Watts area. He responded quite accurately that many, and perhaps most, of the functions and services with which the senators were concerned were not the legal responsibility of the city of Los Angeles, but were split up between Los Angeles County, various school districts, special districts and authorities, and the state of California. To the average television viewer, the mayor seemed to have been evading the senators' questions; indeed, one senator remarked that the city of Los Angeles "does not stand for a damn thing." In fact, however, the offspring of metropolitan fragmentation had come home to roost, and the mayor's television performance merely dramatized the results.

A word of caution needs to be added to the general conclusion that local government structure is significantly relevant to an attack on urban problems. To say that governmental structure is relevant is not to say that structure is the *whole* urban problem, or even 50 percent of it. Governmental structure per se guarantees nothing. The voters can still elect incompetent mayors and councils, can still refuse to vote necessary tax increases, can still be misled by demagogues or blocked by conservative community leaders. Such things as financial resources, political leadership, community traditions, and an interested and informed citizenry are also vitally relevant to urban problems.

A more defensible position is that the structure of local government is perhaps ten percent of the problem, if a figure must be picked, but it is an important ten percent. To develop a sensible structure is to remove one important obstacle on the road to urban progress. It guarantees nothing but permits many things that would otherwise be impossible or a great deal more difficult.

The States and Urban Reorganization: A Historical View

Before considering prospects for the future, it is important to consider first what the states have done and failed to do with respect to efforts to reorganize urban government. State laws have been heavily involved in each of the four major devices proposed for significant structural changes in the government of growing urban areas. These four are *annexation, city-county consolidation, metropolitan federation,* and *special districts,* and the state's role in each will be described briefly.

ANNEXATION

Annexation has traditionally been the most commonly proposed remedy for the problems of suburban sprawl and fragmentation. The method was used by the nation's great cities in achieving their present size, and the case for it is strong, from the viewpoint of both the suburbs and the core city. Certain expensive services could be provided at a lower cost than by the suburbs alone; property values would rise; fire protection would be better and fire insurance rates would be lower; voting privileges in central city elections could be secured; the base for financing municipal government would be broadened; the city would bring about a suburban development consistent with its own; and it would be possible to make a unified, area-wide attack on such metropolitan problems as disease, transportation, crime, slums, and juvenile delinquency. Annexation prevents the beautiful, affluent, and independent suburb of Azalea Heights from saying, "We solve our problems of poverty out here; why don't you in downtown Gutter City solve *your* problems of poverty?"

Notwithstanding these persuasive arguments, it has been virtually impossible for the larger cities in the past few decades to keep pace by means of annexation with the population growth beyond its borders. Opposition to annexation is almost always strong in the suburbs, with any one of several arguments being sufficient to secure a negative referendum vote: higher taxes, a corrupt or incompetent central city government, false promises on the delivery of services, and annexation as a devious tax-grabbing scheme. If it has become difficult to annex unincorporated suburbs, it has become virtually impossible for a central city to annex a suburb that is already separately incorporated. Boston, for example, has never been able to annex Brookline, Newton, and Milton. Pittsburgh is surrounded by 181 municipalities, and Detroit by 72. Minneapolis became completely surrounded by incorporated cities between 1940 and 1950. In short, annexation is virtually dead in the older and larger metropolitan areas, particularly in the North and East, as a device for permitting a city to keep up with its growth. State requirements for popular referendum in the area to be annexed are most often cited as the major roadblock.

Annexation is still commonly used by smaller cities, and even by larger cities in some sections of the United States. Several Texas cities have been able to take advantage of home rule charters which permit them to annex by a vote of the city council without a vote of the residents of either the city or the fringe area. Some of the largest annexations in the United States in the past decade have been carried out by Houston, Dallas, Fort Worth and San Antonio. The most spectacular annexations are those by Oklahoma City which has added approximately 553 square miles since 1959. Its 641.1 square miles place it ahead of Los Angeles (463.6) and Houston (446.7) in total city growth achieved by annexation. The state of Virginia has long had a more liberal annexation procedure than most by virtue of its provision for a special annexation court which judges the merits of each attempt, rather than allowing the voters of the city or suburbs to make the decision. The Tennessee General Assembly in 1955 adopted an annexation procedure which borrowed from both Texas and Virginia. It authorizes annexation by a vote of the city council of the core city, subject to appeal to court for approval or disapproval based on standards of community welfare and progress.

In spite of liberalized annexation procedures in these and other states, the overall picture in the 50 states is one of extreme difficulty in using the prescribed state ground rules to accomplish annexation. What was once the natural and common method of achieving area-wide urban government has now fallen predominantly into disuse except in the case of the newer and smaller cities in the United States. Whether this can be laid entirely to the states' restrictive annexation procedures is the subject of some dispute. Certainly there are other factors involved, but most students of local government contend that annexation procedures must bear a considerable part of the blame. Robert Connery and Richard Leach, for example, have argued that one of the principal reasons why the number of governments in southern metropolitan areas has been kept relatively low is that annexation has been easier in the South than elsewhere. A study by Thomas R. Dye sought to test this hypothesis in a large number of attempted annexations, but concluded that the ease or difficulty of annexation procedures under controlling statutes does

not appear to be predictive of annexation, that is, that the permissiveness of the annexation law is not closely associated with success
in annexation. This kind of study, however, apparently fails to take
into consideration the "intimidating effect" of restrictive state statutes that discourage cities from even trying to annex suburban
areas. So it would seem that there is hardly evidence yet to justify
the rather cynical position that liberal annexation procedures do
not facilitate the achievement of annexation in a given state.

CITY-COUNTY CONSOLIDATION

One of the older devices for restructuring local government is the
extension of a city's boundaries to make them coterminous with the
county boundaries and the consolidation of the two governments
into a single unit. It has been alleged that this provides not only the
advantages of annexation but also eliminates one of the major
sources of duplication and buck-passing. Although probably not an
important consideration until more recent decades, a contemporary
advantage given for city-county consolidation is the capacity of a city
to control the development of its rural-urban fringe area.

The obstacles and complications to city-county consolidation are
legion, and most of them have to do with state restrictions over local
government which simply do not fit the new structure. Constitutional requirements for county officers, tax rates, methods of electing
officials, debt limits, and many other provisions have either inhibited
cities and counties from making the consolidation effort, or have
caused countless headaches over court litigation following its adoption. Such obstacles have caused political scientists on several occa-
sions to pronounce city-county consolidation as a thing of the past,
for such museum pieces as Philadelphia, New Orleans, or New York.
However, city-county consolidation refuses to honor its funeral ora-
tions, as evidenced by the merger of Baton Rouge and East Baton
Rouge Parish (1947), Nashville and Davidson County (1962), Jacksonville and Duval County (1967), and Indianapolis and Marion
County (1969).

In each of these cases the state had a vital role to play although
it was, for the most part, a permissive role. In the case of the 1947
partial merger between the city of Baton Rouge and East Baton
Rouge Parish, the role of the state was limited to legislative authorization for a referendum on a constitutional amendment. The
amendment, passed in 1946 in a state-wide referendum, provided for
the creation of a city-parish charter commission. A charter was
drafted by the commission and in 1947 was adopted by a simple

majority of those voting in a parish-wide referendum (7,012 to 6,705). While the role of the state of Louisiana was basically a permissive one, it should be noted that the Baton Rouge plan would undoubtedly have been defeated if the state had required two separate majorities—inside and outside the city—as is so often the case. The resulting consolidation was not a complete one, with an interlocking-directorate device used to make the city's governing body constitute the majority of the parish's governing body. A differential tax rate was provided for three separate districts—urban, industrial, and rural.

Nashville and Davidson County voters in 1962 adopted a single metropolitan government to replace the existing city and county. While it was in many respects traditional city-county consolidation, the proposal was tailor-made to the unique needs of the Nashville metropolitan area. Residents of an expandable "urban services district" receive a higher level of services and a higher tax rate than do those who live in the outer fringe. Most services are labeled "area-wide," however, and are financed by an area-wide "general services district" tax. As in the case of Louisiana, the role of the state of Tennessee was primarily permissive and passive in the development and adoption of Nashville's metro government. However, Tennessee's involvement extended over a longer period of time and into a greater variety of activities. For example, a metropolitan study in 1952 recommended annexation rather than city-county consolidation, primarily because it was felt that the state's constitutional obstacles to consolidation were too great. In 1953 Tennessee's constitution (said to be the oldest unamended constitution in the world) was amended in several ways, including an authorization for the state legislature to provide for city-county consolidation.

Tennessee's enabling legislation for Nashville's metro government, passed in 1957 and amended in 1961, was basically treated as "local legislation," although for constitutional purposes it was made to apply to the four metropolitan counties in the state. Thus it was sold to legislators more nearly as a "local bill" than as urban policy good for the state as a whole. Nevertheless, the state did pass the enabling legislation recommended by the local planning commission in its 1956 "Plan of Metropolitan Government for Nashville and Davidson County." It in effect became state metropolitan policy for Tennessee, because efforts have been made in each of the four metropolitan counties to adopt the authorized form of government. Only in Nashville and Davidson County was the vote favorable and even here the 1962 victory was preceded by a 1958 defeat. The constitutional amendment requires separate majority approval inside and outside the city. Perhaps more important than the state legislature's role in Tennessee has been the favorable action of the state judiciary. The predicted quagmire of litigation and unsympathetic court decisions simply failed to materialize and Nashville's metropolitan experiment has received very sympathetic treatment on most major court tests.

Jacksonville, Florida, became the third post-war case of city-county consolidation in 1967 when voters approved a merger with Duval County. Following a series of financial and political crises in city and county government a study commission recommended to the Duval County delegation to the state legislature a "Blueprint for Improvement" patterned in many ways after the Nashville metro plan. "Metro" was considered to be a dirty word in Florida because of its controversial association with Miami government, and the word "consolidation" was used instead. Again, the legislature's action was in the form of local legislation, in effect requiring only the approval of the Duval delegation. The city-county consolidation charter was actually drafted by the delegation and approved subject to a single majority vote in the whole county. The charter was adopted by a decisive two-to-one majority in August 1967. Tampa and Hillsboro County, without any serious financial or political crisis dramatizing the case for metropolitan reform, had rejected overwhelmingly a similar consolidation proposal earlier in 1967.

The most recent city-county consolidation, and the first in a northern metropolitan area in this century, was approved by the Indiana General Assembly early in 1969 for Indianapolis and Marion County. More intriguing even than the name chosen for the consolidated government (UNIGOV) is the fact that the merger was enacted by the state legislature *without a referendum*. While this constitutes a sharp departure from traditional state ground rules for consolidation, tradition was at least honored with respect to permitting constitutional county officers and incorporated satellite cities and towns to continue their separate existence. Effective date for the merger was set for January 1, 1970.

States have made available with varying degrees of permissiveness two half-a-loaf alternatives to city-county consolidation. One of these is functional consolidation, or the merger of a single service or activity being performed separately by a city and county. A great deal of this has taken place in the past and will undoubtedly continue as ad hoc situations bring appropriate pressures to bear. Whether the consolidation of schools or health for a single metropolitan area contributes to or detracts from the prospects for eventual overall consolidation is the subject of much debate, but most reform advocates agree that it is a lot better than nothing. On a somewhat broader scale the "municipalized county" is recommended as a means of achieving considerably more coordination in a metropolitan area than might otherwise be possible. This involves moving toward the county provision of urban services for those parts of the county unable to provide for themselves, and in many cases the provision of area-wide services. It does not involve the consolidation of units of government, however.

In both of these cases, functional consolidation and the municipalized county, the role of the state has been predominantly passive, moving to provide enabling legislation from time to time when urban pressures become strong enough and the political opposition does not seem to be heavy.

METROPOLITAN FEDERATION

Still another device commonly proposed, but almost never adopted, for restructuring local government in metropolitan areas is the metropolitan federation. The logical, common-sense case for the federated metropolis is a strong one. Based upon a rough analogy to the relationship between the national government and the states the metropolitan federation would consist of an area-wide government to perform those functions which transcend municipal boundaries, and of component municipalities which would perform purely local functions. Federation has often been proposed for the larger and older metropolitan areas where annexation has been found politically infeasible or otherwise undesirable, and where city-county consolidation is inappropriate or unacceptable. It is argued that the metropolitan federation provides for the best of both worlds—(a) grass roots, community control and (b) area-wide decision making, research utilization, and administration in those cases where the larger community interest is vital.

In general, state governments have done very little either to encourage or permit the establishment of metropolitan federations in the United States. One of the more infamous cases of state foot-dragging occurred in the late 1920s when Pittsburgh and Allegheny County seemed clearly ready to establish a metropolitan federation. Last minute legislative maneuvering made it necessary to secure a two-thirds majority vote in a majority of the municipalities in the county in order to obtain adoption. In a landmark referendum in metropolitan history, in June 1929, the proposed charter was defeated in Allegheny County because it failed to secure a two-thirds vote in a majority of municipalities. The overall vote was highly favorable, 87,847 to 40,973, but it obtained a two-thirds majority in only 48 municipalities, whereas 62 were needed.

The best known examples of metropolitan federation are the governments of Greater London and Metropolitan Toronto. In each case the structure was established by Act of Parliament without the requirement of a popular referendum of any kind. The Toronto federation was created by the provincial parliament in 1953, consisting of the city of Toronto and its 12 suburban satellite cities. It was actually a compromise between complete amalgamation (annexation), proposed by the city of Toronto, and complete independence as strongly defended by the suburban cities. The result was a legislatively imposed two-tier government with selected area-wide functions being allocated to the central government. After more than ten years of operation a Royal Commission on Metropolitan Toronto recommended in 1965 additional centralization of certain functions as well as the merger of the 13 cities into only four. Only part of these recommendations were accepted by the provincial government, and effective in 1967, the 13 cities were merged into six, and welfare administration and much of school operating costs became responsibilities of the metro government. The active and authoritative role of the provincial government in systematically restructuring local government in a metropolitan area is, for the most part, unheard of in contemporary American state government.

The closest thing to metropolitan federation which we have in the United States is the metro government of Dade County and Miami. Voters there narrowly adopted (44,404 to 42,619) in 1957 a two-tiered form of metropolitan government which incorporates, to a limited degree, the principle of federation. The heart of this plan is the retention of the existing municipalities—Miami plus 27 suburban cities—to perform purely local functions, and the allocation of "essentially metropolitan" functions to Dade County. Political opposition and financial limitations have made it impossible for Dade County to assume anything like the package of area-wide functions hoped for by the original advocates. In practice, Dade County's metro is more nearly a "municipalized county" than it is a federation of municipalities, since the cities as such are not represented on the board of commissioners. But even with its lawsuits, recurring referendum fights, and financial limitations, this new approach to governing a metropolitan area has offered new hope and has stimulated the imagination of many other cities.

Once more, in the case of Florida and the Dade County metro, the role of the state involved a stand-pat, show-me attitude toward the area seeking reform. Constitutional and legislative changes were made grudgingly and many would say inadequately, and only when local pressures became strong enough. Dade County's financial difficulty relates to a state court decision refusing to grant the new metro government the financial powers of both a city and a county. As a result it is obligated to perform both city and county functions with, for the most part, only the taxing authority of a county.

FRAGMENTATION BY SPECIAL DISTRICTS

By far the most popular reorganization device, as measured by adoptions, is the special district, a separate unit of government created with boundary lines drawn to coincide with the boundaries of the problems to be solved. It must be created upon proper authorization by the state, but the procedure prescribed is often far more simple than that of creating a municipal corporation, and usually requires no vote by the residents of the area affected. It is easy to see why special metropolitan districts, limited to a single function of government, are so popular. Very little difficulty is experienced in using this device to cross seemingly insurmountable political boundary lines. For example, the Golden Gate Bridge and Highway District is a unit of government with a territorial jurisdiction including all five San Francisco Bay area counties, all of another county, and part of a seventh. Normal opposition to metropolitan reorganization proposals by professional politicians is considerably eased because special districts usually eliminate no jobs and seldom disturb the organization's grip on city hall. When it comes to suburban politicians, ad hoc authorities are exceedingly popular because they lessen the pressure for annexation to the core city.

Special districts are often created for financial reasons, such as enabling an existing unit of government to evade established tax and debt limits, or for equalizing the tax burden over an area wider than that of existing units. Finally, special interest groups almost universally prefer the independent-authority approach for their "pet function" of government over having it integrated with the rest of the city or county government. Thus, transit people prefer mass transit to be operated by an independent authority, parks people prefer the park and recreation system to be operated by an independent authority, public housing people prefer that low-cost public housing be operated by an independent authority, and so on *ad infinitum*. Special districts are consistent with the desire of specialized groups of citizens to watch one function of government very carefully, to the exclusion of all other functions, and this gives strong impetus to the multiplication of special-district government in the United States.

In very limited terms and context a strong case can be made for the special district as a useful device in helping to govern the metropolis. From a broader perspective, however, special districts are vulnerable to serious criticism on a number of scores. Such districts frequently reduce geographic fragmentation for a particular function at the expense of complicating the problem of functional fragmentation—that is, the problem of administering closely related functions in separate watertight compartments. They actually add to the layers of government and make it more difficult for citizens to hold their government accountable. States have generally ignored the problem of supervising the work of special districts and have left the problem of public accountability for such authorities for the most part unanswered. Roscoe C. Martin has sharply criticized the widespread use of special districts, listing several ill effects: it separates the program from the mainstream of city affairs; it purports to "remove the program from politics" but in actuality it tends to replace the general politics of the city with a more narrow, less visible, less public politics of a special clientele; and, finally, it "tends to atomize local government," making comprehensive planning of local programs a virtual impossibility.[5]

Alan Campbell has cited another tendency inherent in the state's open-door policy toward the creation of single-purpose units of government. He suggests that the purpose selected in the creation of a special district is usually more related to the "hardware services" of government—transportation, water supply, and sewage disposal, rather than to the "software services"—education, health or welfare. Apparently the necessity for broader jurisdictions to provide hardware services is more clear-cut, and, furthermore, they are the kinds of services demanded by the more politically powerful middle and high-income voters. Campbell also suggests that software services do not so obviously require crossing governmental boundaries and do not possess political support as do the other services.

A SUMMARY EVALUATION

In summary, the role of the state in meeting metropolitan area pressures for local government reorganization has been predomi-

[5] Roscoe C. Martin, *The Cities and the Federal System* (New York: Atherton Press, 1965), pp. 178–179.

nantly negative, grudging, road-blocking, or simply indifferent in its general stance. The specific roadblocks to local government reorganization are seldom the same in any two states, but the categories of roadblocks can be counted on as existing in the overwhelming majority of states. Referendum requirements, for example, are almost always a difficult hurdle to get over, either in the type of majority required, the number of separate majorities required, or the time and frequency of elections required or permitted. Such requirements may have made sense in the days of an overwhelmingly agricultural and rural or small town society, but are hardly attuned to the contemporary realities of complex, interdependent metropolitan areas. Similarly, the rigidity of constitutional requirements affecting local government officers—their method of selection, term of office, duties, compensation and their "mergeability" with other offices—is a characteristic in whole or in part of the reorganization difficulties faced by most cities in the United States. State governments, either passively or actively, have been a party to arbitrary limitations on local government taxes, indebtedness, powers, and administrative structure, as well as on changes related to annexation and consolidation.

Small wonder, then, that state governments have been on the receiving end of sharp criticism and broad-gauged attack as either obstructionist or irrelevant to modern urban problems and needs. An oft-cited article by Charles Press and Charles Adrian, "Why Our State Governments Are Sick" (*Antioch Review*), is a case in point, with the argument being made that "state government is suffering from an overdose of the small-town political ideology, a viewpoint that no longer is appropriate for contemporary society and business." They contend that the major deficiency among decision makers for state government is "timeliness." Alan Campbell has summarized the negligence of states with respect to local reorganization as follows:

> On the whole, the states have not seen it as their function to encourage basic governmental reorganization at the local level. They have, in some instances, aided the establishment of advisory regional planning authorities and, on occasion, have permitted the establishment of metropolitan-wide functional districts. With one or two exceptions, however, these actions have never been taken in order to bring about a basic new governmental system at the local level.[6]

Even a state governor has agreed with this basic indictment of this

[6] Alan K. Campbell, "States at the Crossroads," *National Civic Review*, 55 (November 1966), p. 559.

particular role of the states: "Municipal or local governments, of course, are the creatures of the state; and it is in this area that the states presumably could make the greatest contribution. And yet, it is interesting to note that it is here that the states have done the least." [7]

Even when there has been an apparent response by the state to urban pressures for help, the state seems to have been unaware that many of its actions in reality complicate the overall urban problem rather than alleviate it. For example, as Campbell has pointed out in the article quoted above, both federal and state aid programs frequently support the inadequate status quo of local governmental structure by providing financial assistance to what would otherwise be ineffective and uneconomic units. The tendency of state assistance to a specific function to result in the creation of special districts with their many independent islands of authority has already been mentioned. Finally, even when the states have passed reorganization enabling legislation which is entirely permissive in character, experience indicates that far more is needed in most cases than mere permission. Indeed, permissive legislation is often publicized by the press so effectively as a solution to the problem that it is harder for reform leaders to sustain the necessary spirit of urgency in their movement for reorganization. States should have had enough experience to know that permissive legislation alone is not enough to achieve widespread local government reorganization. Only where a systematic combination of "carrots and sticks" has been developed and used, such as for the massive consolidation of school districts throughout the United States, has significant reorganization been achieved.

It does not seem unfair to say that state government decision makers have not really been sufficiently interested in a systematic restructuring of the government of metropolitan areas.

Prospects for Affirmative State Role in
Restructuring Urban Government

If one were to use the past as a basis for forecasting the future role of the state in local government reorganization, the prospects for a new, affirmative role would be exceedingly dim. But not all of the signs are negative. Some things are beginning to happen in some states that offer some encouragement, and it is important to look at

[7] Philip H. Hoff, Governor of Vermont, speech to the National Conference on Public Administration of the American Society for Public Administration, Miami Beach, May 21, 1969.

these before making a final assessment of the prospects. These are things which constitute a break with the traditional, passive, rural-oriented stance of state government toward urban reorganization.

NEW STATE INITIATIVE

Beginning with less coercive devices and proceeding to more coercive or authoritative ones, the discussion which follows presents a wide spectrum of state approaches to urban reorganization.

Special State Study Commissions—Increasingly in recent years state legislatures or state governors, or both, have created special ad hoc study commissions to focus exclusively on the question of the adequacy of local government organization in large urban and metropolitan areas. Connecticut, for example, established a "Commission to Study the Necessity and Feasibility of Metropolitan Government." While it reported in 1967 that metropolitan government was neither necessary nor feasible in that state, much of the commission's thinking was incorporated into an enabling law establishing a State Department of Community Affairs. About the same time, the Virginia legislature created the Virginia Metropolitan Areas Study Commission which recommended a multiple and flexible approach to the problem of governing metropolitan areas. The state of Texas commissioned the Texas Research League to conduct a metropolitan area study of that state's 22 metropolitan areas. Its report in 1967 gave strong emphasis to the role of intergovernmental cooperation and regional planning, and urged state encouragement and financial assistance to the creation and operation of councils of government.

Other urban study commissions have been created primarily on the initiative of state governors, as in the case of the Michigan and Washington governors, or in the form of joint legislative committees, such as in California in 1967. The latter was charged with the responsibility of making recommendations concerning a regional government for the San Francisco Bay area.

State Offices of Local Government—There seems to be a rapidly growing consensus in state government circles that all states should have some kind of agency for local affairs. The rapid birth rate of such agencies since 1960 has been one of the more dramatic and visible manifestations of growing state recognition of their increasing urban responsibilities. Close to 20 such agencies had been created by 1968, but only five of these were established prior to 1966. Their names and forms vary considerably from state to state, including such titles as State Department of Community Affairs, State Department of Urban Development, State Office of Local

Affairs, Governor's Assistant for Urban Affairs, and Office of Intergovernmental Cooperation.

Tennessee's Municipal Technical Advisory Service, established in 1949, is one of the earliest and most highly developed of its kind, but it has been more oriented toward university assistance to cities than state-level coordination of governmental programs. The New Jersey Department of Community Affairs is one of the most ambitious, receiving an appropriation of six million dollars for the 1968 fiscal year and a governor's recommendation for more than twice that amount for 1969. Objective observers of the growth of these new agencies are careful to warn against any assumption that the mere establishment of such an office means that a state is becoming actively involved in the solution of urban problems. One New York observer, for example, has pointed out that that state has such an office but its perception of its role seems to be the preservation of the status quo rather than the introduction of basic governmental changes. Its reports demonstrate strong interest in protecting the present local jurisdictional system in the state of New York. Commissioner Kolesar comments on these agencies at greater length in Chapter 5.

State Encouragement of COGs and Metropolitan Planning— States have generally been very receptive to the newest form of cooperation in the metropolis—the voluntary association of local governments. These councils of governments (COGs) usually consist of a council of elected officials designed to facilitate discussion and study of common problems. Some of the earliest ones were organized in Detroit (1954), New York (1956), and Washington, D.C. (1957). The Association of Bay Area Governments (shortened to an unromantic ABAG) was organized in the San Francisco area in 1961 and moved vigorously into the field of regional planning. The COGs got their big boost from the federal government—not from the states—when the United States Housing and Urban Development Act of 1965 authorized financial assistance for planning, and when the 1966 Demonstration Cities and Metropolitan Development Act required that certain applications for federal aid must be approved by a designated area-wide planning agency.

With only nine COGs at the end of 1965 the number has risen steadily so that the number in mid-1969 was variously estimated at more than 100, depending on the definition. The COG is alternately praised by its advocates as the wave of the future and viewed by its opponents as a toothless tiger or—even worse—a protector of the inadequate status quo. It seems clear that a COG can be anything from an Elks Lodge to the beginning of a potent metropolitan government.

Liberalization of Annexation Procedures—Laws to make it easier for central cities to annex the surrounding suburban fringe have been passed by a few states in recent years. It is sufficient to provide a spark of hope for more liberalized annexation procedures but is hardly widespread enough to be classed as a strong trend. In addition to the example of several states cited earlier, the state of Oregon has recently moved to encourage annexation. This new law authorizes cities to annex contiguous territory without an election or consent petitions upon a showing to the State Board of Health that a condition exists in the land to be annexed which poses a threat to the public health, and which could be alleviated by city services. No state has seriously tackled the job of annexing suburbs which are already separately incorporated, however.

Stricter Controls on Separate Incorporations—Closely related to the problem of core-city annexation of its suburbs is the state's policy toward the separate incorporation of these satellite cities. An increasing number of states are beginning to discourage this proliferation in the proximity of existing cities, and particularly in the case of large core cities in metropolitan areas. Ohio has imposed a number of more restrictive standards and, in addition, has required new incorporations to have the approval of the legislative bodies of all municipalities located within three miles of the proposed new city. Florida has increased the minimum number of freeholders required for the establishment of an incorporated municipality from 150 to 1,000. Tennessee's enabling legislation for metropolitan governments for its four major cities and counties prohibits any new incorporations in the county between the time of the establishment of a metropolitan government charter commission and the referendum on the charter itself. If metropolitan government is adopted, all future incorporations are prohibited.

More States Looking with Favor on County Home Rule—The role of the county in governing the metropolis has become increasingly prominent in the thinking of students of government, primarily because it has one thing that central cities and suburban cities do not have. This is what is known in the jargon as "adequate areal jurisdiction" but perhaps "space" is just as accurate a description. In addition, as Norman Beckman has pointed out, the county has high political feasibility—it exists, therefore it is feasible—and does not raise the usual fears of creating new units of government. The major difficulty in adapting county government to urban pressures and needs is its traditional horse-and-buggy administrative organization, representational structure, and powers, and this is where state government comes in. An increasing number of states, although still only a minority of the 50, have enacted legislation permitting county home rule, an essential first step in the development of a "municipalized county."

State Cooperation with City-County Consolidation Efforts—In view of the long half century of silence on the city-county consolidation front, the recent activity involving Nashville, Jacksonville, and Indianapolis can only be looked upon as a "rash of adoptions." To be sure, they constitute only a drop in the bucket, but it would not be safe to dismiss this activity lightly. The states' involvement in these consolidations, as indicated earlier, has been limited primarily to passive cooperation but this, too, is favorable by comparison with earlier eras. One can only speculate on how many additional consolidations might be achieved if states should replace the policy of passive cooperation with a more aggressive policy of carrot-and-stick incentives.

State Assumption of Urban Functions—One way of achieving area-wide administration of urban functions in badly fragmented metropolitan areas is simply for the state to assume responsibility for such functions. In one sense of the word this is actually *replacing* local government rather than reorganizing it. However, in the heavily populated but geographically small states, such as Massachusetts or Connecticut, it can be argued that state government itself is local government. Indeed, Martin Meyerson and Edward Banfield have pointed out that four-fifths of the Massachusetts people already live in metropolitan areas, and they find it hard to see how the state can fail to become "the equivalent, for all practical purposes, of eight or more metropolitan governments." Over a period of several decades Massachusetts has already become heavily involved in the operation of metropolitan service districts for the Boston area, and similar examples can be found in other states.

REQUISITES FOR AN AGGRESSIVE STATE POLICY

None of the foregoing "bright spots" really constitute what can be called a sharp break with the past. They do not constitute, either in whole or in part, a truly progressive and innovative approach to the problem of urban reorganization, especially at a time when the twin pressures for centralization and decentralization in the government of metropolitan areas are increasing.

It is a useful exercise on occasion to ignore political realities and ask the question, "What kind of state policy would provide the urban reorganization called for to cope with the problems of metropolitan fragmentation?" Assuming, of course, that metropolitan fragmentation is one of the obstacles to dealing effectively with the urban crisis, what are the requisites of a "rational" approach by state governments to urban reorganization? Ideally, state governments would create single, expandable, area-wide units of government for each metropolitan community. Smaller, viable sub-governments would be retained where necessary to protect important values of local diversity and to provide a sense of small community representation in the larger metropolitan government. The state would abolish all other units of local government within a metropolitan area. A problem would remain for those metropolitan areas or functions which so seriously spill over area or state boundary lines as to make administration by a single metropolitan government unfeasible. In such cases state or federal assumption of responsibility (in whole or in part) would be required. As unrealistic as all of this may seem, particularly in contrast to the traditional role of state government, it consists of little more than changing governmental structure to conform to the realities of community structure in the United States.

The clear need is for social invention. If the American inventive genius has in the past been able to produce such governmental innovations as a Marshall Plan, a TVA, or an agricultural extension system to meet the challenges of particular eras, we should ask why it is any less reasonable to seek such innovation for the governance of the metropolis.

The two components required for effective state involvement in local government reorganization relate to ends and means. The state government needs a clear official statement of goals or objectives to achieve in the reorganization of local government for urban areas. Based on assumptions concerning the undesirability of local government fragmentation these goals would approximate the "ideal type" described above—a single, expandable, area-wide government for each metropolitan community, combined with viable sub-governments as reasonably required to provide a sense of small community participation.

The second component, related to means or methods of achievement of the goals, is even more critical than the first. An effective incentive system for the reorganization of local government is the *sine qua non* for getting from where we now are to where we would like to be. Political invention of the highest order is required to develop a system of carrots and sticks to achieve the necessary reorganization. Canadian and British experience in reorganizing metropolitan area government without resorting to local referenda might seem very un-American to us, but realism requires the admission that this may be the only effective means. Much of the successful consolidation of school districts in the United States, with all the agonies of the merger of sacred little red school houses, has been achieved without popular referenda. These decisions were no less directly related to the political grass roots than are the current issues of consolidating units of government in metropolitan areas. It is difficult to see why the school-district consolidation procedure should be deemed either un-American or politically unfeasible when applied to the problem of metropolitan fragmentation of general-purpose units of government.

ASSESSING THE PROSPECTS

What are the prospects for achieving aggressive and innovative state involvement in the job of reorganizing local government in metropolitan areas on some kind of systematic, rational basis? Most of the evidence points to poor prospects, particularly in the states of the Northeast, where the hardening of the local government arteries is most severe. New York is probably fairly typical of the northeastern states' attitude toward local governmental reorganization, and Alan Campbell described the lack of support for structural change as follows:

> My own experience as chairman of the Local Government Committee at the New York State Constitutional Convention convinced me that in New York, at least, there is no grass roots demand for general governmental reorganization. Local officials who testified before the committee nearly all supported the status quo. Testimony for major change came only from a few good government groups, and the CED and the National Association of Counties. It is interesting to note that the support of the National Association of Counties was not followed by the State's County Officers Association. (*Address at State University of New York.*)

Prospects in other parts of the United States are probably not so poor as in the Northeast, although there is little cause for optimism, either. The voters in several states have had the opportunity in recent years to adopt new constitutions with provisions designed to facilitate local government reorganization, but have voted them down. It is possible to prove too much from this kind of evidence because many other issues were involved besides local government reorganization. However, the performance of the voters certainly provides no encouragement to advocates of structural change.

The best political guess for the future role of states in local government reorganization is a highly mixed bag with contents varying all the way from states which continue the present tradition of grudging involvement and passive indifference, to a small and select group of states which take the bull by the horns and restructure metropolitan area government much along the lines laid down by the Canadian province of Ontario. Inadequate concern by the states can be expected to lead increasingly to pressure for federal guidelines —as prerequisites for federal aid—calling for a rational structure of local government in metropolitan areas. The increasingly interstate character of metropolitan areas spilling over state boundary lines will continue to strengthen the prima facie case for intervention by the federal government in some form.

A realistic if somewhat pessimistic view of the future in store for local government in metropolitan areas is evolution in the direction of many headless and formless "intergovernmental megalopolities." These would consist of a network of special districts, some single-purpose and some multi-purpose, several counties with increasing but segmental responsibilities, an assorted spectrum of public and private utility-type enterprises, and an elaborate variety of cooperative arrangements with higher governmental levels. Suburban city halls would remain scattered here and there, along with an occasional core city hall, but they would be stripped of many of their former responsibilities and would certainly not be "where the action is." The prospects are good for functional fragmentation to join geographic fragmentation as a major structural problem with autonomous special-purpose authorities looking vertically to state and national agencies for leadership, financial support, and administrative guidelines.

This writer believes that a rational restructuring of local government for metropolitan areas would be far more desirable than the intergovernmental jungle just described. While the political prospects are poor for such a rational goal, it is not an impossible task and the stakes make it well worth the effort. If the states put their minds and wills to it, not a single metropolitan area should be classified as hopelessly fragmented beyond restructuring. Certainly the British parliament was unwilling to accept this verdict for metropolitan London. But even if the top 20 cities in the United States are marked off as hopelessly fragmented, this leaves over 200 remaining as fit subjects for a rational restructuring of local government.

So long as the concept of an inter-dependent metropolitan community still has meaning to the majority of inhabitants in a metropolitan area, it seems elementary to argue that the development of some instrument of area-wide community decision making is not only reasonable but essential to meaningful local democracy. Such a goal for the 1970s constitutes a worthy challenge for state government decision makers.

Roy W. Bahl

4

State Taxes, Expenditures and the Fiscal Plight of the Cities

Urban governments are continuously beset with fiscal difficulties. Simply put, not enough money is generated by local tax bases to meet the immense public service needs which have resulted from metropolitan growth. Naturally, attention turned to the federal and state governments to bail the cities out of this dilemma. And surely the growth of American urbanization is forcing a reorientation of state and federal policy—one that will require at least state government to become urban government. But the certainty of this future pattern notwithstanding, the historical, and indeed current, effectiveness of state government in contributing to resolution of the great fiscal difficulties which accompany urban growth has been, on the whole, woefully poor.

Although a historical view is necessary to understand why state government has not responded more effectively, the main purpose of this chapter is to present an anatomy for state fiscal action. But meaningful prescription requires concise definition, hence we

Roy W. Bahl *is an economist in the Fiscal Affairs Department of the International Monetary Fund. (But the views expressed in this chapter are his own.) Prior to his present assignment, he was a Post Doctoral Fellow in Urban Economics at Syracuse University and Assistant Professor of Economics at West Virginia University. He has written extensively on state and local government public finance and is the author of* Metropolitan City Expenditures: A Comparative Analysis.

begin by dichotomizing the urban fiscal problem in terms of a *balance* and a *level* component.

A fiscal imbalance exists within a certain Standard Metropolitan Statistical Area (SMSA) when the ratio between available tax resources and expenditure requirements is not the same for all political units. Because of governmental fragmentation, the resources-requirements ratio is now weighted, in general, favorably for suburbs and unfavorably for core cities.

The level problem refers to that part of the urban fiscal crisis which is unrelated to government fragmentation. It exists because available revenues of the state and local sector are inadequate to meet public service requirements, and expand less than proportionately to these needs.

In the two following sections the *balance* and *level* issues are explored. In the concluding section we turn to the question of how state government policy may be reoriented to consider the issues of fiscal imbalance and the low levels of fiscal activity.

The Problem of Metropolitan Fiscal Balance

The city-suburb relationship is complex. Generally there is a clustering of middle- and high-income families in the suburbs, while the low-income groups naturally choose housing where they can afford it—in the core city. Moreover, commercial and industrial activity, following the population movement and searching for more space, has also tended to decentralize over the past decade. Such industrial and residential shifts from the cities have simultaneously depleted central city tax bases and forced core city governments to assume the dual responsibility of serving a relatively high-cost, low-income population (much of which is elderly and Negro) and meeting the needs of a sizable commuter population. It is this existence of intrametropolitan, intercommunity differences in the size of the resources-requirements gap which causes a fiscal imbalance, and which distinguishes the fiscal balance from the fiscal level problem. If expenditure needs exceeded government receipts by exactly the same per capita amount in every community within the SMSA (given a constant fiscal effort), there would be a deficit, but not an imbalance. The same is true if there is metropolitan government, since without political fragmentation a resource-requirement gap may arise only from the SMSA as a whole.

The purpose of this section is to define, in broad terms, the determinants of metropolitan fiscal imbalance. Essentially, the argument below turns on the proposition that the nature of the interactions which exist between city and suburb enables a suburban exploitation of the core city. The results of these interactions, or spillover effects, may be grouped as direct or indirect. Direct spillovers result from nonresident, uncompensated use of core-city-provided government services. Indirect spillovers are *reflected* in basic socioeconomic structure differences within the metropolitan region, i.e., in income fragmentation, and result in part from government policies such as zoning and building restrictions.

DIRECT SPILLOVERS

Consider the drain on core-city services which results when non-residents use public facilities. This drain tends to be greater to the extent the central city is a retail sales center (the trip to shop), an employment center (the trip to work), and contains the major libraries, auditoriums, museums, theaters, etc. (the trip for entertainment). Empirical studies have shown with some consistency that per capita spending in (or by) the core city is more closely related to the size of the "contact" population (the sum of residents and nonresidents using core-city facilities) than to the number of people living within the city's jurisdictional limits.[1]

To substantiate the charge of direct exploitation, however, higher service costs imposed by nonresidents would have to exceed the additional revenues generated by this contact population. Cities with metropolitan areas have devised many ways of capturing tax revenues from nonresidents. For the trip to work, occupational taxes have been levied in some Kentucky, Ohio, and Pennsylvania cities. If one accepts the proposition that the commuter-worker receives benefits from and generates costs of city services which are roughly proportional to his earnings, the occupational tax would seem justifiable on equity (equal treatment of equals) as well as adequacy grounds. The commuter-shopper also pays if the core city levies a retail sales tax or owns parking facilities, as do suburbanites coming to the core city for entertainment if an amusement tax is levied. But are these payments by nonresidents sufficient to offset the additional costs which they may generate? If so, the spillovers are compensated, but still the allocation of resources by the loser government is distorted from some optimal level, e.g., the city government may wind up spending more of its budget for traffic control than it would have in the absence of a commuter population.

[1] See, for example, my *Metropolitan City Expenditures* (Lexington: University of Kentucky Press, 1969).

There are less obvious cost benefit considerations which result from direct use of central city services by nonresidents. Suburban commuting results in higher property values (and hopefully higher revenue levels) in the core city because of the greater levels of commercial and industrial activity generated. This higher level of activity may also drain off a part of the unemployment pool—inevitably located in the core city—and thus have the effect of indirectly increasing the property and non-property tax bases. On the negative side, large numbers of commuters impose not only a monetary incremental cost of street maintenance on local residents, but the additional social costs of increased traffic congestion, higher traffic accident rates, a more severe parking shortage, etc.

The nonresident user problem is not unique to the central city. As industry increasingly locates in the urban fringe, the daily outflow of commuters from the central city generates higher satellite government expenditures on behalf of nonresidents. Hence, the potential for *intersuburban* exploitation grows, especially in view of the relatively heavy use of the property tax by suburban governments, i.e., the property tax is not particularly amenable to capturing costs generated by nonresident users.

INDIRECT SPILLOVERS

Direct spillins and spillouts are only a part of the problem. Probably a more important source of the urban fiscal dilemma is the indirect exploitation—caused by a pronounced metropolitan income fragmentation reinforced by a myriad of governmental policies resulting in a divorcing of governmental needs from resources. There is little doubt but that governmental policy has had a major impact on the development of this kind of unbalanced urban structure, primarily in the areas of housing and transportation. As the first chapter in this volume points out, the Housing and Home Finance Agency subsidized the flight to the suburbs with the FHA mortgage insurance, while the continued improvements in metropolitan highway facilities made fringe area sites increasingly accessible and attractive for both resident and industrial use. The ultimate effect of FHA assistance was to make more room in the core city for lower-income migrants and for the population already locked in by either income or racial discrimination in housing.

It is alleged that racially segregated housing has also constrained the Negro from taking advantage of the improved transportation network, i.e., he will substitute higher central city housing for transportation costs because his housing choice is limited.[2] Harvey Brazer makes the point that, "irrespective of whether the commuter 'pays his way' either directly or indirectly, . . . he cannot be said to share in the high costs of services engendered by the increasing concentration there [in the core city] of lower-income newcomers, including the nonwhite population. . . . To the extent that suburban communities, through zoning regulations and discriminatory practices in rentals and real estate transactions, contribute directly to the concentration in the central city of socioeconomic groups which impose heavy demands upon local government services, they are, in fact, exploiting the central city." [3] Netzer attributes wide intrametropolitan variances in fiscal characteristics to variations in the nonresidential component of the tax base, and to public decisions regarding home values and zoning.[4] Overlying all of this is the general propensity of physical planners to view the city as a desirable location for auditoriums, museums, libraries, freeway interchanges, urban renewal projects, post offices and other uses which consume much space and may (temporarily or permanently) bite into the property tax base.

Another reason for intrametropolitan fiscal differences is that some high-income communities make an effort to attract certain kinds of industry and shopping centers (to increase the tax base). At the same time these communities attempt to keep out the lower-income employees with large families (to hold down expenditure requirements). The latter they accomplish with high prices for residential land and by zoning for low density. But intrametropolitan variations in resources, requirements, and the resources-requirements gap do exist, and are apt to grow at an increasing rate. Then it would seem possible that the removal of restrictive conditions on residential locations, i.e., an increase in the residential mobility of core-city dwellers, would tend to reduce these imbalances. Proposed new housing legislation could have such an effect.

David Davies questions whether suburban restrictions impose a negative effect on the central city because it is not certain if

---

[2] J. R. Meyer, J. F. Kain, and M. Wohl, *The Urban Transportation Problem* (Cambridge: Harvard University Press, 1965).

[3] Harvey Brazer, "Some Fiscal Implications of Metropolitanism," *Metropolitan Issues: Social, Governmental, Fiscal,* ed., Guthrie Birkhead (Syracuse University Press, 1962).

[4] Dick Netzer, "The Urban Fiscal Problem" (Institute of Local Government, University of Pittsburgh, Pittsburgh, Pa., 1968).

". . . total welfare in the metropolitan area would increase or decrease if the barriers [suburban restrictions] were removed.[5] This well-taken critique—that the exploitation argument requires proof that total community welfare is increased by the reduction of fiscal imbalances—suggests that the justification for reducing metropolitan disparities must be made on equity rather than efficiency grounds.

In summary, the difference between the city and suburb in per capita financial requirements for a given size package of services arises because of (a) nonresident use of core-city services, and (b) the presence of a higher cost resident population in the core city. In terms of our model, it follows that the per capita cost of providing the same level of services for the city is higher than for the suburb. Since we have said that intercommunity differences in the level of this per capita cost is the basis of the disparities problem, our argument is that fiscal imbalances within the metropolitan region are not a result of some natural growth pattern, but a function of the revealed locational preferences of the higher-income residents in the community and the actions of federal, state, and local policy makers.

THE MEASUREMENT OF FISCAL IMBALANCE

The use of fiscal data to describe intrametropolitan fiscal resource imbalances raises two special problems. First, an analysis of only fiscal differences does not get to the heart of the disparities problem. It assails only the resources dimension of the resource-requirements gap. Nonetheless, this kind of approach does yield some insight into the reasons for different financial abilities and efforts of local governments, and their relative preference among public goods and between private and public goods. Second, core city-suburb comparisons of taxes and expenditures cannot be made solely on an intergovernmental basis because of fragmented functional responsibility. As a consequence, measures in the relevant spatial units must be considered. Sacks and Campbell have used the fiscal activities of overlapping governments as the basic analytical unit in a substantial analysis of intrametropolitan fiscal structure differences among the nation's 36 largest SMSAs.[6] They find per capita total taxes to be greater inside than outside central cities; and though per capita property tax *levels* are about equal, there is evidence that

---

[5] David Davies, "Financing Urban Functions and Services," *Law and Contemporary Problems*, Winter 1965, pp. 127–61.

[6] Alan K. Campbell and Seymour Sacks, *Metropolitan America: Fiscal Patterns and Governmental Systems* (New York: The Free Press, 1968).

TABLE I. City-Suburb Disparities

	Total SMSA	Central City Area	Outside Central City Area			
			Total	Urban Territory	Rural Non-Farm	Rural Farm
SOCIOECONOMIC (1960)[a]						
SMSA population (000)	112,385	58,010	54,873	41,560	11,675	1,637
Percent of total	63.0%	51.4%	48.6%	36.8%	10.3%	1.5%
Median family income	$6,324	$5,940	$6,707	$7,002	$5,830	$4,543
Percent of nonwhites	16.7%	17.3%	5.1%	4.5%	6.1%	6.7%
Percent under 15	58.4%	28.1%	32.9%	32.7%	34.3%	31.0%
Percent over 60	85.5%	14.3%	10.6%	10.7%	9.9%	15.0%
Median school years	11.1	10.7	11.8	12.0	10.6	9.2
FISCAL (1964–65)[b]						
Per capita total local government expenditures	$277	$304	$265			
Per capita current local schools education expenditures	$ 97	$ 82	$113			
Per capita total education expenditures	—	$ 99	$141			
Non-educational expenditures	$179	$232	$132			
Education expenditures as percent of total general expenditures	—	32.6%	53.2%			
Per capita total local taxes	$152	$173	$137			
Taxes as a percent of income	—	7.00%	5.36%			
Per capita total state and federal aid	—	$ 78	$ 78			
Per capita education aid	—	$ 17	$ 28			

Source: Advisory Commission on Intergovernmental Relations, *Fiscal Balance in the American Federal System* (Washington: GPO, 1968), Ch. 3; and U.S. Bureau of the Census, *U.S. Census of Population: 1960. General Social and Economic Characteristics, U.S. Summary*.

[a] Based on all 212 SMSA's in 1960.
[b] Based on 37 largest SMSA's in 1960. Fiscal data reported for outside central city. Includes *total* outside central city area which lies within the SMSA.

effective rates are significantly greater in the central city. The Campbell and Sacks results show central governments spend relatively more for direct benefit (none-educational) services than do suburban governments, whereas the latter spend a proportionately greater amount for educational services. By 1964–65, non-aided education expenditures in the suburbs were some $31 per capita greater than in the central city. The distribution of state and federal aids magnifies this per person difference of $42 (see Table I). However, the central city devotes more to non-educational spending—including the heavily aided welfare, highway, and housing-urban developmental programs—a finding consistent with our thesis that city budgets bend with the direct and indirect effects of the suburbs.

The data in Table I suggest that intersuburb socioeconomic diversity is almost as substantial as that between central city and outside central city. Accordingly, the diversity in fiscal behavior is substantial. Margolis has noted that (in the San Francisco Bay area) lower-income dormitory communities make a greater effort in terms of their incomes, but still fall far behind the public service levels in the high-income dormitory communities.[7] He finds both groups make a lower effort than either the central city or business suburb. The distribution of public funds among alternative functions also varies across suburbs, with some lower-income municipalities behaving predictably like the core city in terms of observed preference for non-educational, direct-benefit services. Sacks provides additional evidence of public finance imbalance among suburban communities in the form of a great variation in taxable property per school child among New York State municipalities (60 to 1), among Cleveland School Districts (15 to 1), and among Cleveland municipalities.[8] Further, in the Cleveland study, significant negative relationships may be observed for both per pupil expenditures and per pupil property tax rates.

The Problem of Inadequate State Revenue Structures

Having defined the metropolitan balance problem and hypothesized its root causes, we may turn to the companion issue of an insufficient level of public resources. Basically, our argument takes the following course: (a) that state-local expenditure requirements

[7] Julius Margolis, "Municipal Fiscal Structure in a Metropolitan Area," *Journal of Political Economy*, LXV (June 1957), pp. 225–36.

[8] See Seymour Sacks and William Hellmuth, *Financing Government in a Metropolitan Area: The Cleveland Experience* (New York: The Free Press, 1961).

expand at least in proportion to income, (b) that combined state-local revenue systems are by and large not able to generate sufficient tax increments, and (c) for a variety of reasons federal-state-local intergovernmental fiscal arrangements accentuate rather than reduce the problem. Since the focus of this chapter is on the state government's role in resolving the urban fiscal crisis, the following discussion is heavily slanted in that direction.

EXPENDITURE NEEDS

If a state's revenue structure is adequate, it will expand automatically in some desired proportion to expenditure needs; and if we assume changes in the demand for public services to be related to changes in the income level, we would be led naturally to argue that the revenue structure of the state tax system may best be gauged by its income elasticity. (A tax is income elastic if the natural growth in revenues is proportionately greater than the growth in income. If revenues increase less than proportionately to income, the tax is said to be income-inelastic. Then the elasticity coefficient is greater than 1.0 if the tax is elastic, between zero and 1.0 if it is inelastic, and exactly equal to zero if it is of unitary elasticity. It should be emphasized here that the elasticity measure refers to natural revenue increments and not to those induced by rate or base changes.)

We might speculate why the expenditure (revenue) response to income should be more than proportionate. First, there is a general tendency for increased scope of government to accompany rising income levels, even for the developed states of this country. A less impressionistic reason for an elastic expenditure-income relationship is that the demand for higher public sector wages may bid up government costs at a greater rate than the overall rate of growth in personal income. Certainly the events of the last few years indicate the operation of a wage rollout effect from the private to the public sector, which in all probability will continue to effect increases in government costs.

But third, there is a productivity imbalance between the public and private sector which will require government to contribute an increasing share just to keep up. That is, the relatively capital intensive private sector tends to increase its physical output per unit of physical input at a greater rate than the relatively labor intensive public sector. This means that even with constant input costs, government's share of total output will decline. Simply put, it will take an increasing amount of each privately earned dollar for government service levels to remain even constant.

REVENUE ELASTICITY

The above arguments are intended as support for the contention that state revenue structures *should* increase more than proportionately to income; specifically, that the average one per cent increase in personal income should be accompanied by a more than one per cent increase in revenues. There are two possibilities for achieving such response in the state tax system: automatic changes and discretionary changes. The use of the latter—periodic legal rate and base adjustments—to maintain an adequate level of state-local government services is an inefficient if not dangerous process for several reasons. First, state legislatures often move slowly, a fact which is certain to result in lagging levels of public services and facilities. Second, the uncertainties associated with frequent tax structure changes are not always an inducement for the location of industry—a subject which is on the minds of state policy makers. Generally, periodic discretionary changes represent a piecemeal approach to revenue structure formation, a process which over the long run is unlikely to generate an integrated approach to state economic development. The management by crisis approach is most likely to be unplanned, and fraught with undesirable features.

The objective ultimately sought in state tax policy, then, is an automatic, elastic response to income. Because of the difficulties in distinguishing between "automatic" and "discretionary" effects, there is a paucity of empirical work on the interstate comparison of total tax base elasticity. However, in a 1968 study by the Advisory Commission on Intergovernmental Relations the results of numerous individual studies were compared; and when these estimates were applied to the actual tax structures of the states, the overall tax structure-income elasticity was found to vary from a low of 0.7 (unity is 1.0) in Nebraska, where reliance on the property tax has been historically heavy, to a high of 1.4 in Oregon, where reliance on the individual income tax has been historically heavy (see Table II).[9] Therefore as of 1967, Oregon's automatic tax response to income change was estimated to be twice as great as Nebraska's.

The main reason for this wide variance is the presence or absence of an individual state income tax. All of the top 25 states have a meaningful personal income tax. To the contrary, no state with an income elasticity below unity has an effective individual income tax. In terms of the historical source of state tax increments, an esti-

[9] Advisory Commission on Intergovernmental Relations, *Sources of Increased State Collections: Economic Growth and Political Choice* (Washington, 1968).

TABLE II. *Income Elasticity of State Tax Structures, by States, 1967*[1]

Low to Medium Elasticity (0.7 to 9.0)			Medium to High Elasticity (1.0 to 1.29)			High Elasticity (1.3 and above)		
State	Weighted elasticity	% of tax collections included	State	Weighted elasticity	% of tax collections included	State	Weighted elasticity	% of tax collections included
Nebraska	0.7	56.0	Alabama	1.0	82.1	Minnesota	1.3	66.9
Connecticut	0.8	65.7	Arizona	1.0	71.4	New York	1.3	74.6
Florida	0.8	75.0	Delaware	1.0	62.4	Virginia	1.3	77.1
Maine	0.8	79.8	Kansas	1.0	77.8	Idaho	1.4[3]	74.4[3]
New Jersey	0.8[2]	67.8[2]	Maryland	1.0	81.0	Oregon	1.4	71.4
Ohio	0.8	75.2	Nevada	1.0[3]	80.4[3]			
S. Dakota	0.8	81.1	N. Dakota	1.0	67.5			
Texas	0.8	61.4	Oklahoma	1.0[3]	63.7[3]			
Illinois	0.9[3]	84.4[3]	Alaska	1.1[2 3]	27.8[2 3]			
Michigan	0.9	69.2	California	1.1	70.3			
Mississippi	0.9	81.2	Colorado	1.1	78.3			
N. Hampshire	0.9[2]	61.8[2]	Georgia	1.1	83.8			
New Mexico	0.9	63.6	Indiana	1.1	85.9			
Pennsylvania	0.9	67.4	Kentucky	1.1	77.9			
Rhode Island	0.9	72.6	Louisiana	1.1	52.3			
Tennessee	0.9[3]	71.4[2]	Missouri	1.1	51.9			
Washington	0.9	81.8	N. Carolina	1.1	74.6			
W. Virginia	0.9	87.3	S. Carolina	1.1	80.8			
Wyoming	0.9	61.9	Vermont	1.1	73.6			
			Arkansas	1.2	76.3			
			Hawaii	1.2	93.0			
			Iowa	1.2	77.9			
			Massachusetts	1.2	71.6			
			Montana	1.2	66.7			
			Utah	1.2	76.7			
			Wisconsin	1.2	73.0			

Source: Advisory Commission on Intergovernmental Relations, *Sources of Increased State Tax Collections: Economic Growth vs. Political Choice* (Washington: GPO, 1968), p. 10.

[1] Includes individual income, general sales and selected sales taxes.

[2] Excludes individual income tax receipts.

[3] Elasticity may be slightly overstated since rate increases were not totally excluded from general sales elasticity estimate.

mated 53 percent resulted from political or legislative actions, the remaining 47 percent accruing because of the automatic response of states' tax bases.

TAX STRUCTURE, TAX LEVEL, AND DEVELOPMENT POTENTIAL:
A DIGRESSION

Overlapping any evaluation of the state's revenue structure in terms of allocative and redistributive considerations is the relatively complicated question of how the public sector affects industry location choices. This question is relevant in any evaluation of any change in state tax structure.

Much attention has been paid to tax levels as an influence on industry location, but almost always with the same result—taxes are marginally important. The conclusiveness of this research notwithstanding, state legislators almost everywhere believe in the powerful attractive and detractive potential of taxes—this belief being periodically honed by the business community. Often the effects of this illusion on state tax policy are profound.

The intent here is not to dredge up the old arguments but rather to suggest the potential effects of tax-expenditure policy for attracting industry. At least three considerations would seem relevant. First, if there is a marginal importance to tax considerations, a tax burden which varies with methods of doing business could act as a locational deterrent to adversely affected firms. This suggests that states considering adoption of general business taxes would do well to consider seriously the neutrality of such tax measures. Second is the general tax atmosphere, i.e., is there a general dissatisfaction with the current revenue structure, and is there pressure for wholesale revision? If the state tax structure has a high elasticity, sufficient revenues will be generated automatically and there will not be need for regular discretionary action. Hence, a viable personal income tax may be a necessary prerequisite for effective business taxation.

Third, there is the possibility that the effect of fiscal policy on the attraction of industry is as important on the expenditure as on the revenue side. Firms may be hesitant about locating in areas where the school system and other public services are inadequate. If this is true, industry may be prone to shun a particular location not because taxes are too high, but because they are too low.

THE FEDERAL ROLE

The federal income tax system, in contrast with state and local systems, offers substantial income elasticity. Inevitably, then, we are confronted with the possibility that through an intergovernmental arrangement of sorts, the proper federal role may be to bail the state-local sector out of its fiscal dilemma. This possibility is discussed in the final section.

Under the present intergovernmental system, the federal-state-local fiscal overlap occurs because of a system of conditional grants-in-aid and a program of direct federal expenditures. The impact which this system has exerted on the urban fiscal dilemma is not easily unwoven, but a fair number of weaknesses are readily apparent. First, whether federal money is effective in resolving urban public finance difficulties depends heavily on the method by which the state passes the money through—be it grants-in-aid or the assumption of direct functional responsibility. Because there is evidence that state government generally discriminates against core cities in favor of both suburban and non-metropolitan areas, federal assistance may not be a significant disparity-reducing measure. Second, the distribution formulae for federal funds have the (increasing) net effect of being income equalizing—being more (negatively) associated with per capita income differences than (positively) with urbanization differences.[10] This result, be it an effect of political over-representation or no, is strong evidence that the federal grant system is not meeting urban needs.

But the most serious indictment of all is the serious bias against the state-local sector in general. The data in Table III demonstrate that the level of per capita direct federal expenditure in states is generally three times or more greater than per capita grants-in-aid. If we concede that federal grants have greater value for states than direct federal spending, there is cause to question the intentions of the federal government toward the urban fiscal problem.

Remedial Fiscal Policies

We have defined the urban fiscal problem above in terms of the basic urban imbalance and the state fiscal weakness, but we must also turn to the question of remedial policy. Throughout, it is important to keep in mind the kinds of problems needing remedy —namely the creation of metropolitan fiscal balance, and the creation of a stronger overall fiscal position by redefining and strengthening of the role of state government. There would seem to be four

[10] A summary of these results may be found in my and Robert J. Saunders' "Factors Associated with Variations in State and Local Government Spending," *Journal of Finance,* XXI (September 1966).

TABLE III. *Per Capita Federal Dollar Flow to States: Three Year Averages, 1965–1967 (In dollars)*

State	Grants and Expenditures	Grants	Grants to State and Local Gov'ts	Grants to Individuals	Direct Expenditures
Alabama	545	109	85	24	436
Arizona	665	120	95	25	545
Arkansas	442	128	97	31	314
California	884	90	74	16	794
Colorado	741	135	88	47	606
Connecticut	776	69	55	14	708
Delaware	597	86	70	16	510
Florida	658	66	52	14	592
Georgia	662	96	74	22	567
Idaho	516	150	93	57	366
Illinois	431	71	49	22	360
Indiana	427	69	42	27	357
Iowa	514	144	56	88	370
Kansas	708	163	61	102	545
Kentucky	523	108	87	21	414
Louisiana	518	114	96	18	403
Maine	580	81	69	12	499
Maryland	898	62	47	15	836
Massachusetts	608	86	60	26	522
Michigan	375	66	50	16	309
Minnesota	501	123	73	50	378
Mississippi	472	128	91	37	343
Missouri	647	108	70	38	539
Montana	754	218	128	90	536
Nebraska	658	194	65	129	463
Nevada	643	155	140	15	489
New Hampshire	507	73	58	15	434
New Jersey	505	49	41	8	456
New Mexico	736	177	137	41	558
New York	479	68	53	15	411
North Carolina	495	75	55	20	420
North Dakota	838	292	95	197	546
Ohio	424	65	50	15	359
Oklahoma	627	152	106	46	476
Oregon	457	121	92	29	336
Pennsylvania	432	66	53	13	366
Rhode Island	719	94	78	16	629
South Carolina	549	76	54	22	474

TABLE III. *Continued*

State	Grants and Expenditures	Grants	Grants to State and Local Gov'ts	Grants to Individuals	Direct Expenditures
South Dakota	669	227	106	121	443
Tennessee	469	98	74	24	371
Texas	652	94	59	35	558
Utah	609	136	107	29	472
Vermont	577	144	117	27	433
Virginia	882	73	63	10	809
Washington	707	106	76	30	601
West Virginia	421	111	101	10	310
Wisconsin	372	66	41	25	305
Wyoming	853	273	223	49	580

Source: Roy Bahl and Jeremy Warford, "Real and Monetary Dimensions of Federal Aid to States" (unpublished manuscript, 1969). Direct expenditure data taken from I. M. Labovitz and H. J. Halper, *Federal Revenue and Expenditure Estimates, for States and Regions, Fiscal Years 1965–67*, House of Representatives Intergovernment Relations Subcommittee, October 1968.

avenues of fiscal or quasi-fiscal action which ought to accomplish such ends. The first and most obvious is reforming state tax systems to increase tax structure elasticity. The second is a redistribution of functional expenditure responsibility between state, federal, and local governments which better recognizes differential taxing capacities and spillover effects. The third is a wholesale reform of federal and state aid systems to take into account modern day functional and governmental needs. Finally, the urban problem may be alleviated by permitting, if not encouraging, local government fiscal reforms—another alternative which could affect direct state action. The first two of these possibilities would permit a higher level of public services, while the latter two would improve the fiscal balance within the metropolitan region. Accordingly the focus must necessarily be on these as complementary rather than alternative strategies. Their interrelations may be as important as their direct effects on the problems of urban balance.

REFORMING THE STATE TAX STRUCTURE

The fact that those states which have successfully increased the productivity of their tax systems have used both major tax sources neither proves nor implies that there is some special formula for tax diversity which results in cumulative revenue growth. However, there are two arguments for tax diversity as a way to increase tax structure productivity. The first is psycho-political. At any given time there is a political limit to the increased use of a particular tax. In practice, this limit is dictated, to state government fiscal decision makers, not by some careful examination of overall tax burden, but simply by what other states are doing. Thus a range of five to seven percent seems to be the currently acceptable limit for a general sales tax. Similarly, property tax burdens in certain eastern states have reached a "maximum tolerable limit," for the time being. These kinds of perceived limits naturally result in a search for alternative revenue sources and hence tax structure diversity.

The second facet of the tax diversification thesis has more economic substance, at least in terms of an upper limit for general sales taxation. An empirical study by Legler and Shapiro begins with the assumption that theoretically a sales tax rate increase, *cet. par.*, has the effect of reducing total revenues, though this effect is generally hidden by income increments.[11] Noting the negative relationship between sales tax rate changes and total tax revenues in Illinois, they suggest that Illinois' tax structure could be made more productive by introducing an income tax rather than raising the sales tax rate.

Tax structure diversity is surely a worthwhile state fiscal goal, but the most pressing state tax reform is in the personal income tax area. For 15 states the need is for enactment of a broadly based personal income tax.[12] The remaining 35 states and the District of Columbia have need to reexamine rate and base schedules in an effort to improve the productivity of their income tax systems. The wide variance in the utilization of the income tax is shown in Table IV. The table compares among states the income tax burden on a family of four. Only about a third of the states carry their income tax progression beyond $25,000 and about half stop the progression before it reaches $10,000; hence there is much potential for increasing the elasticity as well as the yield of state income tax systems.

Sales taxes in one form or another are more widely used than income taxes; only two percent of the nation's population reside

[11] John B. Legler and Perry Shapiro, "Economic Growth and Tax Yields Under Alternative Structures," *Proceedings of the Sixtieth Annual Conference on Taxation of the National Tax Association* (Atlanta, Ga., 1967), pp. 56–65.

[12] Here we draw heavily on the work of the Advisory Commission for Intergovernmental Relations, see Wil S. Myers, "Measures for Making the State and Local Revenue System More Productive and Equitable" (paper presented at National Tax Association meetings, San Francisco, 1968).

in non-sales tax states. But specific practices vary considerably. Again, there seems much room for increasing the elasticity of sales tax systems, first by including services within the sales tax base. Since personal service expenditures are claiming a growing fraction

TABLE IV. *Effective Rates of Personal Income Taxes for Selected Adjusted Gross Income Levels, Married Couple with Two Dependents, by State, 1968*

State	Adjusted Gross Income Class			
	$5,000	$7,500	$10,000	$25,000
Alabama*	0.2	0.8	1.4	2.5
Alaska	1.3	1.9	2.2	3.3
Arizona*	0.5	1.0	1.4	3.0
Arkansas	0.3	0.9	1.3	2.5
California	—	0.3	0.9	3.1
Colorado*	0.1	0.9	1.5	3.4
Delaware*	0.6	1.3	2.2	4.9
District of Columbia	0.8	1.4	1.8	3.2
Georgia	0.1	0.5	1.0	5.1
Hawaii	0.8	2.3	3.3	5.1
Idaho*	0.3	1.4	2.1	4.1
Indiana	0.4	0.9	1.2	1.7
Iowa*	0.4	1.6	2.1	2.8
Kansas*	0.7	1.0	1.3	2.4
Kentucky*	0.4	1.6	2.3	3.2
Louisiana*	—	0.1	0.4	1.0
Maryland	0.6	1.7	2.6	3.5
Massachusetts*	0.1	1.6	2.0	2.5
Michigan	—	0.3	0.8	1.8
Minnesota*	2.0	3.3	4.1	5.7
Mississippi	—	0.4	1.1	2.3
Missouri*	0.3	0.7	1.0	1.8
Montana*	0.9	1.5	2.0	3.5
Nebraska[1]	—.04	0.4	0.8	1.5
New Mexico*	0.5	0.8	0.9	1.2
New York	0.6	1.5	2.2	5.3
North Carolina	0.8	1.8	2.6	4.4
North Dakota*	0.3	0.4	0.8	4.1
Oklahoma*	0.2	0.4	0.7	1.7
Oregon*	1.5	2.5	3.3	4.5
South Carolina*	0.4	1.0	1.5	3.9
Utah*	0.9	1.7	2.4	3.5
Vermont	1.3	2.0	2.6	4.0

TABLE IV. *Continued*

Adjusted Gross Income Class

State	$5,000	$7,500	$10,000	$25,000
Virginia	0.9	1.4	2.2	3.3
West Virginia	0.5	0.7	0.8	1.2
Wisconsin	2.3	3.1	3.9	5.9
Median rate	0.5	1.2	1.7	3.2
Federal tax	5.2	8.0	10.4	16.0

Note: In computing income taxes, it was assumed that all income was from wages and salaries and earned by one spouse. For state tax computations the optional standard deduction was used except for the $25,000 income class where it was assumed that deductions are itemized. For federal tax computations (other than the $25,000 AGI class) the following percentages of AGI were used for estimating deductions: $5,000 and $7,500 AGI classes—16 percent; $10,000 AGI class—14 percent. In computing the state tax at the $25,000 level, itemized deductions were assumed to be $3,115. For those states that allow deduction of the federal income tax, the itemized deduction was assumed to be $3,940 in computing the federal tax liability (addition of estimated state income tax less certain deductions not allowed for the federal tax); except that when the state income tax is itself deductible for state income tax purposes, the actual state tax liability was added for both federal and state tax computation. New Hampshire and Tennessee are excluded since their personal income taxes apply only to interest and dividend income; also excluded is the New Jersey "commuters' income tax." Adjusted gross income is income after business deductions but before personal exemptions and other allowable deductions. "Effective rates" are computed as the ratio of tax liability to adjusted gross income.

  * Federal income tax deductible.

  1 Negative rate results from credit allowed for sales taxes paid on food. If the credit exceeds the tax liability, the taxpayer can apply for a refund.

Source: Advisory Commission on Intergovernmental Relations, *State and Local Finance, Significant Features, 1967–1969*, as taken from Wil Myers, "Measures for Making the State and Local Revenue System More Productive" (paper presented at Sixty-First Annual Conference on Taxation of the National Tax Association, San Francisco, 1968).

of the total consumption, their inclusion would make the sales tax base more responsive to economic growth. More to the point, the nature of a state's economic growth should dictate, at least in general terms, the structure of its sales tax system. For example, if a state's growth is intensive (population is relatively constant and per capita income is rising), the cost of excluding services is much greater than in states where growth is relatively extensive (population and income are rising but per capita income is relatively constant).

To recommend sales as well as income taxes opens the possibility that the degree of equity (in an ability to pay context) desired in the state tax system will not be achieved. There are three responses to such a possibility. First, the regressivity may be ignored as is often done on grounds that the federal tax system accomplishes any redistribution that is necessary. A second, and better, possibility for considering the equity of the system is by providing a set of sales tax exemptions ranging from food, to drugs, to children's clothing. Fourteen states presently exempt food, the District of Columbia taxes it at a preferential rate, and 21 states provide complete or partial sales tax exemption for purchase of prescription drugs. Though this system may reduce the burden on the low-income families, it suffers from the weaknesses of administrative complexity, revenue loss through certain leakages apart from the exemptions, and inequitable treatment of certain types of consumers. The third, and possibly the best, method of increasing the progressivity of the overall tax structure is by using the income tax as an equity instrument via a general crediting system—for example, a six dollar per capita credit to income tax liability. Analysis presented in a recent study demonstrates that either the exemption or the credit methods may be used to effectively reduce the regressivity of the sales tax.[13] The income tax credit method may also be used to provide property tax relief for low-income families, e.g., in Wisconsin and Minnesota low-income, elderly homeowners and renters may claim a credit against state income tax liability.

SHIFTING FUNCTIONAL RESPONSIBILITY

But reform of state tax structures will do little to alleviate urban fiscal problems unless there is some method to effectively transfer this newfound wealth to alleviating the urban problems. The activistic state government strategy would be to increase the amount of intergovernmental assistance. The other side of the coin would involve relieving the expenditure pressure on local units, so that their own resources could be used to satisfy public service needs. This latter approach could be implemented by shifting of financial responsibility for local school and public welfare largely or completely away from the local level. The choice of education and welfare as the functions to be shifted has to do with the objective of

---

[13] John Shannon, "Tax Relief for the Poor," *Proceedings of the Sixtieth Annual Conference of the National Tax Association* (Atlanta, Georgia, 1967), pp. 577–94.

diminishing the resources-requirements disparity between the core
cities and their suburbs. If services which bear most heavily on cities
with heavy concentrations of poverty families were transferred to
state government, the public service requirements would be reduced
more in the core cities than in the suburbs. In this fashion fiscal
disparities are genuinely reduced, though not eliminated since resources still vary widely because of income fragmentation in the
SMSA.

Education—There is a strong case for transferring the financing
of education to the state level. First, the wide disparities in the
quality of local schools and the quality of education available to
certain children is at least partially a result of "accidents of property
tax geography." An example of this is the per pupil assessed valuation between the poorest and wealthiest property tax school districts
in Colorado during 1969.[14] The 38.1 ratio found here means that a
38 times greater tax effort is required in the poorer district than in
the wealthier district to provide an equal (dollar) level of support.

Aside from the disparities problem, education has reached a point
of nearly dominating the property tax base (see Table V). By 1969,
school districts will claim more than half of the local property tax.
Already, school districts receive some 58 percent of total federal and
state aid to local governments. As a result of the claim by education,
the lower per capita level of resources of the core-city governments
is impaired most, hence increasing fiscal disparities within the
urban region. It follows that relief from the pressure of education
on local resources would strengthen the fiscal position of the central
city.

Practically, there would seem to be two possibilities for eliminating educational finance disparities and reducing the attendant
unbalanced pressure on the metropolitan property tax base. Fiscal
capacities could be made more uniform via governmental consolidation. This would reduce suburban exploitation of central cities by
allowing a better balance between services rendered and tax revenue.
(The future of this possibility is discussed by Professor Daniel Grant
in Chapter 3.) The second approach is direct state involvement either
through a revamped aid system or the direct assumption of fiscal
responsibility for the education function. Because the former would
require difficult renovation of long entrenched distribution formulae,
direct assumption would seem to offer the best possibility for a

[14] As reported in Mabel Walker, "Financial Responsibility for Education and
Welfare," *Tax Policy* (Princeton, N.J.: Tax Institute of America), XXXVI, No.
4 (April 1969).

TABLE V. *Distribution of Local Property Tax Collection by Type of Government for Selected Years*

Fiscal Year	All Local Governments	School Districts[1]	Primary Units of General Local Government			Townships & Special Districts
			Total[2]	Cities[2]	Counties[2]	
Amount (millions)						
1942	$ 4,347	$ 1,429	$ 2,571	$1,696	$ 875	$ 347
1952	8,282	3,246	4,351	2,711	1,640	685
1957	12,385	5,307	6,052	3,678	2,374	1,026
1967	25,418	12,433	11,006	6,295	4,711	1,979
1969 est.	31,500	15,800	13,480	7,720	5,760	2,220
Percent						
1942	100.0	32.9	59.1	39.0	20.1	8.0
1952	100.0	39.2	52.5	32.7	19.8	8.3
1957	100.0	42.8	48.9	29.7	19.2	8.3
1967	100.0	48.9	43.3	24.8	18.5	7.8
1969 est.	100.0	50.2	42.8	24.5	18.3	7.0

[1] Includes est. amounts allocable to dependent city and county school systems.
[2] Excludes est. amounts allocable to dependent school systems.

Source: John Shannon, "Financing Urban America: Time for a Change" (address before the Municipal Finance Officers Association, Toronto, 1969).

clean break with past practices and hence an effective solution to the educational disparities problem.

On the fiscal side, the transfer of the education function to the state means a transfer of the support for education from property taxes to income and sales taxes. Because the latter tax bases are relatively elastic and generally unhindered by legal restrictions, schoolmen would be freed from the task of selling bond issues and tax increases to the public. Surely this direct benefit of a state fiscal takeover would bring a greater amount of effort to bear on the effectiveness of local educational systems. Finally, if the state did take over the education function, in disbursing funds the state would have to devise some realistic methods to take account of differing local needs, i.e., recognizing that a given dollar expenditure will not buy the same quality of services in all neighborhoods.

The shifting of education finance to the state level is not a radical and untried idea. Some states have moved in the direction of replacing a grant-in-aid system with a basically state-supported foundation program. North Carolina did so in 1931, and Hawaii, South Carolina, and Delaware have made recent efforts in this direction. The Advisory Commission on Intergovernmental Relations has recommended state assumption of the education function as a goal toward which states should work.[15] Recognizing the importance of local policy control over schools and the need for some leeway in meeting unusual financial situations, the commission recommends that local school districts be permitted to supplement the state contribution, but on a limited basis. This limitation could be effected by a statutory provision restricting the use of local property taxing powers for schools to roughly ten percent of the funds provided by the state to the locality during a designated fiscal period.

Welfare—In cases where welfare remains partially a local function (approximately one-third of the states), substantial and badly needed local resources could be freed by transferring financial responsibility for welfare to the state. Moreover, the very nature of the physical distribution of local welfare recipients within the metropolitan area would suggest that such transfer will reduce urban fiscal disparities. In describing this possibility, Campbell notes:

> If welfare in New York were transferred from the units which presently administer it—New York City and outside New York City, mostly counties—the disparity in fiscal effort (local taxes as a proportion of income) between New York City and its suburbs would be reduced from the present 28 percent difference to 11 percent. In other words, in the case of New York City the result would still leave the city with a higher fiscal effort than its surrounding suburbs but would reduce the gap considerably—for the country's 22 largest metropolitan areas the gap would be decreased from 33 to 18 percent.[16]

There is some evidence of movement toward increased state responsibility for welfare: in California where legislation was introduced to assume the welfare function from the county and provide property tax relief, and in Massachusetts where the takeover is estimated to cost the state some $82 million annually.

But if local government is totally unable to meet the fiscal requirements of the public welfare function, state government is in

[15] See John Shannon, "Financing Urban America: Time for a Change" (address before the Municipal Finance Officers Association, Toronto, 1969).

[16] Alan K. Campbell, "Metropolitan Organization, Politics and Taxation," *Municipal Income Taxes, Proceedings of the Academy of Political Science*, XXVII, No. 4 (1968), p. 567.

only a slightly better position. Anyway, if state and local governments must gear welfare programs to meet internal budgetary limitations, the welfare program will certainly be something less than truly national. The case for shifting responsibility for welfare (and Medicaid) totally to the federal government is imposing. First, states have little effective control over welfare programs. The recent Supreme Court decision prohibiting state residence requirements demonstrates this clearly. Second, states' fiscal capacity and willingness to support the welfare function differ widely—Mississippi's average monthly payment is $35 while New York's is $241—and the caseload may vary according to these differentials. There is more than a passing amount of evidence that such regional inequalities have contributed to a net inflow of the low-income to the central city slums. The indirect effects of growing concentrations of poverty on the public economy of a large central city are well documented. Finally, there is the question of the burden of fiscal support for public assistance (and Medicaid) benefits. State and local tax systems are by and large regressive—and even where the personal income tax is used, its progression is generally limited—hence the burden of financing local services falls heavily on the middle and lower middle-income taxpayer. Financing public assistance payments with the federal income tax with its greater progression would surely produce a more drastic, and in an ability-to-pay sense, more desirable redistribution of income.

The call for federal assumption of the welfare function has already been made. Wilbur Cohen, when Secretary of the Department of Health, Education, and Welfare, made such a proposal. The Advisory Commission on Intergovernmental Relations has also recommended full support of public assistance, including Medicaid, by the federal government.[17] The Commission argues in favor of retaining administrative responsibility of the public welfare program at the state and local level. In 1969 a resolution at the National Governors Conference made the same recommendations. By contrast, the 1969 Nixon proposals would continue to leave a major portion of the welfare financing burden with the states.

REFORM OF STATE AND FEDERAL AID SYSTEMS

In the case of education, an alternative to shifting full functional responsibility to the state is the reform of aid systems to take proper account of resource-requirement differences. The fiscal perversity of

---

[17] Shannon, "Financing Urban America: Time for a Change."

state aid systems which often results in a significantly higher per pupil aid to suburban than city districts must be eliminated by re-forming the basic weaknesses of the distribution formulae. The results coming from such perversity may be illustrated by examining the per pupil state aid advantage of suburban over central city school districts in selected New York State areas: Buffalo, $74; New York City, $134; Syracuse, $175; Rochester, $176; and Albany, $186. That this is not a uniquely New York phenomenon may be verified by examining Seymour Sacks' valuable city-suburb analysis in *Fiscal Balance in the American Federal System.*[18]

To use state aid for balancing the urban resource-requirements education gap requires as a first step a marked increase in the level of state assistance, for even in the absence of fragmented local gov-ernment, local resources are generally far inadequate to meet local needs. Distribution methods must be amended in two ways: (a) the allocation criteria must be changed to equalize quality of education services rather than fiscal capacity, and (b) overall fiscal effort rather than education fiscal effort must be used in the allocation formulae. Though most state aid systems violate these maxims to an almost diametrical extent, there are small rays of hope. Though ultimately unsuccessful, an effort was made at the New York State constitutional convention to require the legislature to correct these obvious in-equities by taking into account the special educational needs of each school district and the total tax burden of that district, in addition to, or as a substitute for, property value per student, the factor which dominates the present formula.[19] By adding these two factors, or by substituting them for present factors, it would be possible to direct aid to those jurisdictions where disadvantaged pupils are concen-trated and, further, to take into account the effort the taxpayers in each district are making for both education and non-education pur-poses. While theoretically it would seem possible for states to equal-ize educational fiscal disparities with such measures, the political realities of such action are not encouraging. State legislators can generally be expected to support proposals that will aid their dis-tricts and to oppose bitterly attempts to redistribute their district's wealth to poorer jurisdictions.

Even apart from education, state aid programs do not offer great

---

[18] Advisory Commission on Intergovernmental Relations, *Fiscal Balance in the American Federal System,* Vol. II (Washington: GPO, 1968).

[19] See Alan K. Campbell, *Governing Metropolitan America: Reform, Politics and Structural Change* (paper presented to Urban Problems Seminar, State Uni-versity of New York at Buffalo, 1967).

hope for directly reducing urban fiscal disparities simply because they are not often concerned with the traditionally urban functions, e.g., police, fire, sanitation, street maintenance, etc. Indirectly though, a combination of greater state fiscal responsibility for education and public assistance could free funds which would raise service levels for the non-aided functions, though not necessarily by a greater amount in cities than in suburbs. But hope for such indirect assistance may be wishful in light of the enormous complications raised by the Balkanization of metropolitan government.

Then, there is the even more complex question of federal-state-local interrelations, specifically the issue of how the urban fiscal dilemma might be resolved in the event of a meaningful federal revenue-sharing scheme. Two elements of federal-state-local fiscal relations may be strengthened by some form of revenue sharing. First, the expected annual level of the federal flow of funds to state and local government may be increased. Such a plan might allow sub-national governmental units to capitalize on the greater elasticity of the federal income tax. Second, the goal of allocative efficiency may be better served if the revenue sharing involves block, or unconditional, grants rather than an extension of the more narrow conditional grants which presently exist. The potential of the general purpose grants for resolving the fiscal ills of American cities rests in part on the ability of state governments to oil the wheel precisely at the squeak. Federal assumption of welfare financing, state assumption of education financing, federal revenue sharing, and a program of general purpose state-to-local grants based on some true measure of need would move the intergovernmental system a giant step toward the goal of fiscal balance.

But the "pass through" problem is the important element of any new program of federalism. The growing suburban domination of state legislatures and the predictable economic-man type behavior of such suburban politicians on behalf of their typically middle class constituents has been much of the root cause of the unrealistic urban role which the state government has played. To insure that the relative advantage of suburbs over central cities is not further increased, a realistic revenue-sharing plan will have to depend on more than the social altruism, or even the sound economics, of such legislatures to resolve the "pass through" problem. Surely the one condition which must be imposed is that federal revenue sharing be urban aid rather than state aid. One possibility here is to specify the minimum fraction which must be channeled to central city governments. The 1969 Nixon proposals based such a minimum fraction on the rela-

tive level of general revenues currently generated by urban governments. While there are many virtues to such an allocation procedure,
no direct account is taken of need differentials, e.g., inter-urban differences in the incidence of low-income families. Nor is the higher
tax effort in the core city considered. The Nixon proposals also
called for a greater share to be retained by the state government
where the education function is financed through special district
mechanisms. In such cases, if the shared revenues are to be partially
used to support a shifting of the education function to the state,
there must be assurance that the allocation of direct state expenditures to the city school districts will properly reflect the greater
concentration of fiscal need there.

Finally there is perhaps the most basic problem with federal intergovernmental policy—in the absence of some ongoing claim on
federal income taxes by state-local governments, federal funds will
continue to be assigned to what may well be low priority needs relative to those of state-local governments. In recent years, per capita
direct federal expenditures in states have exceeded grants-in-aid to
states by several times. And over all of this lies the gargantuan and
growing federal budgetary appetite of the military-industrial complex.

Even in the event of cessation of the Vietnam hostilities, it is
regularly stated that an enormous "peace dividend" is wishful thinking. The Nixon revenue-sharing proposal, though hopefully the
necessary beginnings of a relevant federalism, are woefully weak in
magnitude. If the share of automatic federal revenue increase to be
allocated to the states under this plan is any indication, the budget
priority of the state-local sector is relatively low.

INCREASING LOCAL GOVERNMENT REVENUE POTENTIAL

Yet another alternative for attacking the fiscal problems of urban
areas involves enhancing the revenue-raising potential of local governments, particularly central cities. Three facets of local government finance are relevant here: property taxes, non-property taxes,
and debt-raising ability. The state has much to do with making
possible such local fiscal measures as are required to redeem deteriorating local governmental conditions.

The use of local income and sales taxes is primarily to enable local
units of government to capitalize on a tax base which is more responsive (than assessed property values) to economic growth. Embodied in this thinking, however, is the possibility of capturing the
costs of non-resident use of core-city services by levying a user charge

for public services. For the most part, it is not possible to assess a specific user charge for the service, e.g., what is a unit of police protection. Nonetheless, realizing that some benefits may leak uncompensated out of the community, city financial planners have installed occupational and retail sales taxes to be levied at the point of economic activity rather than at the place of residence. But such measures may not provide long-term salvation for fiscally pressed cities since the centrifugal movement of employment and commerce continues and eventually will deplete even the sales and income tax bases. In the absence of major reforms in metropolitan governmental structure, the heavier use of local income and sales taxation may provide little more than stop-gap relief. However, *in addition to* major state fiscal reforms, these taxes can provide superior alternatives both in terms of equity and yield—to increased local property taxes.

Theoretically, the removal of all fiscal responsibilities for education and welfare could be a proxy for greater local taxing power in that much of the property tax base would be freed for other purposes, or would be reduced. In addition, local units could be aided via a revenue-sharing plan with the state income tax (as is done in Maryland) or with a system of unconditional grants financed from the state income tax. In this manner the greater elasticity of the state income tax may be tapped but local decision-making autonomy retained. The success of such a program in reducing metropolitan fiscal disparity would be greatly dependent on the allocation methods used by the state—namely, the use of proper indicators of public need would be dictated.

There are numerous reasons to relieve the pressure for heavier use of the local property tax. The declining property tax base of central cities offers much of the explanation of the fiscal difficulties of urban America—the property tax base just does not offer the kind of automatic expansibility which would accommodate growing public expenditure pressures. Another defect is the negative effect of present property tax practices on the incentive for the private redevelopment of urban areas. In addition to relieving the pressure for increased usage of the property tax, the state government may take at least three steps re local use of the property tax. First, state restrictions on rate levels could be abandoned, thereby providing localities with more flexibility but thereby also condoning heavier use of the tax. Second, it could assure assessments at full market value (as was done in Kentucky), increasing the flexibility and reducing discriminatory effects, but also condoning heavier use of the tax. Third, the state could encourage a more effective use of the property tax for development purposes via a heavier tax burden on land and a lighter one on improvements, but at a cost of reducing the already low long-term expansibility of the base.

Finally, states could directly and indirectly improve the local governments' position by taking a more realistic policy regarding local debt. Local debt limits which are expressed in terms of assessed valuation of property should be rethought in terms of a more appropriate measure of the income-earning capacity of the city and the current quality of the local infrastructure. Moreover, since the credit-rating process does, and under present conditions should, work in a fiscally perverse fashion—the highest interest cost is paid by those cities least able to afford it—some program of state subsidization should be considered.

Conclusions: Guidelines for Public Policy[20]

Such a mammoth assignment of the role of the state in resolving the urban fiscal problem can hardly be dealt with in such summary fashion as above. Though the unmentioned (in this chapter) relevant considerations are many, one would seem particularly relevant for mention in this concluding section: the relative merits of an aggregative vs. a piecemeal approach. Historically the approach has been piecemeal. Summarily, one could identify almost any number of public programs or plans which are geared to effect the urban fisc: (a) increased local taxing powers, (b) federal assistance to physically renew the core city, (c) state assistance programs, and (d) the creation of metropolitan government, consolidation, or some other scheme to implement the areawide provision of public services. Ideally, the jumbled set of interrelated effects on fiscal balance of each policy would be unwoven and a clear net effect of the aggregate of government policy could be identified. But (a) each governmental program has a multiplicity of direct and indirect effects, some of which may not even be measurable, (b) the interdependencies among the governments and among the individuals in the SMSAs which give rise to the disparities problem are so complicated that the final impulses of any change in public policy do not seem traceable, and (c) the sheer number of governmental programs and natural growth factors which conceivably could affect the fiscal

---

[20] A more complete treatment of this subject is contained in my forthcoming *Land Economics* paper "Public Policy and the Urban Fiscal Problem: Piecemeal vs. Aggregate Solutions."

balance of a metropolitan region is immense, and only with complete enumeration could a net effect be described. These considerations would suggest that if the current piecemeal approach did move the metropolitan fisc toward balance, it would not be through design.

If the approach is to be aggregative, the state government alone would seem in a position to coordinate total reform. Hence the discussions of remedial policy in this chapter center around necessary state government actions.

The following, then, are guidelines for an effective state policy, given the nature of the urban fiscal problem:

(1) State governments should increase reliance on the personal income tax, either by introducing a personal income tax or by strengthening existing systems via increases in the rate progressivity. State sales taxes, which provide a needed diversification in tax structures, should be reexamined, particularly with an eye toward expanding coverage to include services.

(2) Financial responsibility for the education function should be shifted almost exclusively to state government. Public assistance, including Medicaid, should be supported exclusively at the federal level.

(3) A system of federal revenue sharing should be instituted to assure the state-local sector of an adequate share of the federal income tax. Whether functional transfers as described in (2) above do or do not occur, state aid formulae should be amended to reduce rather than increase city-suburb disparities. In the absence of a reasonable pass-through provision, there will be nothing remedial about revenue sharing.

(4) Local reliance on non-property taxes should be encouraged, a system of state-local revenue sharing or general purpose state non-educational grants being attractive alternatives. Finally, local property tax reforms should be encouraged in the direction of promoting physical renewal.

John N. Kolesar

5

The States and Urban Planning
and Development

The states' perception of the urban crisis has been neither quick nor clear. Their initial perception was to view the urban crisis as a series of problems affecting a specific class of local governments. The traditional response based on this perception was to treat urban areas according to well-established principles for meeting a problem in any other distressed area: a little rechanneling of tax funds here, a bit of expert assistance there, a dash of home rule for one place and a jigger of regional coordination in another. With a little fine tuning, the public and private mechanisms were supposed to put things on the right course for the long haul. Infinitesimal change was acceptable because infinite amounts of time were available.

But events of the 1960s showed that the time available was disconcertingly finite. Moreover, the traditional minor adjustments had been more often discussed than enacted. Many of those that had been effected seemed to have disappeared into the muffling embrace of the public and private bureaucracies without having any beneficial effect on life in urban society. Often solutions somehow were transformed into problems. Zoning laws spawned by "The City

JOHN N. KOLESAR *is deputy commissioner of the New Jersey Department of Community Affairs where he was previously chief of the Office of Public Information. Mr. Kolesar came to that position with a background of 16 years as a news reporter and editor. In 1966 he won a national science writing award from the American Academy for the Advancement of Sciences.*

Beautiful" movement helped form thousands of non-communities and cemented American society into rigid compartments. Urban renewal destroyed more housing and neighborhoods than it renewed. Welfare came to be hated by both those who received it and those who paid for it. Cities seemed unable to get enough home rule to work their way out of their own problems, but the suburbs had more than enough to maintain enclaves. Regional and metropolitan government was politically out of reach but regional agencies with narrow functional responsibilities were salable and helped drain the already low supply of government potency. All the while, urban development accelerated, an irresistible, cancerous growth that government action irritated and aggravated and distorted, but neither stemmed nor swayed.

A New Response

In the 1960s, in some states, a new kind of non-traditional response began to form. Dimly perceived, without a consistent overall strategy, these responses sought to break away from the old vertical lines of program function, the minor tinkering with governmental machinery, and to treat the urban crisis through a direct, comprehensive attack. The new response was more pragmatic and activist. At times, it produced ad hoc government organisms that fell outside the ordinary channels of the federal system—in New York an Urban Development Corporation took shape, in New Jersey a Hackensack Meadowlands Development Commission was created, in many places the Model Cities programs drew the states into new ways of confronting the urban crisis. These new agencies caused uneasiness for those who liked their organizational charts neat and clean, but their creation made it possible for some states to go straight to the heart of urban development without having to cut through layers of organizational sediment that had piled up in the traditional government mainstream.

COMPREHENSIVE LOCAL AFFAIRS AGENCIES

An important phase in the direct action response to the urban crisis was the creation of state departments of urban, local or community affairs. The origins of these departments lie in one of the traditional responses, i.e., provision of technical assistance to local governments. Governor Richard J. Hughes of New Jersey summed up this concept somewhat disparagingly in a speech in 1968 with the phrase "super information booth." Essentially, the original idea was to create unobtrusive state agencies which would blushingly provide assistance and information on technical matters to local governments, all the while being careful to imply no lack of competence on the part of sensitive local functionaries. New Jersey has had a Division of Local Government for half a century providing technical assistance on local budget and debt matters. Its original name was far broader than its powers. Ironically, its title has been narrowed to the Division of Local Finance in the state's Department of Community Affairs while its role has been broadened. New York's Office of Local Government, established in 1959, is an agency limited largely to the technical assistance function. However, New York State has been a pioneer in carrying out direct action urban programs for 40 years, working through a variety of agencies. (In Chapter 3, Professor Daniel Grant also expresses some views on these agencies.)

FROM HUD TO CHUTZPAH

The creation of state agencies devoted to local, community or urban affairs received formal impetus in a report by the Council of State Governments to the National Governors Conference in 1956 recommending that each state set up an agency to determine the needs of metropolitan and non-metropolitan areas. The idea was endorsed by the Governors Conference and later by the United States Conference of Mayors, the National League of Cities, and the National Association of Housing and Redevelopment Officials. The creation of the federal government's Department of Housing and Urban Development (HUD) in 1965 was based on a parallel concept and undoubtedly lent more force to similar action by the states.

In itself, creation of a separate government agency to deal with a specified set of problems is a traditional response. What was new in the urban affairs agencies was the unconscious assumption that the urban state of living in itself had become a problem, aside from the standard categories of governmental functions like health, welfare, education, transportation and finance. The assumption and its implications were only vaguely felt, however.

Beginning in 1966, the urban affairs agencies, frequently entitled "Department of Community Affairs," were created by one state after another. Pennsylvania's was the first cabinet-level agency into operation in 1966. Within three years, half of the states had such agencies, ranging from small advisory bodies to large-scale, active departments with broad program responsibilities. The Pennsylvania, New Jersey and Connecticut departments of community affairs, all created in

1966 and early 1967, had the broadest range of powers and were frequently used as models for creation of such departments in other states. All three involved a merger of existing agencies with new ventures for their state governments.

The Pennsylvania department combined such functions as technical assistance to local governments, the war on poverty, local planning aid, housing assistance, recreation and conservation aid, mass transit aid, a state Model Cities program, and urban renewal assistance. New Jersey's department lacked the mass transit and conservation programs but had all the other functions of the Pennsylvania department and in addition carried out such functions as local finance supervision, programs for youth and the elderly, day care demonstration centers, and a wide variety of experimental programs, particularly in housing and remedial education. Connecticut's department had a similar basic package of programs tied closely to comprehensive community development action plans. The Pennsylvania department had $47.3 million in appropriations for 1969, Connecticut $41.3 million from bond issues and appropriations, New Jersey $26 million from appropriations and bond issues, plus the bonding power of a housing finance agency operating at a $25-million-a-year pace. In addition, there were varying amounts of federal and foundation funds channeled to the departments.

The New Jersey department can be considered representative of the new agencies. It was the largest in terms of staff, with about 400 employees in 1969, an indication that it emphasized direct program action more than the other states and relied less on the formula aid programs which require smaller administrative staffs in comparison with appropriations. Creation of the department was first proposed by Governor Hughes in 1961 but it took five years to win the approval of an unenthusiastic legislature. The department began operations March 1, 1967, under the direction of Paul N. Ylvisaker, whose experience as director of public affairs for the Ford Foundation put him in the front rank of the nation's urban practitioners.

The department inherited a mixture of attitudes and reputations with the agencies pieced together for its creation. The Division of Local Finance was known as a dependable, stolid rampart against fiscal recklessness in local government. The Office of Economic Opportunity, the oldest such state agency in the nation, had already compiled a reputation for extemporaneous tradition-busting. The Division of State and Regional Planning had a solid rating within its profession but wore the standard "dreamer" label pinned on planners by outsiders. The new Office of Community Services, with its technical assistance and Model Cities programs, was viewed variously on the local scene as a bunch of upstarts and a valuable place to get both financial and professional help. The Division of Housing and Urban Renewal, with a battery of new housing programs, was looked at with plain suspicion. The department's statutory assignment contained built-in conflicts with longstanding state bureaucracies. Its activities crossed normal functional lines and many of its staff were firmly convinced that challenging established institutions was essential, if state and local government were to be made workable.

The result was an expectable amount of hostility from fellow bureaucrats, both at the state and local level. As an official of another stage agency confided to his counterpart in the Department of Community Affairs during the first year of its existence, "When one department has to go into another department's territory, it tips its hat and politely asks, 'May we come in?' You guys knock the door down and zoom in on motorcycles." Events added to the controversial reputation. Major combat between black residents and police occurred in Newark, Plainfield and other New Jersey communities in the summer of 1967. The infant department, with a high proportion of black employees and state government's closest working contact with the black community, was drawn into a central role in providing emergency services and setting up communication between ghetto residents and the legal authority. Commissioner Ylvisaker found himself risking life, limb and reputation when he leaped in front of National Guard armored personnel carriers in Plainfield to delay a search of black residents' homes until some of the heavy armament could be removed to cut down the potential for provocation. Further bloodshed, but not controversy, was avoided.

Less than a year after its establishment, the department found itself the target of a bill in the legislature which would have dismantled it. However, the abolition measure was condemned widely in the press and by a sizable number of legislators of both major parties. The bill died and the department survived. The sponsor of the measure, a legislator with a reputation for sincere conservatism, later said passage was never the intention. The new department needed chastening for its overly expensive ambitions, he explained. In other states, similar agencies also found themselves operating in the outer regions of legislative tolerance. Many of them were greatly disappointed by lack of financial and statutory support.

The New Jersey department's "motorcycle" reputation dwindled in some areas as its largely youthful staff learned some of the discreet rules of bureaucratic operation and some of the bureaucracies became resigned to seeing the Department of Community Affairs apparently everywhere. But the nature of the job made controversy a way of life for such departments. Operating on the urban frontier, without a clear product to advertise, with no consensus strategy to provide cover, treading across levels and lines of government, challenging dearly held views on race, home rule and even motherhood, such departments could not achieve safety without surrender.

NEW YORK TAKES ANOTHER APPROACH

New York State, which had long led the other states and often the federal government in attacking the urban crisis, chose not to set up a comprehensive community affairs department like those in its neighboring states of Massachusetts, Connecticut, Rhode Island, Pennsylvania, New Jersey and Ohio. Instead, it carried on most of the same functions through a variety of separate agencies. There were some advantages to its method of operation. Its Office of Planning Coordination, operating as part of the governor's office, was in a position to move freely across lines of government without generating the animosity and lack of response that plagued HUD and some of the state community affairs departments. The same freedom applied to the Office of Urban Innovation, established by Governor Rockefeller in 1968. The disadvantage was that such offices lacked some of the leverage obtained through direct ties with operating programs. In New Jersey's Community Affairs Department, the Office of Program Development not only devised new programs, it operated them through the pilot stage before they were spun off to other line agencies. Presentation of a fait accompli, rather than a proposal, to a line agency has some advantages in maintaining the vitality of a new program.

New York had long been the nation's leader in construction of low and moderate-income housing. Its legislation was the model for other states which engaged in housing construction programs through limited dividend and non-profit corporations. Its Housing Finance Agency law was copied by other states in the 1960s and its Division of Housing and Community Renewal operated urban renewal and housing assistance programs similar to those which formed a major part of the line functions of community affairs departments in the other states. Still other agencies carried on New York's human resources programs, which were numerous enough to require a 161-page catalog to describe. Thus, while New York did not follow the developing trend toward comprehensive urban affairs agencies, its multi-faceted approach was as direct and activist as the others. Given strong personal involvement of the governor's office, there was no reason why New York's approach would not work as well as the others, although with a different set of strengths and weaknesses.

LIMITATIONS OF LOCAL AFFAIRS AGENCIES

One limitation of the community affairs agencies was that beyond some high-sounding but ineffective language about "coordination" of other agencies inserted into their statutes, they had little to say about some of the most important urban programs—welfare, taxes, road construction, health care, etc. It would not have been practical to assign all of these functions on a statewide basis to one department. For instance in New Jersey, which was almost entirely urban, every state department, including even the Department of Agriculture, had a role in urban affairs. The vision of an all-encompassing, planned attack on urban problems led a few states to venture into creation of new mechanisms.

Comprehensive, Planned Approaches

THE MODEL CITIES PROGRAM

One of these new approaches was centered on the Model Cities program, which originally was conceived with traditional, direct federal-city ties, omitting the states as participants. The Model Cities program was born as a natural evolutionary step beyond the urban renewal and anti-poverty programs. But the assumptions and internal logic of the Model Cities program gave it some potential characteristics of a new departure, rather than just an eclectic collection of physical and social programs. The Model Cities process, which involved a comprehensive human and physical resources plan drawn up for a sizable urban neighborhood, created governmental relationships which required constantly escalating commitments of the government agencies. It was a difficult process to let go of.

The Demonstration Cities and Metropolitan Development Act of 1966 required "widespread citizen participation in the program," a phrase which did not sound as sweeping as the "maximum feasible participation" by the poor required in the earlier War on Poverty legislation. In implementing the general phraseology of the law, HUD issued a program guide in 1967 stating, ". . . there must be some form of organization structure, existing or newly established, which embodies neighborhood residents in the process of policy and program planning and program implementation and operation. The leadership of that structure must consist of persons whom neighborhood residents accept as representing their interests."

As the program developed, the HUD guidelines produced a kind of two-headed control of the Model Cities programs. In many cities, neighborhood representatives were elected formally and won veto power over the actions of the city demonstration agencies, who were employees of the regular city administration. In some cities, the neighborhood planning councils began to take on the role of a statutory city council. Some councils demanded and received separate planning staff assistance to give them the technical base for responding to the proposals emanating from the city demonstration agency staffs. Some Model Cities programs ran into serious delays and others foundered completely because of inability to make the two-headed system work. But many got safely through the first years of the program under dual leadership. Officials of the Nixon administration in 1969 sought to clear up some of the ambiguity with statements aimed at putting the mayors in charge. For instance, Robert H. Baida, Deputy Assistant Secretary of HUD for Model Cities and Governmental Relations, said in a speech, "The Model Cities Program is not to be controlled by citizen groups. Control and responsibility rests with local government. Unfortunately, this administration inherited a philosophy in many areas in the country dedicated toward extensive citizen control." But whether citizen control of Model Cities programs could be eliminated quietly by statements from on high remained to be seen. Many a mayor was likely to find it easier and safer to accept the status quo.

In the beginning, the Model Cities process at the federal level was almost entirely the province of the Department of Housing and Urban Development. However, HUD's coordinating function was of little real value in putting together the pieces needed from other departments. The Urban Affairs Council created by the Nixon administration soon after it took office raised the level of coordination above the cabinet level. In no time, men like HUD Secretary George Romney were talking of expanding the Model Cities program citywide and making it the major delivery system for federal aid to cities. Once the huge fiscal and administrative implications became apparent, however, the talk dwindled.

THE STATES AND MODEL CITIES

While the states were not originally part of the Model Cities design, they could not be kept out for long. For one thing, many federal aid programs, particularly those of the Department of Health, Education and Welfare, were channeled through the states to the cities. For another, the Model Cities program implied an across-the-board attack on urban problems, even if only within a narrowly circumscribed geographic area. If such a broad programmatic approach was to be carried out, the states had to be involved.

Pennsylvania and New Jersey were among the first states to get into the Model Cities program, providing through their community affairs departments assistance to cities in financing and preparing their proposals for submission to HUD. The difficulties of coordination at the state level duplicated the experiences of HUD at the federal level. Governor Hughes of New Jersey created the first state urban affairs council a few weeks after the federal council was established. The assignment was comparable to the federal council's —to coordinate urban programs above the cabinet level, with the Model Cities program as the first specific target. Governor Shafer of Pennsylvania created a similar council later in the year, as did such other states as Wisconsin and Minnesota.

MODEL CITIES: ADVANTAGES AND DISADVANTAGES

The full implications of the Model Cities program were not translated into results in the first three years of the program. The planning process, which had the potential of directing government and private programs to fill the full range of needs of the residents of an area, in most cases produced only a collection of warmed-over anti-poverty and urban renewal proposals. Government agencies at the local, state and federal levels were all unable to achieve a fully coordinated response to the plans. And the funding, almost entirely federal, was at much too low a level, threatening to starve the performance out of the program.

Nevertheless, the Model Cities program did avoid some of the flaws in traditional urban programs. It broke down some of the old categorical channels that sent funds from Washington to the cities. It relied heavily on the consumer of public services to determine his own needs and select the strategies for filling them. It sought to apply a rudimentary form of systems analysis in designing the programs. It provided flexible, block grant financing aimed at matching programs with resources. And it forced muscle-bound bureaucracies to loosen up a bit.

EXTENSIONS OF THE MODEL CITIES APPROACH

One reason the Model Cities program may have struck a responsive chord with some of the states was that it resembled programs of planned urban development they had begun themselves. Pennsylvania embarked in 1968 on a Partnership Cities program, which commits the facilities of state government to a planned program designed cooperatively with the local government involved.

Connecticut's Community Affairs Department engaged in an even more ambitious systematic attack on community problems. It was given authority to require localities to draw up comprehensive community development action plans as a condition for receiving state grants. The planning process was spelled out in detail and included both physical and human resources planning. The grants covered varying percentages of the cost of such categorical programs as urban beautification, neighborhood facilities, housing code enforcement, urban renewal, harbor improvement, tax abatement, anti-poverty programs, and industrial and business projects. However, some unconvinced local officials complained that the program involved too much unproductive paper work during the lengthy planning process and merely repeated the rote statements typical of requirements for federal programs.

ATTEMPTS TO BROADEN PLANNED URBAN DEVELOPMENT

The Model Cities program, Pennsylvania's Partnership City program, and Connecticut's Community Development Action Plan all basically involved a broad-scale attack within a limited geographic area. For center cities, this was a significant limitation. For instance, it was not possible to draw up a plan for solving the narcotics problem within one Model Cities neighborhood. Nor was there any chance for a long-term answer to housing problems in a city ghetto area if all demolition, relocation, rehabilitation and construction had to take place within the confines of one neighborhood or even one city. Limiting geography reduced some of the infinity of variables in defining needs but it also closed some of the possibilities for real solutions.

The inherent limitations of trying to deal with urban problems within a narrowly contained geographical area had long been recognized. It was this recognition that led to proposals for construction of new communities, regional government or statewide comprehensive planning. While there had been frequent discussion of such concepts, the states had done little but talk about them. Most often, state involvement in controlling and carrying out such complete urban development programs was blocked almost immediately by home rule arguments. However, several states started ambitious urban development programs that met the home rule issue head-on in the late 1960s.

THE URBAN DEVELOPMENT CORPORATION

New York State, in another of its pioneering efforts, created an Urban Development Corporation in 1968. It was the most powerful statewide instrument for urban development created in the nation. The corporation was given authority to issue one billion dollars' worth of revenue bonds. Coupled with anticipated private financing, the corporation was expected to generate at least five billion dollars' worth of physical redevelopment. Its powers included housing construction, urban renewal, and commercial and industrial development and, in fact, enough authority to provide the physical facilities for an entire community. Two allied corporations were also created by the same package of legislation. One corporation was a private agency with power to lend funds to private enterprise for renewal of blighted areas and to finance development and research. The other, the Urban Development Guarantee Fund of New York, was given authority to guarantee loans made by private lending institutions to residential property owners and small businessmen unable to obtain financing elsewhere. The two allied corporations existed only on paper for more than a year, however.

Among the most significant characteristics of the Urban Development Corporation were the direct involvement of a state agency in urban renewal, the use of a public benefit corporation to exercise broad powers which had previously been considered the province of government, and the authority to override local zoning regulations in carrying out the corporation's functions. The authority to disregard local objections in renewing substandard areas was the most controversial feature of the legislation. The law required cooperation and coordination with local plans, but ultimately the corporation's nine-member board of directors could override local objections by a two-thirds vote. Passage of the law was obtained by the Rockefeller administration April 9, 1968, the day of the Reverend Martin Luther King's funeral. There were some home rule protests from local officials, most notably from Mayor John Lindsay of New York City. Chosen president and chief executive officer of the UDC was Edward J. Logue, who had acquired a reputation for producing results as head of two of the nation's most successful urban renewal programs, in New Haven and Boston.

The corporation in its first year of activity did not use its power to override local objection. It entered municipalities only upon

invitation. One local leader, quoted by Barry R. Fischer in MONI-
TOR, official publication of Associated Industries of New York
State, Inc., said, "I'd just like to see UDC march into some suburban
area and impose their will. It would take a year for the political
smoke to clear and UDC would lose, not the locality." In truth,
UDC's early activities were devoted largely to housing construction
in center cities. Early in 1969 it acquired 2,100 acres of land in the
town of Lysander, about 15 miles northwest of Syracuse, and an-
nounced plans to develop a new community of 16,000 population.
Like agencies in many other states, the UDC found new community
development a tempting method of starting with a clean slate in
dealing with the problems of urban development.

The UDC was not without critics who held no great allegiance to
home rule. Some urban experts thought it was not making the most
of its powers. Others questioned the fact that UDC was created as an
additional agency in New York's urban affairs attack, without any
attempt to coordinate it with existing agencies or to fit it into a
comprehensive urban strategy. There was some disappointment at
the minor role either given to or accepted by private enterprise. But
the UDC was a state instrumentality with a capacity to accomplish
much that had been impossible before. As such, it was the envy of
officials in other states with less adventurous urban policies.

A REGIONAL DEVELOPMENT AGENCY

A state action of comparable boldness and significance was New
Jersey's creation of the Hackensack Meadowlands Development
Commission. The law, enacted in January 1969 after years of pushing and pulling in the legislature, created a state commission with
broad master planning and development powers over 28 square miles
of marshland only five miles west of Manhattan. The marshland
had been passed over for three centuries in the development of the
New York metropolitan area because technology was not up to the
task of building on the soggy ground at reasonable cost. It was used
largely as a dump by 128 communities and is one of the most un-
sightly areas on earth. However, with advanced technology, an investment of some $300 million would allow the land to be reclaimed
for urban development worth several billions. In recent years, development of low-profile, low-employment uses, such as warehouses,
had been spreading into the Meadowlands, which lie in 14 municipalities and two counties. The local governments were engaged in
competition to attract whatever development they could, to help
spread the burden of New Jersey's extremely high local property

taxes. Short-range fiscal considerations overrode any thought of long-range benefit or protection of the environment. The legislation was enacted only over angry opposition based on the home rule tradition. Even after enactment, the battle was not over. Local officials challenged the constitutionality of the law in court.

The state-appointed commission was created as a semi-independent arm of the Department of Community Affairs, and Commissioner Ylvisaker was appointed Chairman of the seven-member agency. The commission's plans were to be worked out in cooperation with the 14 municipalities, and the 14 mayors were given a veto power by majority vote. But the commission had the ultimate power to override the mayors' vetoes by a five-sevenths vote. The commission's powers included authority to draw up a master plan for the Meadowlands, set construction standards, oversee the reclamation, act as a redevelopment agency, sell revenue bonds to finance its activities and assess private property for beneficial public improvements it installed. One of the most significant features of the law was a unique system for sharing property tax benefits from new construction. The value of new development is pooled and each municipality shares in proportion to its acreage in the Meadowlands District. Thus actual location of a specific tax ratable would not affect the revenue to any municipality. The tax-sharing pool eliminated the competitive underbidding for ratables.

Development of the Meadowlands was envisioned as a massive project which would take decades to accomplish. It involved a total planning effort that would strain to the limit the state of the art of urban development. It combined all of the difficulties of developing a new community with those of redeveloping an area ringed by some of the most urbanized communities on earth.

The Need to Change the Ground Rules

New York's Urban Development Corporation and New Jersey's Hackensack Meadowlands Development Commission represented high stages of evolution in the states' attempts to deal directly with the problems of urban development through agencies capable of carrying out planned, coordinated strategies. But as powerful and unique as these agencies were, they were in no way a final answer to the question of what the states' proper role in urban development and planning should be. Given the scale of urban problems in New York and New Jersey, neither the Urban Development Corporation nor the Meadowlands Commission represented a solution. It would be more accurate to consider them large-scale pilot projects. Possibly the most significant feature of such mechanisms was that they both depended on dispensation from some of the ground rules which hamstring the states' efforts to deal with urban problems. In order to make these agencies effective, it was felt necessary to exempt them from some of the customary tax, home rule and organizational restrictions. Outside their spheres of activity, the old ground rules continued to prevail, acting as a drag on the states' chances of coming to grips with the problems of urban development. If such agencies achieved success, there was a strong prospect that they could represent no more than a dry seat on a sinking lifeboat.

There are inherent difficulties in direct-action responses to urban problems. As Jay Forrester points out in *Urban Dynamics,*

> . . . the massive action program, if it does nothing about the underlying causes of difficulty, simply comes into conflict with the operation of a system which is already set at cross purposes. The internal forces in most social systems are so powerful that they will likely dominate any effort to treat symptoms, if treatment does not reach to the true structural causes.

Reaching true structural causes is, of course, a frustrating business, laden with political risk. Many times it lacks the quick humanitarian rewards of direct action programs. Applications for grants to federal and state agencies are replete with statements that the program proposed will produce results with "high visibility." Quite often, such programs also produce results which soon become invisible.

Another limitation of the direct-action response is that it led to more action than anyone could handle. Programs and projects multiplied in bewildering complexity. This impelled a search for "coordination," a search that seemed destined to inevitable failure. As long as the basic system of government and private actions worked to deepen the urban crisis, direct-action programs aimed at the ever-multiplying symptoms were bound to proliferate and defy anyone's coordinating capacities. Many direct-action programs were competitive both in terms of objectives and in consumption of resources, whether human, financial or physical.

Lingering in the background was the ever-present hope that a comprehensive planned urban strategy could be developed to solve the difficulties with coordination and duplication. Unfortunately, much of this planning tried to wrench basic forces out of shape and pin them neatly to a map. Many maps and glossy reports resulted, but few comprehensive plans ever got beyond that stage. There is reason to believe that the problems were far more comprehensive than any plan could ever be.

Finally, direct-action programs that avoid changing the ground rules relieve the pressure on established institutions to make fundamental changes. Remedial education courses conducted by poverty programs allow school systems to go on using the methods that produce dropouts. State or federal aid to cities can paper over basic defects in local tax systems. A police community relations unit can leave the main body of a police force to go its way generating animosity in the community. As Forrester puts it, "An action program changes the system balance so that the system relaxes its own internal pressures. As the outside effort picks up the burden, more and more is left to the outside effort."

THE STATES' ROLE IN CHANGING GROUND RULES

Thus, there would seem to be little chance of easing the urban crisis unless the basic ground rules can be changed to reduce the overwhelming forces that work against both direct action and planned development. The states, of course, have only one piece of the action in setting the ground rules. The urban crisis is intertwined with crises in race relations, poverty, alienation, class conflict, technological change, and population growth; it is a phrase describing the plight of modern, post-industrial man; it is with us now and it is the coming thing. Viewed that way, the urban crisis may seem too much for the states and maybe everybody else. It is certainly much too big a bundle of troubles to be affected by traditional responses based on the idea that a specific class of local governments need a little special attention. Nor could such non-traditional instruments as New York's Urban Development Corporation or New Jersey's Hackensack Meadowlands Commission be multiplied enough times to bring them up to the scale of the problems. New York cannot turn over all urban development to a public benefit corporation nor can New Jersey declare itself a regional development district to be master-planned by an appointed commission.

But if direct action applied from outside and above seems to be an insufficient answer, it is possible that internal changes in the fundamental systems of the urban environment would provide enough leverage to stop the descending spiral. The changes would have to be the kind that result in a better physical environment and human services from the consumer's standpoint. When it comes to leverage needed to achieve that kind of change, the states occupy a critical position. As the basic particle in the federal molecule, they control many of the important links in the chain of private and public actions that could lead to real improvement in the urban environment.

The states hold power over these important ground rules:
They specify the internal workings of urban tax systems.
They set conditions that determine cost and use of land.

They have major influence over the internal content of basic services like education, transportation, health care, public safety and justice.

The states exercise their control over these basic ground rules of urban life through laws creating local property tax systems, state grant-in-aid programs, zoning laws, housing codes, teacher certification requirements, public school systems, colleges, universities, highways, transit systems, health codes, medical licensing, insurance rating systems, air and water pollution codes, the courts, police training requirements, etc. The interaction of these laws determines what happens inside school classrooms, how municipalities grow and decline, how people get to work, where factories locate, how medical bills are paid, where and what kind of housing gets built, how good the air is, whether the water is drinkable. Many of these laws have not been considered to be involved in the urban crisis. But many of the symptoms of the urban crisis are really signs of general defects in the quality of public services and controls. The defects seem to show up in urban areas because that is where the pressure is greatest. Putting an urban patch on a universally weak fabric merely shifts the strain to some nearby point which cannot bear up. If the states are to do their part in producing tolerable urban development, they must produce movement at the critical leverage points they control.

STATE TAX SYSTEMS

One of the most crucial of these leverage points is the tax system which states prescribe for themselves and their local governments. The high level of taxes makes them important determinants of private action. In their scramble to raise money, the states have ignored in large part the effect their policies have had on private activity. All too often, when the states turn to their tax problems, they view them only as a case of maladjustment between levels or classes of government. They rarely get into the internal workings of the taxes, to see what kind of private actions they stimulate.

The property tax is subject to more absurdities than any of the other major sources of revenue for state and local government. It counteracts most of the good intentions of zoning and planning laws. It drives industry away from the areas that need it most. It promotes creation of slums and impedes renewal. It is a disaster for the elderly and the poor. It adds to pressures that make downtown black and boondocks white. It generates a series of vicious spirals. Yet, when states turn to property tax reform, they generally produce only some tidying up of administration (undoubtedly needed) or efforts to counteract its gross imbalances through injections of aid from on high. Meanwhile, the tax is allowed to go on fueling the problems that create the needs which are never filled.

Short of abolition (which might not be a bad idea), the property tax must be internally readjusted to produce at least neutral results. It might even be possible to convert it into an asset by readjusting it to stimulate private actions that go in desirable directions. Unfortunately, there is little research and even less experience in that kind of adjustment. Heavily urbanized states with high property taxes, such as Massachusetts, California and New Jersey, may be forced into such efforts. (For a lengthier discussion of tax structure, see Dr. Roy Bahl's comments in Chapter 4.)

CONTROL OF LAND USE

A second important leverage point within the control of the states is the planning and zoning structure. With the exception of Hawaii and Alaska, both special cases, planning and zoning have been handed over by the states to local governments. In local hands, land use control has become a prized captive of the home rule tradition, a kind of security blanket to ward off threatening strangers. In an effort to combat rising property taxes, developing suburbs used restrictive zoning to keep out people, mostly poor people and, above all, black people. Lot sizes and living area specifications were used to legislate minimum prices for housing. The result was homogenized, compartmented non-communities. At the same time, justifiable defenses against deterioration of the environment seemed unable to hold up against the pressures. The states found that the adventurous housing construction programs they established in the 1960s were blocked in the suburbs by the zoning laws they had passed in the 1920s. They were forced to build in the center cities. Land costs made high-rise apartments the only feasible course, in spite of everyone's intention not to build any more high-rise apartments for families. In the suburbs, the large lot sizes spread people at low densities, raising the per capita cost of utilities and services. As a defense, the lot sizes were increased further. One New Jersey county on the suburban fringe of the New York metropolitan area

found in 1969 it had overdone its restrictive zoning. Taxpaying industries were moving out because they could not pay their help
enough to buy any housing within 30 miles.

A few states have made tentative efforts at regaining some of the
land use control powers they handed away, but political reality
stifles decisive action. Statewide planning is largely advisory and
there is relatively little coordinated control by states over even their
own construction and capital facilities. Some steps have been taken
to achieve regional or countywide land use planning, although federal requirements for regional planning failed to produce anything
basically different. In New Jersey, legislation initiated by the Community Affairs Department was proposed in 1969 to revise the local
planning and zoning system and install the rudiments of a planning
system for state-owned facilities. The local planning system would
not be fundamentally changed, except to ban use of zoning as an
exclusionary weapon and to require localities to pay more attention
to the effect of their actions on their neighbors. The state's control
over its own facilities would be exercised through use of a land bank
system to purchase sites in advance and through designation of critical areas around such facilities as highways, airports, reservoirs,
parks and forests, to protect the public investment. The legislation
ran into an immediate home rule backlash. However, a few more
thoughtful critics challenged the legislation on grounds that it was
too conservative, and in the long run their view was more likely to
be upheld in retrospect.

Massachusetts in 1969 enacted a law which tried to break through
local zoning barriers against low-income housing. It created an ap-
peals board within its Community Affairs Department with power to
overrule local decisions which raised insurmountable obstacles to
groups seeking to build housing for lower-income groups outside of
central cities. Whether such a procedure could actually produce
low-income housing in suburban areas remained to be seen.

A broad-scale court attack on local zoning was undertaken in 1969
by such groups as the National Committee Against Discrimination
in Housing and the National Association for the Advancement of
Colored People. They based their attack on grounds that the zoning
laws had been operated to deny equal protection of the law to racial
minorities. They expected to carry their challenge to the United
States Supreme Court eventually. If they were successful in chipping
some pieces off the traditional zoning structure, as seemed likely,
the very foundations of the structure could be placed in jeopardy
(not necessarily an unmitigated evil).

QUALITY OF URBAN SERVICES

A third major leverage point controlled by the states is their ability to specify the internal qualities of services which constitute much of the urban environment. In a rural society, the environment was largely in private hands and the sum total of private actions was not likely to create a crisis. But in a highly technological, urban society, where specialization has reached a high level, cities live constantly on the edge of crisis. The urban resident is critically dependent on a whole series of specialized services—transportation, health care, water supply, garbage disposal, air pollution control, education, public safety. Well-publicized instances of breakdown in these services in the 1960s constituted the most obvious symptom of what became known as the urban crisis.

The conventional wisdom holds that while the quality of public services may be subject to localized deterioration, it is otherwise acceptable. For instance, according to this viewpoint, health care among the affluent is acceptable but is inadequate for the poor; education is bad in the cities but is tolerable in the suburbs; police protection is adequate in rural areas but not in the ghetto. There is an underlying fallacy to the assumption that public services are internally sound, except when put to the test of an urban environment. This is really not different from saying our reservoirs are adequate, except when there is a drought.

The unfortunate consequence of perceiving only localized deterioration of public services is that it leads to localized remedies, which can do more harm than good. The statement that children educated in city schools suffer in comparison with their peers in suburban schools seems statistically unchallengeable. Statistics also show that teachers in suburban schools are paid better and the school buildings are newer and better-equipped. The suburbs are able to provide these things because they spend more money per pupil than do the cities. Therefore, the reasoning goes, it is necessary to get money to the cities so they can spend as much per pupil as do the suburbs. Usually, the prescription of localized remedy stops right there. Apparently, there is an assumption that given better buildings and higher pay, good teachers will depart their jobs in the suburbs and enlist in the uplift of ghetto children. Of course, the suburbs might decide not to bid farewell to their best teachers, but simply use their superior tax resources to raise their pay scales to reestablish their accustomed advantage, meanwhile vowing to put a stop to this sort of thing at the next session of the legislature. Or it may turn out that when the superior suburban teachers reach their brand-new ghetto classrooms, they are unable to think of anything to do that their predecessors didn't try.

In fact, is the product of the suburban school system so eminently satisfactory? Is there basic soundness in a school system that can distill the joy out of music, art and literature, all inventions designed originally to please? It is likely that the suburban pupil does better simply because he has more going for him outside school than does the pupil in a city ghetto. Education is not synonymous with the classroom. Cash poured in from outside is not likely to produce benefits over the long-range unless it is accompanied by changes both within the educational system and outside of the schools.

In the same way, health care for the poor probably cannot be improved long-term merely through attempts to put them on an equal financial footing with the affluent in the medical market place. First, it is unlikely that there is enough money anywhere to actually bring about such an equality. Adequate medical care, provided with all the inefficiencies and quality defects inherent in traditional medical business practices, would be prohibitively expensive if extended to those of moderate and low income. There is no guarantee that the health of poor people would improve appreciably if such care were available to them. Better health among the affluent is probably due as much to the life style affluence supports as it is to the availability of doctors, nurses, hospitals and medication. If anything is likely to improve health care for the poor, it would probably also improve it for the affluent. The widespread introduction of preventive medicine techniques, for instance, could be a useful change for people of all income levels. The fee-for-service system might have to be abolished to make preventive medicine an actuality.

Similarly, more highways are not likely to solve transportation problems. Nor is more professionalization or better pay for police the whole answer to the apparent deterioration in public safety. If enacted alone, such steps are likely to aggravate problems.

Direct Action on the Ground Rules

In any effort to change the ground rules that affect the quality of urban life, the states can learn much from their first traditional responses and their later efforts to deal with urban development through direct action.

In their traditional responses to the urban crisis, the states often chose as their subjects for action the fundamental systems that govern the quality of the urban environment. But their actions were tentative, fragmented and too superficial to have any real effect.

When states began taking direct action on urban development, their responses were often forthright and comprehensive, but they left most fundamental processes untouched; typically, they were demonstration projects, exceptions to rules which continued to prevail.

What is needed is the boldness and energy of the direct action response applied to the subject matter of the traditional response.

PLANNING FOR THE UNPLANNABLE

Efforts to take direct action on the ground rules of urban development should not be conducted as a piecemeal probing for better quality in government services. The efforts can and should be the subject of comprehensive planning, but planning of a different sort than the kind usually practiced by state governments.

Planning on the state level, where it exists at all, has been preoccupied with land use. The result, too often, has been an attempt to achieve impossible goals through irrelevant means. With maps and census statistics comprising much of the technology, attempts have been made to control the location and flow of population through land policy. The apparent assumption behind such planning is that if everyone could be placed properly in the landscape, the economic and social pieces would necessarily fall into place.

As states become involved in urban development, they find more and more of their fundamental governmental processes pulled into the network of interaction. Land use is only one of these processes and it is not always the most important one. It is these processes and their interaction which should be the subject of planning for urban development.

If the basic processes of state government were well-calculated to stimulate private actions that move in the right directions, it should not be necessary to adopt anything as inherently rigid as the zoning structures that result from planning which is land use-centered. The goal should be to design processes that leave the end results open to the spontaneous choice of a well-informed consumer. Like the rhythm section in a jazz band, the states can set the basic tempo and harmony, allowing spontaneity to do the rest. Order can be achieved without undue resort to rigidity and sorting out.

One reason state comprehensive planning has been preoccupied with land use is that until recently its perceived needs required little else and the technology permitted little more. Before the states became involved in the urban crisis, state planning typically dealt with location of highways, institutions, open space, and other physical facilities—all of which could be converted into problems of land use. At the same time, most of their social and economic services and regulatory programs were initiated in response to specific crises and generally were subject to little planning of any kind.

But planners themselves have shown increasing dissatisfaction with a narrow land use role and have begun to seek out new technologies. Electronic data processing, systems analysis and program-planning-budget systems are all being explored as methods of extending planning to the social and economic actions which states carry on all the time without benefit of planning. They make a new kind of planning possible.

The program-planning-budget (PPB) system, made famous when introduced in the United States Defense Department by Secretary Robert S. McNamara, is on its way to becoming a major tool in government planning. Traditionally, government policymaking starts with the questions: where are we now and where can we go from here? The PPB system starts with the questions: where do we want to go and how can we get there from here? Starting with this concept, there is erected a PPB system of goal-setting, consideration of alternatives, cost-benefit analysis, selection of programs, and budgeting, accounting and evaluation, all aided by flows of information from electronic data equipment.

There are possibilities for achieving rational state policies from such techniques, but the dangers are great also. The PPB system can be operated dishonestly or negligently to produce bad planning. Its operation is not automatic; selection of goals and program alternatives requires at least as much imagination and clear-headedness as the traditional methods. It is possible to start with preconceived budget notions and construct plausible goals and objectives to act as window dressing for the kind of decision-making process that asked: where are we now and where can we go from here?

In addition, the PPB system relies heavily on cost-benefit analysis, which favors so-called "hard" programs, like highway construction, over such "soft" programs as job training. If this bias were to affect state policies, all sorts of mischief would result. Cost-benefit analysis can be manipulated to produce almost any desired answer. For instance, new freeways are often justified on grounds they will save carefully calculated amounts of gasoline for drivers; meanwhile, the oil lobby presses for more freeways. Either there is something wrong with the assumption in the cost-benefit analysis or there are unsuspected strains of altruism in the petroleum industry. It is likely that if a proposed freeway were to increase gasoline consumption, the added motor vehicle tax revenue would be claimed as a benefit.

But budget-making is one of the fundamental processes of state government that must be pulled into any comprehensive approach to urban development. The PPB system represents the kind of technology that must exist if state planning is to become more than an adjunct to the real estate business.

THE WELL-INFORMED CONSUMER

Planning for urban development that leaves the ultimate choices to be made by well-informed consumers must place heavy reliance on a price system that reflects real costs accurately. Such a price system does not prevail now. Instead, prices, particularly those for government services, do not reflect actual costs and do not provide accurate bases for decision. This is true of small things, such as privately marketed plastic containers which are cheap for the manufacturer to make and the consumer to use, but are expensive for government to dispose of. It is also true of big things, such as highway or urban renewal construction, where many of the real costs for destruction of housing and businesses are shifted to other parts of the economy.

Some costs are now wrongly allocated among government programs, i.e., housing program costs which are actually part of the price of a highway that plowed through a city neighborhood. Other costs are debited to the government when they belong to the private sector, i.e., apparent increases in taxes for solid waste disposal which are actually part of the cost of advances in the technology of plastics production. Some government costs are concealed by shifting them to the private sector, such as the loss of good will suffered by a merchant whose store and clientele are wiped out by urban renewal. Such a faulty price structure provides bad information for planners and policymakers in government and for consumers in the private sector. It is usually the "soft," intangible costs—the destruction of a neighborhood, damage to ecology and environment, social dislocations—which are hardest to measure and easiest to conceal. Because of this, such values are written off at zero in the cost-benefit calculations and are disregarded in the private and public market place.

If the vogue for systems analysis of government programs and services takes hold, it could provide the basis for a realistic price system. Thus, an analysis of New York City's streets, bus lines, subways, bridges, tunnels, and elevators that viewed these facilities as part of one system for moving people might result in realistic cost-benefit calculations. Policymakers and consumers might then be able to make a valid decision on whether it is cheaper to raise the subway fare, tunnel and bridge tolls, or real estate taxes.

Another necessity in such a price system is recognition of quality. The new planning technologies can be seriously distorted through selection of units of output that seemingly possess virtues of objectivity, but actually stress quantity at the expense of quality. Thus, health care programs that measure output in patients treated or education programs that measure pupils per dollar are really measuring only input. Patients treated negligently or pupils educated badly should not be counted on the benefit side of the ledger; they are costs.

CHALLENGING THE ESTABLISHMENTS

Proper use of the new technologies equips the states to engage in kinds of planning they have not done before. It can produce greater knowledge of the interaction of processes conducted by intuition now. Decisions can be made to redirect fundamental processes of government so that quality and diversity are emphasized.

Undoubtedly, decisions by the states which involve changing the ground rules that underlie government programs and services will run head-on into deeply entrenched establishments. Teacher groups are allies when governments propose channeling more tax funds into education. They can become enemies when the consumer proposes changes aimed at improving quality or expanding diversity in education. Medical doctors have come to accept the government as the source of some of their fees, but change in the fee system itself is not likely to be acceptable. All the establishments resist efforts to penetrate the solid barriers of professionalism and specialization they have erected over the years. Frequently, creation of sub-professional employment categories offers a solution simultaneously to problems of poverty, racial discrimination and manpower shortages in technical fields, yet just as frequently such solutions are resisted by the establishments as threats to professionalism. Professionalism and specialization are highly prized by producers of services, but may not be of such great value to the consumers of these services. They also contribute to the sorting out of society by income, age, residence, race, occupation and class. They help stifle diversity and mobility, necessary ingredients of a tolerable urban society.

The political risks in challenging the establishments are great. But there is little chance that the fundamental processes that contribute to the deteriorating quality of urban life can be changed unless the establishments are confronted. They are, in fact, being challenged on many fronts—by community action agencies, Model Cities neighborhood councils, college students, Ralph Nader, black militants, muckrakers, hippies, unfrocked priests, and dissidents within the ranks. It is a noisy, confusing process, and quality often becomes a casualty. But through the noise and fumes, the states should perceive that the establishments are under attack for reasons that are not unrelated to the daily concerns of state government.

Conclusion

The states have at last come alive to the urban crisis. With a handful leading the way, they have stirred themselves to take direct action on the problems of urban development. Some of those actions have displayed boldness and innovation which may yet rescue the states' reputation as incubators of good ideas. But lying unexplored and unexploited is the great body of ground rules which the states set intuitively and which help produce much of what has become known as the urban crisis. Until they turn hot enthusiasm and cool minds to these ground rules, there can be little real headway made against the tide of the urban crisis.

John M. DeGrove

6

Help or Hindrance to State Action?
The National Government

Flexibility and adaptability have been the hallmarks of government in the United States from the very beginning. The allocation of functional responsibility among the three levels of government—national, state, and local—is no exception. Given this flexibility, there has been a natural parallel concern with maintaining a balance of power in the federal system among its major components. For much of our history, this concern was confined to questions of state versus national government power. More recently, with the drastic expansion of national-local relations since World War II, and especially since 1960, the concern has involved all three levels of government. This chapter has as its prime purpose an assessment of how national government action, chiefly via the grant-in-aid device, can move the states more squarely into the mainstream of urban action. That such movement is necessary if states

JOHN M. DEGROVE *is Dean of the College of Social Science of Florida Atlantic University, where he was previously chairman of the political science department. He has been a consultant to state and local governments on problems of structure and function and was a member of the President's Commission on Urban Problems which completed its report in 1968. Dean DeGrove has in preparation a study of political leadership patterns in selected urban communities and is co-author of* City Managers in Politics: An Analysis of Manager Tenure and Terminations *and* The Urban Political Community: Profiles in Town Politics.

are to remain as major partners in the federal system is generally admitted. The alternative may well be two sturdy, full-length legs —and one short, frail one—undergirding the federal system.

SEPARATION VS. SHARING IN FEDERALISM DOCTRINE

Much of the traditional writing on the nature and function of the federal system in the United States has focused on legalistic interpretations of what functions should be performed by which level of government. There was typically an assumption, explicit or implicit, that whole functions had to be assigned to the national or state governments, after which the excluded level had little or nothing to do with performing the function. In a recently published study of federalism, titled *The American System,* prepared by Morton Grodzins and edited for publication after his death by Daniel J. Elazar, what amounts to a major reinterpretation of the past, present, and projected future of the federal system is made. Grodzins first developed the sharing thesis in *Goals for Americans,* published in 1960 under the auspices of The American Assembly. He stated flatly that "the American federal system has never been a system of separated governmental activities. There has never been a time when it was possible to put neat labels on discrete 'federal,' 'state,' and 'local' functions." To Grodzins, American federalism is a system of sharing, a "marblecake" rather than a "layer cake." Its principal feature is and has been the mutual interaction of national, state, and local governments to solve problems that steadily increase in complexity and intensity.

There is a general acceptance of the Grodzins thesis as the correct interpretation of the current and future, if not the historical, nature of the federal system. The Advisory Commission on Intergovernmental Relations, which has emerged in the last decade as the major assessor and interpreter of the federal system, seems to accept the premise as both what is and what should be. The premise includes the proposition that while local governments legally are creatures of the state, politically they are full partners in the system.

FEDERALISM AS A DOCTRINE IN 1969

The nature of much of the debate concerning the federal system seems, as we review it today, almost a product of another world. It was a world in which domestic problems were pressing to be sure, but not so pressing as to shunt aside ideological and legalistic debates. As late as 1956, President Eisenhower was talking about turning the clock back, and he seemed to faithfully represent a rising tide of objection to the steady expansion of national government programs, based on both constitutional and public policy grounds. The trend seemed for a time strong enough to force the national government back into a narrow and rigid frame in which "state and local governments individually would determine the need for new governmental activities." The movement seemed to reach a peak in 1957, when the National Governors Conference eagerly responded to an Eisenhower suggestion that led to the establishment of the Joint Federal-State Action Committee charged with the responsibility of pinpointing programs and revenue sources that could be shifted from Washington to the states. The inability of the committee to develop any major shifts, and the cool reception for the modest proposals made, were indications that talk, not action, would dominate the debate over de-escalating federal grant programs.

The sweep of history has left the nation with no time and at least a declining inclination to indulge in such debates. The rising crisis of the cities, fed steadily by our inability to make even strong beginnings at solving the maze of problems that flow from the collection of so many low-income Americans, including a majority of all black Americans, in the nation's great cities occupies an increasingly large part of our time. Surely, most would agree that the central question is no longer how to scale down the efforts of the national government—though most would agree that major improvement in the effectiveness of that effort is needed—but how to raise the level of state effort to a full partnership role in dealing with urban problems. Federalism in 1969 is more than ever pragmatic, and new patterns are emerging as the national government vastly expands its long-standing policy of returning a portion of the rich "take" from the income tax to state and local governments via grants-in-aid.

THE PATTERN OF PROGRAM GRANTS: 1787 TO 1960

In elaborating on his theme that "the American federal system had never been a system of separated governmental activities," Morton Grodzins traced the development of federalism through four periods: (a) questions without answers—before 1797; (b) federalism and adjustment—1787–1800; (c) the period of cross-currents—1800–1913; and (d) the triumph of cooperative federalism—1913–1948. To Grodzins, the system of sharing responsibility for meeting public problems was evident across all four periods. The early land grants gave way to money grants based on the estimated value of land, which in turn became annual cash grants. The first continuing cash grant coincided closely with the closing of the frontier. Congress in 1879 authorized aid for teaching material for the blind, a program still administered by the Department of Health, Education, and Welfare. In the last two decades of the nineteenth century, three more programs involving annual grants of money were approved, beginning with aid for agricultural experiment stations in 1887.

The categorical grant system as it exists today is usually traced back to 1862, the year Congress enacted the Morrill Act to aid states in establishing land grant colleges.[1] The assistance was in the form of land, but the strings attached to the grants were clear-cut and rather specific. The objectives of the program were spelled out, and use of the funds restricted accordingly. Annual reports were required. The irrelevance of the constitutional issue today in determining the expansion or contraction of the national government's grant program should not obscure the fact that just that issue probably did slow significantly the movement of Washington into the cash grant field. National government assistance to states in developing "internal improvement" projects was restricted to land, where the constitutional mandate to dispose of the national domain in the public interest seemed clear. Attempts to provide grants of money for such things as roads and aid to veterans, however, ran into vigorous constitutional objections. While the national government gave away millions of acres of land for aid to such things as wagon roads, canals, and railroads (Florida alone received almost 20,000,000 acres of land under the Swamp Lands Act of 1850), efforts by Congress to augment a cash grant system typically ran into presidential vetoes. Presidents Monroe and Jackson vetoed bills providing funds for roads, and Jackson in 1832 turned down Henry Clay's proposal to give money grants to states to support both roads and education. The perspective of history, of course, reveals these constitutional anxieties as a minor interruption in a long-term trend that has gained strength over the years.

The Advisory Commission on Intergovernmental Relations (ACIR), in Volume I of *Fiscal Balance in the American Federal System*, presents a survey of the development of the categorical aid system. The first two decades of the twentieth century saw the addition of two major programs, one of special interest because

---

[1] Throughout the chapter, I have drawn on the published and unpublished materials of the Advisory Commission on Intergovernmental Relations. I am greatly indebted to Commission Executive Director William Coleman, Elton K. McQuery and others for their help.

of its incentive objective. The rising popularity of automobiles created a road crisis, and the national government responded by enacting in 1916 the first of many succeeding bills to assist in managing the automobile explosion. Bills to aid vocational education and rehabilitation followed in 1917 and 1920, with the major purpose being to lure the states into providing vocational training through their local governments to meet certain manpower skills generated by World War I. The two pieces of legislation represented the clearest example to that date of using the grant as a stimulating device.

Developments during the Depression focused on new welfare and economic recovery programs aimed at reestablishing economic stability in the nation. ACIR reports that 17 of the 95 "broad" grant categories existing today (there are more than 400 individual categorical grants) were adopted during the 1931–1945 period. A variety of welfare, health, and housing programs of immediate or potential significance to the nation's urban areas, and especially to its great cities, were included.

During the 1946–1960 period, new programs tended to concentrate in the health, education, and welfare areas, with important additions in transportation (aid to airports, the interstate highway system) and pollution control. The steady addition of new grants has meant a shift from time to time in program focus. The welfare focus of the 1930s kept almost two-thirds of the grant payments in the health, labor, and welfare fields through 1955. After that, the massive infusion of new money via the Federal Highway Act of 1956—$2.25 billion additional in highway grants by 1960—shifted the aid emphasis to commerce and transportation.

A brief review of the development of the national government's categorical grant system sets the stage for the cloudburst of new national government grant programs after 1961, a significant portion of which were aimed at bringing the dollar power of Washington to bear on the agony of the cities. Ten grant programs were approved prior to 1930; 17 during the 1931–1945 period; and 29 during the 1946–1960 period. While the 1950s look relatively mild in terms of grant program expansion when compared to what has happened in the 1960s, a number of major new programs, many of key importance in the development of urban programs by Washington, were approved. The 1949 approval of urban renewal legislation and an expanded commitment to public housing, aid to education in "impacted" areas, urban planning assistance, and water pollution control all stand high on the list of the most critical needs of the cities. The stage was set for the hyper-active sixties in the development of the categorical grant system.

Contemporary Patterns in National Grant Programs

THE GENERAL EXPANSION AND PROLIFERATION OF GRANTS

It is against a setting of rapid escalation that the incentive or stimulation possibilities of the national government's grant programs will be examined. If a prime objective in our society is to bring all states, or at least the larger industrial-urban states, into full partnership status in confronting urban problems, then surely logic would argue that the expanding role of the national government's grant program offers major leverage possibilities. One does not have to be a complete economic determinist to agree that, at least to a degree, power follows dollars. How extensive has been the expansion of the use of the grant device? How could it be modified to promote a larger role in urban affairs for state governments? Are there other, non-grant approaches that could be followed by the national government to strengthen the states in urban problems? Questions such as these will be assessed in the remainder of this chapter.

The avalanche of new grant programs during the 1960s was clearly an effort by the national government to respond to the plight of the cities. It took place within a setting of continued state neglect of their urban, and especially their large-city, children.

The new programs concentrate overwhelmingly in two departments—Housing and Urban Development, and Health, Education, and Welfare. Many of these programs go to the heart of city, and especially larger-city, problems. Open space, air pollution, model cities, special support for ghetto schools, the various components of the poverty program, basic water and sewer facilities, and a wide variety of health services are only a partial listing. Many of these new programs bypass the states, and send aid directly from Washington to local governments.

The impact of the "creative federalism" expansion of grant programs on the allocation of fiscal responsibilities in the federal system is impressive. The outburst of activity meant that grants-in-aid as a proportion of total national government spending rose from 4.6 percent in 1955 to over 10 percent in 1968. Grant programs from Washington to state and local governments represented about 11 percent of total state-local revenue in 1957. A decade later, the total had increased to over 17 billion dollars, representing 17 percent of state-local revenue. Comparable estimates for Fiscal 1970 range from 20 to 25 billion dollars, with the percentage of all state-local revenue rising to over 20 percent. One long-range assessment of fiscal needs and resources calls for a fairly rapid movement to a full one-third of all state-local revenue being supplied from the "top" of the federal system. President Johnson's estimate that national government grants might total $50 billion by 1975 simply moves in that direction.

DIRECT FEDERALISM

A distinguishing feature of the "grant explosion" of the 1960s was the expansion of direct assistance from Washington to local governments. A second and closely related feature was a shift in program focus. After the massive infusion of dollars that resulted from the Federal Aid Highway Act of 1956, the prime emphasis in terms of dollars in the grant program moved to commerce and transportation. The trend of the 1960s, as ACIR puts it, "has been to place the principal emphasis of federal aid once again on health, labor, and welfare." Major efforts to deal with the hard problems of the large cities were a prominent part of this shifting emphasis.

Direct federalism may be identified as direct payments from the national government to local governments (or even private individuals and institutions). Prior to 1960, 25 programs—beginning with the low-rent public housing program in 1967—had been adopted under which funds could go directly from Washington to the local government. From 1960 through 1966, another 43 such grants were adopted. In 22 of the grants, there was no state role in the grant process. All of this, of course, has meant a very substantial increase in national government dollars for urban areas. Other programs that flow through the states but are vital to the nation's cities have also been greatly increased. Thus, of the total grant-in-aid funds in Fiscal 1968 of $17 billion, an estimated $10 billion was spent in Standard Metropolitan Statistical Areas (SMSA). This is not to say that the funds were distributed wisely in terms of central city versus suburban needs, nor that the total closes the dollar gap between needs and service demands in the nation's metropolitan areas. It is to say that in the general "role adjustment" by major actors in the federal system to meet the crisis of the cities, the national government has forged a new partnership with the cities, especially the larger cities, of the nation.

A detailed analysis of the growth of direct federalism published by ACIR in *Fiscal Balance in the American Federal System* suggests at least two conclusions about the significance and consequences of the expansion. *First,* it seems clear that the surge of funds directly from Washington to the cities has its roots in the continued failure of most states to support states' rights arguments with cold cash. This alone might not have produced the spurt of action by Washington, but when combined with the rising protests and riots in the cities, action was swift and extensive. A *second* conclusion is that for the first time, grant programs are shifting away from their historical bias in favor of rural and suburban areas, and toward the problems of the central cities.

Direct federalism represents a commitment by the national government to the metropolitan areas, and especially to the problems that haunt their central cities. Thus, an examination of the character of many of the new direct grants shows that they represent a catalog of the toughest problems facing metropolitan America today: air pollution (1963); neighborhood youth corps (1964); equal employment opportunity (1964); community action program (1964); aid for educationally deprived children (1964); solid waste disposal (1964); water and sewer programs (1965); law enforcement assistance (1965); and model cities (1966). Many of the problems occur in all sections of the nation, but the twin forces of density and poverty make them a crushing burden for the cities. Washington has responded to the call for help. The states' response to date has been weak and incomplete.

THE POSITIVE IMPACT OF WASHINGTON GRANTS
ON STATE-LOCAL STRUCTURE AND POLICY

One theme that runs through almost all recent assessments of the federal system is that national government involvement in state and local affairs, primarily through the grant approach, has strengthened state government. There seems to be little or no "hard" data to support the proposition that dollars from Washington are making hollow shells of the state. The data suggest, on the other hand, that the grant program generally, and the vast expansion of it during the 1960s, has had at least three positive impacts on state and local government. First, the hardpressed metropolitan areas, and especially the larger central cities in the Midwest and Northeast, have received some relief in their losing battle against rising costs and rigid fiscal resources.

The data marshaled to support the disadvantaged position of

the central city are convincing. Central city taxpayers already shoulder a significantly heavier burden than their suburban cousins— 7.6 percent of personal income as opposed to 5.6 percent. This figure reflects the fact that central cities have been trying harder in the face of declining tax resources. Striking support for an assumption long supported only by fragmentary data is provided by ACIR data showing sharply higher costs for services for the central cities as opposed to the suburbs. Education is the exception. Here the suburbs typically have indulged their superior fiscal resources to spend significantly more per capita for schools. Thus, the special needs of poverty areas are not met in education. The 37 largest central cities spent $232 per capita for non-educational municipal-type services. The comparable figure for suburbia was about $100 less per capita. The reasons are not hard to find. Central cities are faced with the triple handicap of services for daily in-migrations from suburbia, a greatly higher proportion of "high cost" citizens, and a higher density that increases many municipal costs such as fire, police, and sanitation. Increasingly this disparity is showing up among rich and poor suburban towns.

The sum and substance of the matter is that the 228 metropolitan areas in the United States have most of the nation's wealth, but they also have most of its social and economic problems. The resources are there, but the fiscal balance that would make the resources available to the greatest areas of need is not. If the ACIR study is correct in saying, and I believe it is, that "State, local and federal legislative action is necessary and urgent to bring fiscal needs and resources of our urban governments into better balance," the implications for intergovernmental relations in this country are far-reaching. To begin with, fiscal disparities between central cities and suburbia are increasing. Time alone will only aggravate the problem. A conservative estimate of the "tax gap" for the central cities of the 36 largest metropolitan areas indicates a 14 billion dollar deficit in the 1965–1975 decade. If the reasonable assumptions about the continued in-migration of "high cost" families, a declining rate of property tax increase as saturation levels are reached, and the need for increasing the quality of urban services are made, the gap for the 36 large central cities is estimated for the decade at 25 to 30 billion dollars. How can the gap be closed, or at least significantly narrowed? The ACIR study sums it up by saying that "it will have to be done at enormous cost relative to the community's income and tax base unless many of our central cities are given massive infusions of federal and state aid, . . . functions are shifted to the state and federal levels, or if the cities are given more opportunity to tap an area-wide tax base."

Furthermore, the rising percentage of total state-local revenue supplied by national grants means that state governments have been given some relief from the insistent demands of their citizens for added services in the face of tax structures that send revenues up at a considerably lower rate than the growth of the gross national product. This advantage is, perhaps, illusory. Most state governments could raise more money to meet the problems of urban America if they could but marshal the political will to do so. Failure to respond will finally bring about the often predicted decline of the states as a vital part of the federal system.

Finally, the increasing use of project grants as opposed to formula grants has allowed a "zeroing in" on specific problems that have reached crisis proportions. Most such problems occur in central cities. Formula grants go to all states according to a formula set in the enabling legislation. The transfer in turn by the states to local governments may or may not meet the needs of urban areas. Thus, the several programs for aid to roads have long been criticized for short-changing metropolitan areas. Project grants such as urban renewal, model cities, public housing and the great majority of the recent grants involved in the growth of direct federalism specify eligible units of government, but the eligible recipient must then apply for the aid. Within the limits of the authorizing legislation, national government administrators can decide where the money is most needed. Categorical project grants, then, have the advantage of implementing a national policy by dealing with an immediate, pressing problem.

NEGATIVE IMPACT OF FEDERAL GRANTS

As welcome as the new thrust of increasing grant dollars has been to hard-pressed cities (and states), it has not been an unmixed blessing. The extreme proliferation of grants has brought increasing overlap and duplication, leading in turn to confusion and uncertainty on how to struggle through the bureaucratic jungle to the pot of gold at the end of the rainbow.

The impact of large numbers of narrowly categorical grants on state policy and administration has several negative dimensions. The creation of a vertical "functional autocracy" has been encouraged in which functional specialists form a solid alliance among the three levels of government and resist any effort at external controls, whatever the source. Governors have been especially strong in their objection to this trend. The complaint is that the state administrative departments interact with their national counterpart largely independent of gubernatorial control. Cause and effect is, of course, hard to establish, given the fragmented nature of executive authority in so many states.

In the area of planning, the number of grant programs calling for planning is increasing, but this very fact is producing duplication, conflict, and confusion. Planning for a single functional area is often left unconnected to any comprehensive effort to plan, and comprehensive planning requirements are apt to be contradictory. Program coordination is further hampered by the fact that national government regional offices and boundaries for various programs still typically do not coincide. Looming over all else from the point of view of many state officials is the threatening increase in direct federalism. Here state and local officials split sharply. Almost three-fourths of the mayors responding to a 1963 survey by the Senate Subcommittee on Intergovernmental Relations opposed mandatory channeling of all national government grants through the states. On the other hand, almost all (98 percent) state officials and about two-thirds of the school board members surveyed approved of such a requirement.

Negative factors involving local governments that flow from the rapidly growing categorical grant system depend partly on one's point of view. Most would agree, however, that the local government system in the United States is overly fragmented. Until very recently, the national government was matched only by the states in its indifference to the problem. Only under the prodding of ACIR and others has a movement begun to favor governments of general jurisdiction (cities, counties) over special districts as the recipient of grant funds. The Intergovernmental Relations Act of 1968 did include a provision that general purpose governments should be given preference when possible. The problem is another dimension of the functional autocracy disease. Professionals at each level prefer to go their "expert" way free from interference by mayors, governors, chairmen of county commissions or any other political or even policy-planning forces. Thus, a major fault of the whole grant system—widely recognized but so far largely unsolved—has been the inability to bring even a minimal level of coordination among functionally independent programs. Efforts to change the picture are gaining strength, but they have far, far to go.

The question of whether current trends in national grant programs, specifically the great increase in grants directly to local governments, are introducing fundamental changes into the federal system that spell the beginning of the end for state governments as equal—or at least near-equal—partners in a system of sharing is not easily answered. If one accepts the Grodzins view of the politics of federalism—and the data support this position overwhelmingly—the states remain major forces in the system. The changes of the sixties, however, are too recent to evaluate with any confidence. The answer to the question seems to lie more with the states themselves than with any other level of government. Should states continue to make only token commitments to the tough new urban problems, the non-centralized power system that has characterized federalism for more than 180 years might undergo a fundamental change.

THE NATIONAL GOVERNMENT: ORGANIZING FOR
URBAN POLICY MAKING AND ADMINISTRATION

Daniel P. Moynihan, in an address at Syracuse University in May 1969, called for a national urban policy, and listed ten key points that it should encompass. The ACIR has urged the development of a national policy on urbanization "incorporating social, economic, and other considerations to guide specific decisions at the national level which affect the patterns of urban growth." It was further urged, in a 1969 ACIR study, that Congress and the President both introduce organizational changes to assure the development and maintenance of a national urban policy. The proposal included the creation of a new agency in the Executive Office of the President and called for the development of parallel programs at the state and area-wide local levels. Policy planning would then form the framework for rationalizing national government aid to states and localities.

F. N. Cleaveland and his associates, in a study entitled *Congress and Urban Problems* published in 1969, makes clear at least some of the reasons why urban affairs as a field of national policy has been slow to emerge. Urban affairs as a policy field has "definitional and conceptual" problems that have delayed the development of appropriate machinery in the Congress out of which something approaching a national policy might flow. Cleaveland traces the National League of Cities effort to secure the establishment of a joint committee on urban affairs comparable to the Joint Economic Committee, and then points out that this alone would not suffice. He calls for "the establishment of a legislative committee on urban affairs in each house of Congress." As long as the House and Senate conduct vital legislative business through a system of highly specialized committees, any field of public policy for which no legislative committee feels or expresses proprietary concern is doomed to remain dependent on the vagaries of legislative politics. The Advisory Commission endorsed the joint committee approach by recommending that Congress "provide within its standing committee structure a means to assure continuing sympathetic review and study of the progress" in the direction of developing a national urban policy. State government policies and plans were to be developed in a companion effort. Some observers feel much of the problem has been overcome by the de facto conversion of the housing subcommittees in the House and Senate to urban affairs committees where subcommittee members do become experts in urban affairs. Others accept the Cleaveland thesis that a more formal conversion would help speed the development of a national urban policy.

This review of contemporary patterns in national government grant programs highlights a period of flux and change in the federal system in the last decade. The next decade promises to be even more challenging. The change might be thought of in terms of changing roles for each level of government in the marble cake of federalism. The expansion of direct federalism has given local governments unmistakable status as a third component in the system. The national government has become the champion of the cities in attacking the tough urban problems produced by density and poverty. The states remain vital partners in the system, but their future is in question.

The Politics of Fear: State Reactions to National Government Expansion

BROAD POLICY SETTING

Direct federalism has put an increasing strain on intergovernmental relations. States righters cry *foul* and retreat behind constitutional Maginot Lines. State haters assert the immutable irresponsibility of the states to its larger urban children. The National Governors Conference deplores; the U.S. Conference of Mayors applauds. The debate has been intense and often bitter. Out of it, there seems to be emerging a consensus that is acceptable to at least some protagonists on both sides of the issue. If such a consensus is developing, the Advisory Commission on Intergovernmental Relations deserves a large part of the credit. It succeeded in structuring the debate to some degree by setting the conditions under which states could rightfully demand a part in all national government grants to urban areas. The conditions were simple and to the point: federal grants would channel through the states when, and only when, "a state (a) provides appropriate administrative machinery to carry out relevant responsibilities, and (b) provides significant financial contributions, and when appropriate, technical assistance to the local governments concerned." Any reasonable application of these standards would at present make possible direct federalism in a wide range of programs in a large majority of the states. The Advisory Commission believes that "a consensus is beginning to emerge among state officials that if a state chooses to remain aloof from the problems toward which the federal aid is directed, then local units should be free to participate in the federal program and deal directly with federal agencies concerned." The principle is simple: buy in or stop complaining about being left out.

If the consensus is with us, it has only a shaky foothold in some jurisdictions. "Economy firsters" who utilize a states' rights banner under which to oppose substantive government action at any level take a hard line on the matter of direct federalism, and generally oppose the expansion of the grant program either direct to local governments or through the states. The evidence provided by Cleaveland and his associates on the nature of congressional voting on a series of key urban issues over the period 1955–1964 is striking. In five of the seven cases,

> the roll call votes demonstrated a dominant pattern of party voting. The evidence was clear: all five cases involved legislation sponsored by the Democratic Congressional leadership, and in every instance rural and small-town Democratic members voted in much larger proportions to support these urban bills than did the Republicans from urban and suburban districts. This predominance of party influence over constituency influence strikingly confirms the finding of much research on Congress that political party is most likely to be the decisive factor in Congressional voting.

A more balanced assessment of state performance in meeting the crisis of the cities admits to grave deficiencies. Philip H. Hoff, former Governor of Vermont, in a paper delivered at the 1969 National Conference of the American Society for Public Administration (ASPA), stated that: "In honesty, I think we have to acknowledge that in the past the states have not done all they could or should have about the urban problems in our country. It is clear beyond dispute that, prior to reapportionment, the cities got the short end of the stick." The ACIR, certainly an organization friendly toward the states, makes no bones about the inadequacy of the performance of most states to date. While exceptions are noted, the ACIR report on fiscal balance states that:

Wholesale involvement and participation by most of the states in the functions of urban government continues to be the exception rather than the rule. At present, 37 states are assisting financially in the federal airport construction program, and 20 are participating financially in building local sewage treatment facilities. However, only 11 are assisting financially in programs of urban renewal; 10 in urban mass transportation; and 4 in local hospital and medical facilities construction. One of the crucial questions regarding the crisis in the cities—indeed in American federalism—is whether the states will forfeit their responsibility for financing major urban services to the national government.

Alan K. Campbell suggests just that possibility. After documenting the fact that state grant-in-aid programs tend to favor the rural and suburban areas at the expense of the central cities, Campbell suggests that "it may be that a pattern is developing whereby states will tend to aid suburban and rural areas, while the federal government will make up the difference in the central cities."

The political implications of such a development are, to say the least, far-reaching. Yet, we are well along the road to just such a fundamental alteration in the nature of the federal system. Many representatives of the central cities have lost patience with what they consider state unwillingness to respond to their problems. The only solution they see is national government help direct to the cities. The attitude is illustrated in a paper presented to the 1969 ASPA Conference by John J. Gunther, Executive Director, United States Conference of Mayors. Gunther holds that "after all, there has been very little movement toward constructive involvement by the states in helping cities meet the challenges of the urban crisis." Gunther went on to oppose in the strongest terms any revenue-sharing or block grant system of national government help to states, on the precise grounds that the money would never get to where it was most needed—the cities.

The hearings conducted by the Senate Subcommittee on Executive Reorganization entitled *Federal Role in Urban Affairs* produced considerable sentiment similar to Gunther's view. Senator Joseph S. Clark testified that, "I have always been for bypassing states because I was a mayor and not a governor." He went on to assert that, "I think, actually, that state government is the weak link of American government today. I think that both the federal government and most of the local governments, at least in the larger cities, are more

sophisticated, more mature, in their dealing with these problems."
Mayor Ivan Allen of Atlanta felt that "what is decried by many as
'federal encroachment' has been the salvation of Atlanta."

Given the feeble performance of most states with regard to most
urban problems to date, it is hard to fault the skepticism of local
officials, and especially of big city mayors, that states will ever generate the political will that must precede wholesale commitment. Yet
even the most cynical big city mayor can agree that the states could
do much if they would. Certainly there is evidence that the sleeping
giant of state government is beginning to awaken and respond to
the urban crisis. Yet all too few follow the admonition of the Advisory Commission that states "begin to pay part of the bill for urban
development, housing code enforcement, mass transit, and other
major urban functions just as they have been paying for years a part
of the bill for state agricultural experiment stations, county agents,
and rural roads."

One reason for the growth of project-type grants in dealing with
urban problems is undoubtedly the reluctance of most states to
move in the urban area. Perhaps the time has come to stop thinking
of states in the aggregate and treat them individually. If the "buy-
in" principle enunciated by the ACIR is followed literally, just
such a development would occur. The national government "would
become selective in laying down patterns of intergovernmental relations . . . and . . . stop treating states like New York, Pennsylvania, and California in an identical fashion with Alabama, Mississippi, and Wyoming." Thus, perhaps it is not necessary for all
states to awaken to the urban challenge at once. States vary widely
in their political climate and in degree of urbanization. The proposals described below to prod the states into relevance might well
be designed so as to leave room for laggards and still maintain a
balance of power in the federal system.

*National Government Action to Expand State Programs for
Urban Areas*

THE POWER OF THE GRANT DOLLAR

For all the rhetoric surrounding the Nixon proposal of 1969
to inaugurate a revenue-sharing proposal, there seems little possibility that such a plan, even if expanded vastly beyond the scale
proposed by the President, would replace in whole, or even in
significant part, the present system of categorical aids. It is far more

likely that the categorical aid program will be refined, simplified, and consolidated in many areas, but that it will continue and expand. At least two factors support this assumption. First, the scope of urban problems, the backlog of unmet needs, is so great, the need for solutions is so pressing, that any other course of action is almost unthinkable. Just as arguments about which level of government should perform which function have been made largely obsolete by the rising tide of urban problems, so the same tide renders essentially irrelevant the debate over whether categorical aid or revenue-sharing programs should channel the flow of Washington dollars to state and local governments. Both will be needed, and other approaches will probably have to be added, including some version of a tax credit plan that will stimulate more states to tap the income tax as a source of revenue.

National government grant programs have grown dramatically in size and variety in the last decade. By way of summary, in 1927 national and state grants provided only ten per cent of all local government revenue. By 1967 the figure had increased to about one-third, and the national government portion was growing rapidly. Federal aid to state and local governments has increased tenfold in the last 20 years, fourfold in the last ten years, and doubled in the last five years. Such aid increased from about 11 percent of total state-local general revenue a decade before to over 17 percent in 1967 and an estimated 20 percent or more in 1970. Total national grant funds for Fiscal 1970 were estimated in the $20 to $25 billion range. There were few signs in 1969 that Mr. Nixon and the Republicans would change this trend, which one observer saw leveling off at the end of the 1970s at about one-third of all state-local general revenue.

If the national government is to continue expanding the flow of dollars to state and local governments, the time seems ripe for a reassessment of not only the general efficiency of the programs but of the possibilities of better achieving major national goals in the process of expansion. Increasing—massively increasing—the involvement of the states in the problems of the cities is a major national goal. Further, the achievement of this goal can be hastened by a more systematic use of an incentive-disincentive-restricted grant approach utilizing categorical, broad functional, and revenue-sharing programs.

THE FERMENT IN GRANT APPROACHES

A major justification of the categorical grant approach has from the beginning been that national goals could be achieved through this approach. Thus "strings" of varying tightness and number have always characterized the system. Some have truly contributed to national goals. Others have done little in that direction, but much to satisfy the endless appetite of bureaucratic red tape. Almost all have had one thing in common: they have served narrowly functional national goals, such as abating water pollution or improving the supply of housing, rather than broad policy objectives, such as a broad multi-functional attack on improving the quality of the urban environment.

The rapid expansion of the categorical grant system has been accompanied by a rising chorus of voices calling for its reform. In recent years the voices have not come alone from those who see the grant program as a threat to state-local independence, but have included many who favor the system and wish to see it expanded. The repeated efforts to return large areas of the grant program to states and their localities seem too far removed from reality to merit serious treatment. Suffice it to say that the Kestnbaum Commission labored long and came up with little along that line, while the subsequent Joint Federal-State Action Committee recommendation to return full responsibility for sewerage treatment facilities and vocational education to the states, as minor as it was in the total picture, was opposed by the National Governors Conference, local officials, and the Congress.

Responsible voices for reform have developed a number of proposals that are gaining support. Some have been referred to above. All involve greater coordination among grant programs. All call for a simplification of the present maze of categorical grants. Most agree that the role of elected officials at every level—governors, mayors, and county executives—must be strengthened in developing a national, state, and regional urban policy. There have been, then, persistent demands and rising support in recent years for additional sharing approaches to accompany the rising tide of national dollars. The major new approaches suggested have been broad functional grants; general support grants involving a revenue-sharing plan; and a tax credit scheme under which states would be "persuaded to make greater use of the income tax."

Broad functional grants amount to a consolidation of what are often dozens of fragmentary grants in a given functional area into one or at least fewer broad functional programs. Such a consolidation was achieved, at least temporarily, by the Partnership in Health Act of 1966. The general support or revenue-sharing approach involves returning a part of the rich tax take by Uncle Sam to state and local governments. There are many versions of this approach, but most are based on a per capita formula that adds an adjustment for variations in tax effort. A prime issue with revenue sharing has been over whether it should have a "mandatory pass-through" feature—that is, whether all or some local governments should receive a portion of the money either directly or by the money flowing automatically through the states. The tax credit scheme, simply stated, would allow the state income taxpayer to deduct a specified amount paid in state income taxes from his federal tax bill.

It seems clear that the nature of the debate over which of these approaches to use has shifted and that support for a "mix" is increasing. The debate on whether to venture into new sharing approaches was for a time cast in a "total replacement" framework. That is, the revenue-sharing plan was put forward as (or was assumed to mean) a total replacement for all categorical grants. The ACIR has pushed hard to support revenue sharing as an alternative, not a replacement, for the categorical grants. It has taken the position that the President should have the authority, subject to a congressional veto, to reorganize categorical grants along broad functional lines. There is much merit in both the broad functional and revenue-sharing proposals. Both offer new opportunities to further "persuade" states to become more relevant in urban affairs. Both offer further levers by which to improve local government structure. The consolidated categorical grants would make it possible to continue "zeroing in" on specific hard problems of urban areas such as housing and poverty. In combination, broad categorical grants and a revenue-sharing plan could bring a large net increase of aid money to both states and localities, and it could do so in such a way as to maintain a balance in the federal system.

There are those who decry the "strings" that are now attached to federal aid as an undue intrusion by the federal (and sometimes state) government into the affairs of the lower unit of government. We need have little patience with needless bureaucratic red tap that needlessly complicates and endlessly delays grant programs. However, it can also be argued that neither the federal government nor the states have attached enough conditions of a broad policy nature to the grants that channel money from higher levels of government to lower levels. Two areas of needed action will serve to illustrate the point. One involves motivating states to put significantly greater amounts of money into the tough problems of the cities. The second concerns the issue of using grants to force a rationalization of the tangle of overlapping and duplicating governments at the local level. The fundamental national purpose that is involved is to coax, persuade, assist, or otherwise drag states into far more relevance in meeting the crisis of the cities.

NEW GRANT APPROACHES AND STATE URBAN POLICY

Incentives of one kind or another are not new in the grant program picture. Indeed, in a sense the entire categorical grant system has as one major purpose the stimulation of states to share in meeting the problems occurring within their borders that have national significance. Grants, either project or formula, typically have a cost-sharing or matching requirement which must be satisfied in order for funds to pass to states and localities. An apportionment procedure in formula grants provides for dividing the money among states and localities. This formula often provides for varying amounts on the basis of need or fiscal capacity. Population and per capita income are often relevant variables.

The practice of apportioning funds on the basis of program need and financial ability, increasingly common since 1930, often has had equalizing factors built in. Thus in matching requirements, the straight 50-50 arrangement may be replaced by a scale ranging from one-third to two-thirds, depending on the ratio of the state's per capita income to that of the United States. Further, Congress has sometimes abandoned the 50-50 matching formula without varying state matching requirements, presumably to further an overriding national purpose. The first major example was the Interstate Highway System, with a 90 percent national/10 percent state ratio. The Elementary and Secondary Education Act of 1965 provided 100 percent national government grants to school districts for aid to culturally disadvantaged children. Economic development grants may go as high as 80 percent national in areas of major economic distress. Obviously, a willingness to vary the national government percentage can be used to "persuade" states to commit funds to a particular functional area.

A more direct use of the incentive approach has increased in recent years, especially in connection with the project grants that target pressing problems, more specifically urban problems, for attention. Most incentives to date have been all too modest, but they at least indicate the possibilities. Most appeared in the 1960s. The open-space land legislation in 1961 offered an incentive for area-wide planning for urban area open space by increasing the maximum federal share from 20 percent to 30 percent if the recipient of the aid was an area-wide government, or participated in an area-wide open-space plan. The incentive was ended in 1965.

The Federal Aid Highway Act of 1963 as amended in 1965 tempted states to limit billboards along federally aided roads by adding one-half of one percent to the dollar value of projects covered by national standards where states adhered to the standards. In 1965, the 25 states that had taken advantage of the billboard incentive were allowed to continue, but for the remaining 25 states, beginning January 1, 1968, the incentive changed to a disincentive in that ten percent of the allotment of any state would be withheld if states had not made provision for "effective" advertising control along both interstate and primary roads. The 1965 Elementary-Secondary Education Act offered an incentive during 1967 and 1968 to agencies eligible to receive basic grants for educating children from low-income families. The incentive was based on the increase in educational spending by the local government units the previous year. The incentive was repealed in 1966 as unworkable. The Public Works and Economic Development Act provided for increases up to ten percent if the project was in an economic development district and was consistent with the overall plan for the district.

The incentive approach that most directly involves the "state spur" technique was included in amendments to the 1956 Water Pollution Control Act adopted in 1965 and 1966. The federal share maximum of 30 percent could be expanded to 40 percent if states assumed at least 30 percent of the cost of the pollution control project. If the state had adopted enforceable water quality standards for inter- and intra-state waters, the state share could be lowered to 25 percent, while the federal share could go to 50 percent. If the pollution control project conformed to an areawide plan, another ten percent in federal funds could be added. Determining cause and effect is always risky, but the evidence to date strongly suggests that the effort to lure more state dollars into the critical and very expensive water pollution area has been successful. The number of states sharing the cost of local sewage plant construction when the incentive was adopted in 1965 was eight. The ACIR reports that by September 1967 it had increased to 20, and in five other states such action was under consideration.

As calls are going forth from all sides for a reassessment of the grant-in-aid system, it seems time—and past time—for the national government to take a long, hard look at the flow of dollars to state and local governments as a way of moving states to where the action is—in the cities. Many will argue that the states cannot afford to substantially increase their help to urban areas. For some states this may be true, but for many it is not true. Unless a state is making full use of the range of tax programs available, including the sales tax and an aggressive use of the state income tax (individual as well as corporate), it cannot argue inability as an excuse for its failure to join the partnership in fighting urban problems. The reason must be ascribed, rather, to a lack of will. A tough-minded Congress could go far toward improving the balance in the federal system by using the incentive approach to persuade states to assume their rightful responsibilities toward urban areas.

The restricted grant takes a different approach toward using the federal aid programs as a spur to state action. Instead of offering incentives (or disincentives) to bring about a policy objective, grants are simply not made available at all unless certain conditions are met. The approach is already widely used in the grant program, especially in the project grants so common in the 1960s expansion of grants to urban areas. Urban renewal, model cities, public housing, and the like require that certain conditions must be met before the state or local unit can be eligible to receive a grant. This principle could be used to bring greater order out of the tangle of local government units, at least in metropolitan America. The logical source for new conditions on grants that simply bar funds to local government units below a minimum size would be the state. The logic of the situation, however, has not produced very much action. Indeed, the evidence seems clear that both federal and state grant programs to local areas have had just the opposite effect.

They have tended to prop up artificially what are essentially nonviable units of government too small in area, resources, or both to carry out even the most minimal definition of urban functions in a satisfactory way. State grants tend to favor smaller units of government in the countryside or suburbs over the larger cities. Federal grants have tended, at least until the 1960s, in the same direction, and in addition often favored special districts over local governments of general jurisdiction.

The Douglas Commission in its final report took a step in the right direction by recommending that:

> Congress promptly adopt legislation under which, beginning five years after its enactment, the eligibility of local governments in any metropolitan area to participate in federal grant programs would be contingent upon there having been completed, within the preceding ten year period, a comprehensive official study of local government structure within the area carried out either directly by the state or states con-

cerned or by a public agency authorized by state law to carry out such a study, and including the publication of findings and recommendations.

The ACIR was even more explicit in its call for state action:

> The Commission further recommends the amendment of formulas providing state aid to local governments so as to eliminate or reduce aid allotments to small units of local government not meeting statutory standards of economic, geographic and political viability.

Both recommendations are to be commended, but they are only the beginning. Congress should move immediately to eliminate grants to local units of government that fail to meet the viability standards developed by the ACIR. No doubt some reasonable time period to phase out the ineligible units will be necessary. It seems highly unlikely that we will ever achieve the Committee for Economic Development objective of an 80 percent reduction in units of local government unless some such approach is adopted. The states have, in fact, already shown the way with regard to the multitude of tiny school districts that existed in this country just a few short decades ago. By using a number of techniques, including incentives, disincentives, and an outright ban on aid to districts below a certain minimum, the number of school districts in the nation was reduced from 109,000 to 22,000 over a 25-year period. The reduction percentage coincides with the CED figure of 80 percent. A direct parallel between school districts and other units of local government is not suggested, but the analogy has some validity.

There seems to be widespread and growing support for sweeping consolidation of the more than 400 categorical grant programs into much fewer broad functional grants. A beginning was made in 1966 when the Partnership in Health Act authorized consolidation of about 20 categorical grants in such areas as heart diseases, tuberculosis, venereal disease and cancer. Authorizations, appropriations, and requirements were consolidated. President Johnson in 1967 directed the Bureau of the Budget to pinpoint other areas for similar action. Such action will not come easily. Functionally based interest groups interact with the professional bureaucracy to resist such change. If the change is to come, Congress through legislation and the executive through administrative rules should place as a first priority item the inclusion of incentives for greater state action such as those provided in the water pollution area. The extension of such a principle, for example, to a consolidated grant program for housing would seem in order.

REVENUE SHARING: REVOLUTION OR EVOLUTION
IN THE FEDERAL SYSTEM?

It may be that some version of a revenue-sharing plan ranks as an idea whose time has come. Proponents of the general idea have become more and more numerous in recent years. They have appeared from every part of the political spectrum, and from both major political parties. The concept has been supported by those who favor a scaling down in the present categorical grant programs, and by those who favor an expansion of those programs. The Advisory Commission on Intergovernmental Relations and the National Commission on Urban Problems have both endorsed the idea. President Nixon has joined the ranks and proposed a version of the plan to Congress. What is it, why is the idea so widely supported, and what impact would its adoption have on the federal system? The answers to these and related questions are far from simple.

Revenue sharing is an old idea, but its recent popularity can be traced to a proposal put forward in 1964 by a study group that included Walter W. Heller, ex-chairman of the Council of Economic Advisors, and Joseph A. Pechman of the Brookings Institution. The group argued that a revenue-sharing plan should be an addition to, not a replacement for, the categorical grant system, since "categorical and general-purpose grants have very different functions, and these cannot be satisfied if the federal system were limited to one or the other." The fundamental purpose of revenue sharing is to "share" with the states part of the rich harvest reaped by the national system of income taxes. This system produces increased revenue at a faster rate than income rises, whereas state and local revenue systems typically grow more slowly than income growth.

At least three major questions may be raised about methods of implementing a revenue-sharing plan, even if one accepts the approach in principle. The questions are: (a) should there be a "pass-through" feature that channels some of the funds to local governments? (b) should strings of any kind be attached to the grants? and (c) to what extent should equalizing factors be built into the distribution formula? Interest in revenue sharing rose to a peak in the 89th and 90th Congresses. In the 90th Congress alone, 110 members sponsored 90 different bills including some 35 versions of the basic revenue-sharing approach. A review of the key features of these bills illustrated the ramifications of the questions noted above. The Advisory Commission identified five factors that tended to distinguish the bills: (1) basis of sharing; (2) allocation factors; (3) provision for local sharing; (4) expenditure controls; and (5) relationship to national government categorical grant programs.

A clear majority of the bills provided for sharing from one to five percent of the national income tax collections, with most using tax collections in determining how much to set aside for distribution. Six used taxable income in determining the amount set aside for distribution. Fifty-six of the bills used some combination of per capita income, population, and revenue or tax effort as allocation factors.

The original Heller-Pechman Plan made no provision for a "pass-through" arrangement to local governments, urging instead that all revenue go to the states. The decision was based on the difficulty of working out an equitable local sharing procedure, and on the assumption that states would use much of the money to help local governments. Many local spokesmen, especially in the larger cities, objected strongly to any such omission. It was later recognized by the authors of the plan that a "pass-through" feature might be desirable. Local protests had their effect, since over half of the bills introduced in the 90th Congress included a provision for local sharing. One provided for direct sharing with metropolitan areas of 1.5 million or more.

None of the bills went directly to the problem of correcting the resource-needs gap between central cities and suburbs in metropolitan areas. A per capita income distribution formula would be mildly equalizing in nature. A more effective way to use revenue sharing to reduce fiscal disparities in metropolitan areas, as pointed out by the ACIR, would be to base the local share on non-educational expenditures. Such an approach would give more money to the larger cities than to their suburbs.

One of the great attractions of revenue sharing for state governments has been the prospect of "no strings" grants, but this proposed feature has also been the source of much opposition to the plan. Nine bills provided for no controls at all, but varying degrees of control for a variety of purposes were included in the others. The most stringent controls were included in the Reuss Bill (HR 1166) which tied the funds to the development and adoption of state and local government modernization plans.

A strong minority of the bills, 28 out of 90, called for cuts in the categorical grant programs, but only three had specific provisions for such a reduction. A sampling of the provisions of selective bills introduced provides some feel for the variety of provisions that can be encompassed under the revenue-sharing tag. Senator Javits' bill restricted the areas in which the money could be utilized to health, education, and welfare. The revenue-sharing fund was made up of one percent of taxable income, with 85 percent distributed on the basis of population and relative tax effort, and 15 percent used to supplement the shares of below-average per capita income states. A local pass-through provision had to be submitted by each state each year, taking into consideration population, density, per capita income, and other factors. The Tydings bill included the unique provision for aid to metropolitan areas of 1.5 million or more who request an allocation. A commission on federalism was authorized that would handle the distribution. Where a direct allocation went to a metropolitan area, the state still got from the area two-fifths of what it would have gotten without such an allocation.

The data on bills introduced make it clear that while there is widespread support for some form of revenue sharing, ideas as to how to go about it also vary widely. It is equally clear that the possibilities of using the revenue-sharing approach as an incentive or restricted grant device have been accepted by some members of Congress. It should not be overlooked, furthermore, that resistance to the revenue-sharing approach still exists. Much of the resistance may be tied to a fear that approval would not include a mandatory pass-through for urban areas, or that it would mean a cut in categorical grant programs. Certainly most mayors would oppose either development.

Two commissions that have studied and made recommendations on the question of revenue sharing both favor the approach and seek to serve national goals in implementing it, but the goals to be served are somewhat different. The ACIR has recommended a grant-in-aid "mix" including categorical grants, broad functional grants, and general support payments under a revenue-sharing plan. While the recommendation itself is something less than specific on the matter, the discussion following the recommendation makes it clear that a prime objective is to have the general support payments distributed in such a way as to close the resources gap between central city and suburb. The Commission notes, in *Fiscal Balance in the American Federal System*, that "if federal general support were distributed to local governments on the basis of non-educational expenditures, it would go a long way toward relieving the central city 'overburden' due in large part to the concentration of low-income persons in the major cities." The pass-through issue is left open by the Commission, except to say that if such a provision is made, any money used by local governments should be in conformance with state comprehensive plans.

Three members of the Commission, including its chairman, dissented in whole or part. Chairman Bryant, former governor of Florida, felt that there was too much uncertainty about the effect of the revenue-sharing plan on the federal system to approve it. Secretary of the Treasury Fowler favored more flexibility in grants and a move toward broad functional grants, but felt that it was too soon to choose among many proposed methods of giving additional help to state and local government. Mayor Arthur Naftalin of Minneapolis objected only to the state government comprehensive plan provision, since "states have yet to demonstrate a sufficient sense of urgency about urban problems let alone develop the competency to make this state planning requirement work."

The Douglas Commission made revenue sharing a major factor in its final report, *Building the American City*. Chapter 5 of the report, "Overhauling Federal Aid for Urban Needs: A Revenue Sharing Plan," spells out the details. While the central proposal was a revenue-sharing plan, the recommendations stressed two other objectives: (a) to maintain and support more generously the categorical grant programs "that help disadvantaged persons in urban areas"; and (b) to strain out of present grant programs provisions that "tend to discriminate against major cities and urban counties." The sharing plan itself was based on the annual allocation of a percentage (not specified) of a state's net taxable income, allocated to states on the basis of population with an adjustment for relative state-local tax effort. The pass-through provision was mandatory, and such funds would go only to "major municipalities and urban counties on a basis determined by their respective shares of all state and local tax revenue in a particular state."

The proposal for "selective direct local sharing" was the unique feature of the Douglas Commission proposal. "Major cities and urban counties" were defined as cities of 50,000 or more and counties above 50,000 with at least half the population urban. In 1960 there were 310 such cities and 407 counties containing some 122 million persons, or two-thirds of the total population. The Commission opposed pass-through grants to all local governments because of the "tremendous administrative complexities" of providing a share of the pie for some 80,000 local units of government, and because it would "sustain and entrench many local governments that are far too small to represent viable units."

The variety of approaches in implementing a revenue-sharing plan makes it clear that a "no-strings" approach leaving states free to do as they please with the funds is not a necessary part of the package. The contention here is that the traditional narrow administrative strings that clutter the bureaucratic landscape ought indeed to be kept out of any such plan, but that broad national urban policy objectives ought to be built into it. As a minimum these broad objectives should include *restrictions on the size of local government units eligible for aid,* so as to actively promote larger, general purpose, local governments. An allocation formula similar to that proposed by ACIR should be included that will *assure a closing of the resources gap between the central city and the suburbs.* Consideration should at least be given to including *a provision that no state can qualify unless it is making a minimal fiscal effort toward solving metropolitan problems that shape the crisis in the cities,* including at least compensatory educational funds for disadvantaged children, substantial sums for the various components of the poverty program, housing, urban renewal, model cities, air and water pollution, and mass transit. Any funds accumulated because of ineligibility of a state under these criteria would be distributed to the remaining eligible states. Finally, no state should be eligible for funds unless provisions had been made and implemented for an ongoing process of comprehensive state, regional, and metropolitan planning. (For a discussion of other aspects of revenue-sharing, see Chapter 4.)

MEETING THE URBAN CRISIS: THE FULL-FUNDING APPROACH

A clear long-range trend in the federal system in the United States is the slow but steady movement upward of the responsibility for providing the dollars for the never ceasing service demands of the urban society. It is increasingly true that "more money is raised at the top than is spent there, and more is spent at the bottom than is raised there." Given the capacity of the federal system to resist over-centralization in spite of this trend, it is probably a good thing. The national level is by far the most efficient collector of dollars, and it does it far more equitably than any other level. Local governments stand at the other end of the continuum. Expanding state and local revenue through traditional grants and revenue sharing is one way of using the superior taxing ability of Washington to help state and local governments. Another approach is for the national government to take over much larger proportions of the funding of certain high cost services. The function most frequently mentioned in recent years is welfare. The Advisory Commission on Intergovernmental Relations has proposed that the national government assume all cost of public welfare and medicare, involving an estimated six billion dollars in added costs. President Nixon's 1969 public welfare proposals moved part way in that direction. Certainly this approach seems preferable to placing heavier burdens on state and local tax systems that are typically heavily regressive in nature.

An Assessment

As the road to the present urban hell was paved, many major sins of omission and commission can be ascribed to the states. Cities and suburbs, counties, townships, and boroughs alike are, after all, legal creations of the state. The deadly combination of restricted annexation and unrestricted incorporation; the chaotic and uncontrolled mushrooming of special districts; the limitations upon municipal taxing and borrowing power; the deliverance of all important police powers of zoning, land use and building regulations into the hands of thousands of separate and competing local governments—these are but a few of the byproducts of decades of state governments' nonfeasance and malfeasance concerning urban affairs. . . .

The political landscape has been strewn with defeated governors, mayors, and county officials who courageously committed suicide at the polls by doing what had to be done to increase the resources of government to meet, at least in part, the escalating service demands from an insatiable (and largely unappreciative) public.[2]

Many may look aghast at the proposals in this chapter to broaden rather than end the strings attached to national government dollars that flow to the state and local levels. Without question many of these strings in the past have been unduly rigid, endlessly complicated, hopelessly confusing, and often contradictory. The approach here includes support for a drastic re-shaping of the present categorical grant programs in the direction of consolidation, simplification, and standardization of such things as matching formulae where such action does not interfere with meeting a significant national purpose.

What is proposed is that narrow technical strings be largely replaced with a combination of incentive and restrictive measures that will allow the pursuit of broad national urban policies. Such an approach will never emerge if the proliferation of categorical grants goes on apace, and revenue-sharing plans simply pass dollars to state and local governments without broad controls that will assure the

---

[2] ACIR, *Urban America and the Federal System* (Washington: G.P.O., 1969).

furthering of basic national urban policies. A first order of priority, perhaps, is to articulate a national urban policy at the top of the federal system, and promote—even demand—similar comprehensive planning action at the state and local levels. Congress and the executive branch have a heavy responsibility to continue hopeful beginnings in this direction.

A. James Reichley

7

The Political Containment of the Cities

To ask why the states have not done more to help their cities is, of course, to raise a question of political power. The simple answer is that the cities have been unable either to persuade or compel the states to give them the help they feel they deserve and need. The question then becomes, why not?

When one entity of government fails to take beneficial action that is desired by another, it must be because the desired action is too difficult, or because the first entity is not sufficiently motivated to act, or, most usually, a combination of the two. Representatives of the state governments have understandably tended to emphasize the first of these causes. We would like to do more for our cities, they are inclined to say, but we simply do not have the money. They have received in this plea the perhaps unexpected support of a considerable number of political scientists and economists.

The editor of this volume, for instance, has shrewdly observed that the graduated income tax has enabled the federal government to concern itself with "program politics," while the relatively fixed incomes of the states have tied them to a "tax politics," which consumes a disproportionate amount of their governmental energy. The peripatetic Daniel Patrick Moynihan has argued that the "basic equation of American political economy" rises out of the fact that

---

A. JAMES REICHLEY *is associate editor of* Fortune *magazine. He was previously legislative assistant to Senator Kenneth Keating of New York and legislative secretary to Governor William Scranton of Pennsylvania. He is the author of numerous magazine articles, two novels, as well as* The Art of Government *and* States in Crisis.

for every one percent increase in the gross national product, the income of the federal government goes up one and one-half percent, the income of the cities about half of one percent, and the income of the states somewhere in between. The whole design of the Heller plan was to help correct this imbalance.

There is a great deal of truth to this argument. Lack of funds *does* make it difficult for the states to help their cities, or for that matter to do anything else. Failure of state tax structures to keep pace with the demand for services has inhibited consideration by governors and legislators of means to deal with the urban crisis. It would be a mistake, however, to exaggerate the purely fiscal as opposed to the political causes of this dilemma.

THE POLITICS OF STATE TAXES

The tax structure that a governmental entity employs is, after all, the result of political decisions, regularly reaffirmed. The federal government derives enormous revenues from the graduated income tax because it has been able and willing to maintain this form of taxation. (Even so, the federal government has not been spectacularly eager to make its resources available to the cities. Federal aid to cities has been rising more rapidly than state aid in recent years, but in 1967 local government was still getting more than ten times as much financial assistance from the states as from the federal government. Dr. Moynihan has had better luck than Dr. Heller at getting a proposal for federal revenue sharing with state and local governments onto the national agenda, but the prospect for implementation of this idea in any substantial form still seems very much in doubt.) Most states have adopted some form of income tax, but rates are much lower and graduation is less than in the federal model. Moreover, a number of the most important states have so far enacted no income tax whatever. In 1962, only 18 states had no personal income tax. But the holdouts included seven of the ten most populous states, and ten of the 18 states which were more than 70 percent urban in 1960. In 1967 Michigan enacted its first income tax, followed by Illinois in 1969. But in the summer of 1969, anti-income tax forces still held the upper hand in such key dominions as Pennsylvania, Ohio, Texas, New Jersey, Florida, and Connecticut.

Failure of many major urban states to avail themselves of the fiscal resources of the income tax was due originally to the power of business lobbies, which were particularly influential in the states in which industrialization had occurred first. By the time labor began to challenge business hegemony in the urban states in the thirties, the bite of the federal income tax was being felt among all but the lowest economic classes. State income taxes became almost universally unpopular, and were opposed by many liberal as well as almost all conservative politicians. By the sixties, business had relaxed much of its traditional opposition to state income taxes, but ordinary voters formed walls of resistance against their enactment where they did not already exist, or expansion in those states which had adopted them prior to 1932.

While voter resistance to state taxes, particularly the income tax, has limited the states' financial capabilities, such funds as are available have not usually been distributed to the advantage of the cities. With the notable exception of New York, most urban states give less per capita aid to their cities than to areas outside the cities. In 1966, such cities as Los Angeles, Philadelphia, Detroit, Cleveland, and Houston received substantially less state aid per capita than the statewide per capita distribution of state subsidies. Differentials of this kind derive in part from factors like the higher percentage of parochial school students in cities, which results in lower per capita subsidies to the public schools. But certainly they also reflect the cities' relative lack of political power.

THE HOME RULE ISSUE

It is not on fiscal matters alone that the cities have been unable to work their wills with the states. As Professor Grad explains, "home rule" has been the battle cry of city delegations in state legislatures for almost a century, but most states still keep tight rein on the operations of city government. If the average mayor sets out to revamp the administrative structure that he heads, he must, as John Lindsay discovered in New York, secure approval for his plans from the state legislature. If he is faced by a riot, he may find himself, like Richard Daley in Chicago in the spring of 1968, without the elementary powers to call a curfew or halt the sale of gasoline. In Boston, the chief of police was appointed until 1962 by the governor of Massachusetts, and the police department of St. Louis is still governed by a board of commissioners appointed by the governor of Missouri.

City hunger to annex tax-rich surrounding suburbs has generally received scant support in state capitols. Since such super-cities as New York and Chicago were created around the turn of the century (often in the mistaken belief that the addition of middle-class constituencies would make them forever Republican), legislatures have usually heeded the demand of the suburbs for continued independence. Proposals for "regional governments," to exercise authority over both cities and suburbs, have not yet received serious consideration in most states. Even regional compacts to deal with specific problems, like transportation and environmental pollution, have been approached with extreme caution in state legislatures.

The other chapters in this book document many more instances in which the cities have received not only less help than they need, but also less than has been granted to other members of the state's family of jurisdictions. It must then follow that the state governments, beside lacking fiscal resources, have not in the past been very highly motivated to give aid to the cities—or, as has been true in some cases, been absolutely repelled by anti-city bias. The questions which must now be asked are why this condition has existed, and whether it is likely to change.

IMPACT OF REAPPORTIONMENT

Under a democratic system of government—even one limited by constitutional and economic checks, like that of the United States —the primary source of political power is votes, which is to say, people. Economic and moral forces certainly play a part in the American political process, but are not consistently effective unless able to gather popular support for the points of view they represent. The individual public official may succumb to a bribe or rise to a moral challenge, but in the end he will fall if his constituents are not similarly tempted or inspired. Physical intimidation, which in most nations in the world plays a decisive part in allocating political power, still limits Negro franchise in some southern states, and still can turn the tide on election day in some backwoods counties and some "controlled" city precincts. At the state level, however, with the important exception of muffling the black voice in the Deep South, it has had no significant effect since the demise of Huey Long in Louisiana. Distribution of political power among regions in most states, therefore, rises initially out of the geographical distribution of population.

If all votes are not counted equally, of course, this rule must be modified. Prior to the Supreme Court's series of decisions on legislative apportionment during the early sixties, over-representation of rural counties in many state legislatures caused serious discrimination against urban voters and their interests. Most states gave some advantage to rural areas in their methods of apportionment, and some states, like California, Texas, and New Jersey, provided in their constitutions for one house, on the model of the United States

Senate, in which representation was on the basis of area rather than of population. In addition, many states, as in the notorious case of Tennessee, which first brought the matter before the Supreme Court, simply ignored constitutional mandates for decennial reapportionment, thereby freezing representation at a period when the great majority of voters lived in small towns or on farms.

Before reapportionment, many city representatives and their sympathizers had come to believe that weighted apportionment was the *entire* cause of the relative impotence of city delegations in the legislatures. Now that the process of redrawing legislative districts on the basis of "one man-one vote" has been almost completed, spokesmen for the cities are having painful second thoughts. Some, in fact, have grown a bit nostalgic for the bad old days of domination by rural squirearchies. "At least you could buy the rural legislators!" Mayor Daley was heard to lament on a day when Chicago was faring badly at the hands of the new suburban leadership in the Illinois legislature. "The chief effect of reapportionment has been to update conservatism," according to Jesse Unruh, who in 1969 was demoted by Republican takeover of the California Assembly from speaker to minority leader. In Cleveland's embattled city hall, Mayor Carl Stokes complained recently, "One man-one vote hasn't changed a thing as far as the central city is concerned. Instead of the farmer with his conservatism and detachment, you now have the man from suburbia, who is as conservative and detached, and sometimes as hostile to the city, as the rural member."

Actually, malapportionment by the time the Supreme Court delivered its rulings was penalizing the suburbs much more than the cities. In some states, like Ohio and Texas, the practice of electing all representatives on a countywide basis in at least one house left suburbs virtually unrepresented. Table I compares representation of some major cities with that of their suburbs in the legislative house with the *least* equal representation before and after reapportionment.

Failure of reapportionment to produce city control of legislatures has left some city representatives undisturbed in their conviction that the day when cities will dictate to the states is not far off. Others, however, have felt compelled to reassess the distribution of real power, based on the size of the population groups within their states.

THE POPULATION BALANCE

The 1960 census, which will govern legislative apportionment in most states until 1972, showed only ten states which were not more

TABLE I. *Comparison of Population to Representation Before and After Reapportionment*

	Percent of State Popula- tion in 1960	Percent in House Before Reapportion- ment	Percent in House After Reapportion- ment
CALIFORNIA SENATE			
Los Angeles, San Francisco,			
San Diego, Oakland	26	10	25
Suburbs	39	12.5	37.5
NEW YORK ASSEMBLY			
New York City	46	43	45
Suburbs	17	11	18
PENNSYLVANIA HOUSE			
Philadelphia, Pittsburgh	24	21	23
Suburbs	24	19	23
ILLINOIS SENATE			
Chicago	35	31	36
Suburbs	27	14	24
TEXAS SENATE			
Houston, Dallas,			
San Antonio, Ft. Worth	27	13	32
Suburbs	9	0	0
OHIO SENATE			
Cleveland, Cincinnati,			
Columbus	19	33	30
Suburbs	16	6	12
MICHIGAN SENATE			
Detroit	21	15	18
Suburbs	27	12	32

than 50 per cent urban. Since the Census Bureau includes all persons living in towns of more than 2,500 inhabitants or in the "densely settled fringe" of urbanized areas in its "urban" category, however, this term is almost useless for purposes of political classification. Certainly residents of small towns of less than 10,000 people sense little political identity with inhabitants of major cities. Also, persons living in cities of less than 50,000 are more likely to feel antagonistic than fraternal toward such giant cities as New York, Chicago, Los Angeles, and Philadelphia, particularly if they happen to share a state with one of the super-cities. Finally, residents of the metropolitan areas outside great cities, whether technically "urban" or "rural" under the Census Bureau's definitions, are generally bound in a common "suburban" point of view.

A more helpful tool for political analysis is the Census Bureau's designation of "Standard Metropolitan Statistical Areas" (SMSA)— generally, cities of more than 50,000, along with surrounding areas "socially and economically integrated with the central city." A very rough classification of political interests based on place of residence can be achieved by dividing state populations into residents of SMSA central cities, inhabitants of their surrounding suburbs, and persons living outside of the SMSAs altogether. This scheme of classification obviously creates categories which embrace multitudes of differences. There is a great distinction in point of view between residents of small cities and inhabitants of the rural countryside, both of whom are included in the third or "outstate" category. Likewise, persons living in cities with populations from 50,000 to 100,000 are operating under social structures essentially different from those which exist in the super-cities. (It may be argued that one of the root problems of the super-cities is that they provide *no* visible social structure to which the ordinary citizen can relate his behavior.) Still, the division into SMSA city dwellers, suburbanites, and outstaters provides a workable basis from which analysis can begin.

As it happens, these three groups were close to equal in the total national population in 1960. SMSA city dwellers comprised 32 percent of the total population, suburbanites 31 percent, and outstaters 37 percent. Not surprisingly, as is shown in Table II this distribu-

TABLE II. *Percentage Distribution of State Populations in 1960*

	SMSA Cities	SMSA Suburbs	Outstate
New York	58	31	11
California	34	50	16
Pennsylvania	32	48	20
Illinois	42	35	23
Ohio	35	34	31
Texas	46	17	37
Michigan	32	41	27
New Jersey	18	60	22
Massachusetts	33	51	16
Florida	24	41	35

tion was substantially different in most of the ten most populous states. (These ten states contained 54 percent of the total population, 62 percent of the total urban population, and 67 percent of the total living in SMSAs. All are among the 18 states which the Census Bureau found to be more than 70 percent urban.)

Among the top ten states, only Ohio approximates the national distribution among the population groups. Only in New York, Texas, and Illinois, however, does the deviation from the national norm significantly favor the cities. Only New York contained an actual majority of city dwellers.

Among the other 40 states, only one, Arizona, had more than 50 percent of its population living in cities. Only in New York and Arizona, therefore, do the cities have the potential strength to dominate state governments without help from the other two groups. In reality, cities in neither of these states have been able to gain a clear upper hand. Not only do city voters divide their support among parties and candidates in statewide elections, but also the potential city strength is split by rivalries among the cities themselves.

In Arizona, there are only two cities of significant size—Phoenix and Tucson. Phoenix by itself comprised 34 percent of the state's population in 1960 and was more than twice the size of Tucson. Fearing total domination of the state by the metropolitan giant, Tucson has increasingly aligned itself with the rural minority. Phoenix, nevertheless, plays a powerful role in state government, and at least recently has set the tone of Arizona politics. Quarrels with the hinterland, however, do not usually come on questions of policy, since Phoenix, the home base of Senator Barry Goldwater, has remained politically quite conservative. Except for supporting a relatively generous state subsidy for education, the city has done little to promote state action on urban problems.

At the other end of the process of urbanization, the cities of New York have made important contributions to the political process which has produced what is surely the most progressive state government in the nation. Never, however, have the cities been able to exercise the dominance to which population would seem to entitle them. New York City, which in 1960 by itself contained 46 percent of the state's population, is overwhelmingly Democratic, but during all but four years since 1939 the state has had a Republican governor. In the legislature, even after reapportionment, the cities have been unable to exercise effective control. This is partly due to the political ineptness of New York City Democrats, but results largely from the historic antagonism felt among the state's other cities toward the great metropolis. Voters in cities like Rochester, Syracuse, and Binghamton support Republican candidates in percentages unusually high for eastern cities at least partly because the Democratic party is closely identified with New York City. This situation has not left the cities powerless—Republicans since Thomas Dewey have taken care to cultivate their urban constituencies—but it has made them petitioners instead of arbiters in state government.

If cities have not become dominant in the two states where they hold actual majorities, it is not surprising that in the remaining states they have had generally tough sledding. The 22 SMSA cities of Texas, which together comprised 46 percent of the state's population in 1960, have had difficulty acting in concert and were hampered by under-representation in the state senate prior to reapportionment. In any case, many of them, like the cities of Arizona, have usually supported conservative candidates and policies. Chicago accounted for 35 percent of the population of Illinois, but since the state has few other sizable cities, the metropolis has had to deal for favors with the suburban and outstate blocs. In only two other states, Hawaii and Nevada—both rather special cases—did cities contain more than 40 percent of the state's total population.

Current population trends will further weaken the position of the cities in state politics. The 1970 census will show the cities slipping well behind the other two geographic groups in population strength. For the first time in American history, more people will be found living in suburbs than in cities. Looking ahead, some projections indicate that by 1985 suburbanites will outnumber city dwellers by almost two-to-one. The effect of this swing to the suburbs has already been felt in statewide elections. Table III shows the shifting distribution of the vote in presidential elections for principal cities and their suburbs in four urban states.

Another trend in demography which will complicate the political problems of the cities is the growing percentages of Negroes in central city populations. Black majorities are projected during the seventies for such important cities as Detroit, Baltimore, Cleveland, St. Louis, and perhaps even Chicago and Philadelphia (not, however, for New York City or Los Angeles). While black governments in the cities will at last give Negroes the power base they have always lacked in American politics, it would be foolhardy not to anticipate tensions between black city halls and the predominantly white admin-

TABLE III. *Percentage of State Vote Cast by Cities and Their Suburbs in Presidential Elections*

	1952	1960	1968
NEW YORK			
New York City	48	42	39
Suburbs	14	18	22
ILLINOIS			
Chicago	41	37	31
Suburbs	19	26	30
PENNSYLVANIA			
Philadelphia	21	18	18
Suburbs	11	14	16
MICHIGAN			
Detroit	29	23	18
Suburbs	19	27	30

istrations in state capitols—similar, perhaps, to the antagonism that existed between Irish administrations in Boston and Yankee governments in Massachusetts during the early years of this century.

The Suburban-Outstate Coalition

The central conclusion that emerges from all of these statistics is that the cities do not now and will not in the foreseeable future have the votes to dictate means for dealing with urban problems to the states. The dream of city politicians in the fifties and early sixties that the cities might some day be able to impose their wills on the states simply will not bear the test of reality. This does not, of course, mean that the cities will have no access to power. If they are not in a majority position, neither, generally speaking, are their suburban or outstate rivals. In only four states, New Jersey, Rhode Island, Massachusetts, and California, did suburbanites in 1960 comprise more than 50 percent of the population. In 24 largely rural states (though including Wisconsin and Indiana) outstaters held a clear majority. In the 20 remaining states, not counting New York and Arizona, some combination of city, suburban, and outstate interests is needed to form a majority. Even where suburbanites or outstaters could theoretically rule alone, divisions within their own ranks almost always force them to seek some outside support. In almost all states, some arrangement of shared power is a necessary condition for government.

Population groups can achieve power in state politics in two ways: through their representatives in the state legislature, or by affecting the results of elections for statewide offices, particularly governor. In the legislature, the city delegations were until recently forced to negotiate for favors with the outstate squires who were dominant in all but a few heavily urbanized states like Massachusetts and Rhode Island. Contrary to general belief, the squires were not always unresponsive to metropolitan needs. For one thing, in the big urban states many of them were aware that they owed their positions to a kind of democratic sufferance. If they had been too outrageous in thwarting the desires of cities and suburbs, rural weighting of apportionment would not have survived for as long as it did. For another, they were often relatively enlightened men, who had made careers as lawmakers and had developed considerable knowledge of and even sympathy for urban problems.

Jesse Unruh, who worked at close quarters for many years with the squires in the California legislature, has observed that they were frequently men of independent judgment, able to continue as legislators without heavy campaign expenditures due to the very population sparsity of their districts. Since reapportionment, Unruh claims, districts are so populous that a successful candidate must either be extremely wealthy or turn to the "special interests" to fill out his campaign budget. The result has been to eliminate a breed of fairly disinterested public servants from the legislature. Mayor Daley's regret over the passing of rural legislators who could be "bought" may spring from a cruder perception of the same phenomenon—men who were willing to help the cities, if they could receive some help in return for projects which would benefit their own districts.

Nevertheless, there is no doubt that the rule of the squirearchies tended to direct state government toward essentially rural values. The things that the states have done best, as Paul Ylvisaker has pointed out, have been the things which rural constituencies could appreciate: superior highways, land grant universities, decentralized public school systems. Distinctively urban problems, though usually not wholly neglected by the squires, were inevitably regarded as being of secondary importance. Most critically of all, the outstate representatives usually practiced the rural virtue of frugality. With the encouragement of the business lobbies that were their frequent allies, they held state expenditures of all kinds, though particularly those intended for the cities, to a minimum. The fiscal straitjackets in which almost all states are still enclosed were thus formed.

The dominance of the squirearchies has now passed, because of reapportionment, in all but the most rural states, but their remaining leaders retain substantial influence. Ylvisaker, who as New Jersey's first Commissioner of Community Affairs has learned perhaps more than he wished to know of legislative behavior, has observed that the skills which the squires acquired during their years of dominance help now to preserve their effectiveness beyond their numbers. In addition, they still comprise from one-fourth to one-third of the memberships of legislatures in most urban states outside of California, New York, and lower New England. In some states, as has already occurred in Maryland, city delegations may find it possible to make common cause with the remaining squires against the rising power of the suburbs. In general, however, the outstaters will probably choose alliance with the suburbs over coalition with the cities.

RISE OF THE SUBURBS

The suburbs, both because their interest generally lies somewhere between that of the cities and that of the outstate, and because the drift of population is so clearly in their favor, now occupy enviable positions in most urban state legislatures. After years of sometimes resentful submission to the authority of the squires, the suburbanites have at last ascended to positions of power. In Illinois, for example, in 1969 not only the governor and state attorney general, but also the president pro tem of the state senate and the majority leader and majority whip of the house of representatives were residents of suburban Cook County. Suburbanites also held key offices in the legislatures of, among other states, New York, California, Pennsylvania, Michigan, and New Jersey.

Despite the complaints of city representatives against suburban indifference and even hostility, the shift from outstate to suburban leadership has probably produced a net gain for the cities. Suburbanites, for one thing, as Moynihan has remarked, "are at least used to spending a lot of money." Resistance to state tax increases is probably not quite so strong in the suburbs as outstate. When Governor Richard Ogilvie pushed Illinois' first income tax through the legislature in 1969, he received much greater support from suburban representatives of Cook County than from their fellow

Republicans downstate. Moreover, at least some of the cities' problems are shared by the suburbs. Mass transit in metropolitan areas, air and water pollution, disappearance of open space near large cities are issues to which suburban voters respond. Moreover, the very proximity of the cities, plus the fact that many suburbanites work in downtown office buildings, forces the distinctive problems of the inner cities upon the attention of suburban representatives. "We know now that a bomb that goes off in the core city affects suburbia," says New York Assembly Speaker Perry Duryea, whose home district is in suburban Suffolk County.

This does not mean that suburban representatives recognize a generally common interest with the cities, or that city-suburban coalitions are likely to appear in many state legislatures. The influence of party, for one thing, works against it. In most urban states outside the South and Southwest, city delegations are overwhelmingly Democratic and most suburban representatives are Republicans. In states with low legislative party discipline, like California, this is only marginally important. But in states with traditions of strong party discipline, like New York, Pennsylvania, and Ohio, the suburban Republicans not only view their Democratic colleagues from the cities with the normal amount of inter-party animosity, but also are strongly influenced by the conservative views of the outstate members of their party caucuses. A further conservative check on suburban Republicans in some states appears to be coming from the new breed of Republican legislators that have begun to be elected from cities like New York and Chicago. In these cities, which for many years have supported mildly progressive and hopelessly outnumbered Republican parties, Republicanism has suddenly begun to gather strength from the new conservatism of white working-class neighborhoods. Since Republican legislators elected from these neighborhoods owe their success to their ideology, they are likely to take a hard line on issues like law enforcement and welfare. Though as yet few in number, they have already somewhat conditioned the policies of Republican leaders in some legislatures.

The deeper reason for the lack of close ties between city and suburban representatives is that their interests on many issues do not really, at least in the short run, which no politician can safely ignore, coincide. The reason that the Democratic Party has so spectacularly failed to penetrate the suburbs in most states is that the Democrats are identified with the crooked politics, dirty and unsafe streets, and racial tensions of the cities, which many suburbanites have deliberately chosen to put behind them. Having reached the suburbs, they are chiefly concerned that the cities' problems shall not follow them. They are willing, within reason, to pay higher state taxes, but they insist that the state give first attention to what they regard as their primary needs. In New York in 1969, when Governor Nelson Rockefeller proposed a five percent across-the-board cut in projected expenditures for all state programs, Perry Duryea and his fellow suburban Republicans in the legislature insisted that most of the cuts in education subsidies be restored, and that the difference be made up by doubling the slice in welfare. The legislators were undoubtedly reflecting the values of a majority of their constituents.

Actually, many outstate and suburban legislators probably go farther in providing help for the cities than is popular in their districts. Richardson Dilworth, former mayor of Philadelphia and now president of the Philadelphia Board of Education, tells of traveling to the capitol of Pennsylvania in the winter of 1969 with a group of Philadelphia businessmen in search of more state aid for the city's schools. Dilworth had threatened that the schools would close before the end of the school year if no additional funds were found. At a meeting with legislative leaders from suburban and rural areas, one of the businessmen argued, "As politicians, you cannot afford to permit the schools of the state's largest city to close for lack of money." This suggestion was greeted with laughter. "As politicians," said one legislator, "there is nothing that would do us more good than to go back and tell our voters that we wouldn't let Philadelphia have another nickel."

The cities' best hope for eventually gaining allies in the suburbs is that the present political unity of the suburban delegations will some day be broken up. The suburbs at present embrace a wide variety of economic levels and life styles. They include communities which range from cloistered rural villages to densely populated industrial slums. Their political unity, as Richard Wade has pointed out, is based almost entirely on their common fear of and opposition to the city. In time, their natural differences may begin to pull them in different directions. Close-in suburbs are increasingly experiencing problems that are similar to those faced by the inner cities. This may eventually draw them closer to the cities politically. Some movement in this direction is already occurring in the suburbs of New York. Democratic candidates now commonly win legislative contests in some districts in Nassau and Westchester Counties. The industrial towns around Detroit also send Democrats to the legislature. In the suburbs of most major Northern cities, however, the Republican phalanx remains almost unbroken. In 1969, not a single Democrat represented the districts of suburban Cook County outside Chicago. Of the 36 legislators elected from the four suburban counties that surround Philadelphia, only two were Democrats. For the foreseeable future, such joint action between city and suburbs as takes place will occur under uneasy partisan truce rather than through intra-party collaboration.

BIG CITY MACHINES

The cities' legislators, though almost everywhere outnumbered by suburban and outstate representatives, are not of course without legislative weapons. Governors seeking tax increases must usually obtain at least a few votes from city delegations, to make up for defectors in the suburban and outstate contingents, and must grant concessions in how the money is spent in return for this support. The ability of city machines to deliver large blocs of legislators strengthens their positions in bargaining. Party discipline, which works against the cities with suburban representatives, is often to their benefit in the legislature at large. Most urban states contain pockets of outstate and even suburban Democratic strength, which as a rule wax and wane in correspondence to the fortunes of the national Democratic Party. When the Democrats are in the ascendancy nationally—or even when their ticket runs well in urban states although falling short of national victory, as occurred in 1968— these pockets combined with the Democratic blocs from the cities will often turn at least one legislative house over to Democratic control.

Since the city representatives, though a minority in the entire legislature, are usually a majority in the Democratic caucus, Democratic control in effect means city control, and much city oriented legislation can be expected to pour forth during these periods. Democrats won control of the Pennsylvania House of Representatives in 1968, for instance, and promptly elected a speaker from Philadelphia and a majority leader from Pittsburgh. Democratic legislative leaders in Illinois are usually selected by the current boss of the Chicago machine. When Democrats gained a majority in the New York Assembly in 1965, antagonism between warring party factions made it difficult to guess from one day to the next who would be speaker, but it was always certain that the victorious contestant would be a representative from New York City. This situation naturally creates a certain amount of ill feeling among Democratic representatives from outstate, whose views are often more conservative than the party line dictated by the cities. When the chips are down, however, at least in the big urban states of the East and Great Lakes region, the outstaters usually follow the will of the machine. Outstate Democratic representatives, in the nature of things, run a higher than average chance of being knocked off in the next election, and many will then be forced to turn to the machine for continued gainful employment.

The machine quality of Democratic politics in most cities, however, probably is more a handicap than a help to the cities in its total impact on legislative behavior. Not only does the machine give suburban and outstate Republicans a useful menace to run against, but also the customs of ward politics seem to produce a rather inferior brand of legislator. Legislative service appears to hold more prestige in the suburbs and particularly in the outstate than in the cities. A seat in the legislature is regarded by most city machines as a political plum—and not a very highly valued one—to be rewarded to a faithful party worker. There is a wonderful story about a Chicago politician who was sent to the United States Congress by the machine when he was well over 70. When asked by Speaker Sam Rayburn why in the world he had come at such an advanced age, and why in any case the machine had seen fit to endorse him, he is supposed to have replied feelingly, "Because it was my turn!" The attitude underlying this anecdote still seems to prevail in the political clubhouses of many major cities. Normally, the machine sees to it that its delegations are led by a few highly skilled parliamentarians, but the majority of the representatives that it sends to the state capitol are, to put it mildly, undistinguished.

Changes in the nature of city politics may before long improve the quality of city representation. Machines are everywhere on the ropes, and would probably vanish altogether if anybody could find some other means for carrying out the onerous chores of ward politics. While legislative elections in the cities are contests of such low visibility that machine candidates still usually triumph, the city legislative delegations have begun to include a growing number of members who claim some kind of identification with "reform." The reform faction from New York City was, in fact, decisive in settling a contest between two rival machine leaders for the post of minority leader in the state assembly in 1969. Since the reformers, whatever else they may be, are usually abler men than their machine predecessors, it is at least possible that they will be more successful at forging productive alliances with legislators from other parts of their states.

On the other hand, reformers are sometimes so intensely partisan that even the flimsy combinations put together on occasion by machine and outstate representatives may become unworkable.

INFLUENCE OF THE LOBBIES

Cities receive some measure of assistance from many of the lobbies and pressure groups that operate on state legislatures. Business lobbies used to spend a good deal of their time balking cities' pleas for financial aid and keeping regulatory powers out of the hands of city governments. During the New Deal years, many state governments were employed by business as defensive buffers against the growing power of the liberal-labor coalition in the city halls and in Washington. More recently, however, the corporate establishment has swung toward the view that state government can play a positive role in cooling the social tensions which threaten continued prosperity, and the business lobbies have changed their behavior accordingly. Also, some business interests, like commuter railroads and the housing industry, have a direct financial stake in state aid to the cities. The new attitude of business has led it to join forces on a number of issues with organized labor, which has always, in a general way, given support to the aspirations of the cities. Even the still formidable farm lobbies are prepared to relax their traditional hostility toward city oriented programs, so long as no challenge is raised against the special privileges which have been written into tax and labor laws for their constituents.

All of these groups still sometimes find themselves opposing the cities on particular issues. Individual business lobbies defend their special bailiwicks: retailers fight credit control laws, coal and steel companies oppose legislation to prevent water pollution, oil companies block use of gasoline taxes to build mass transit facilities. Schoolteacher lobbies, among the most effective in many state capitals, have in some states slowed the progress of the movement to decentralize city schools. Public employee unions use their power in state legislatures to wring concessions from city governments. (Voter indignation against public employee strikes, on the other hand, has led to tough anti-strike laws for government workers in most states.)

Predictably, the lobbies expend a good deal more energy on protecting their special interests than on the common effort to bring more state help to the cities. Most lobbyists operate on the assumption that their influence with the legislature is as fixed as a bank balance. Influence expended on a good cause may be missed, they believe, on the rainy day when the lobby's own vital interests are threatened.

Response from the Governors

On the whole, cities will probably continue to gain more from the favor of executive officers elected on a statewide basis than from their power in state legislatures. This does not mean that the cities will be able to elect their first choices as governor or to the lesser executive posts, or even that the candidates who gain the majority of city votes will usually win elections. Exactly the opposite is likely to be the case. It is no accident that in 1969 eight of the ten most populous states had Republican governors. (One of the two Democratic exceptions, Preston Smith of Texas, was probably more conservative than any of the Republicans.) The controlling political fact in almost every urban state is the majority held by a combination of suburban and outstate voters. Even in New York, as has been noted, where the cities do hold a majority, divisions between New York City and the upstate urban centers generally produce statewide victories for candidates opposed by the metropolis.

The fact that the cities give only a minority of their votes to the winners does not, however, free candidates who have the support of the suburbs and the outstate to ignore the cities. Since none of the regions are monolithic in their votes, and since population strength is fairly evenly distributed among them, the crucial question in every election is how deeply each candidate can eat into the camp of the opposition. In other words, the candidate of the suburban-outstate combination—in practice, outside the South and Southwest, almost always the Republican—is vitally interested in holding down the size of his opponent's majority in the cities. The fact that Republicans have generally been winning elections in the urban states in recent years is due not only to the emerging strength of the suburban-outstate coalition, but also because Republican candidates have succeeded in winning substantial support in the cities themselves.[1]

[1] The election of Republican William Cahill as governor of New Jersey in November 1969 established Republican control in nine of the top ten states. The overwhelming size of the Cahill victory was due to support from the cities as well as the suburban-outstate coalition.

The Republican Party, though a minority in most cities since the New Deal, has never been without resources of urban strength. Some city voters—particularly among white Protestants, small businessmen, and old people—have always remained loyal to the G.O.P. Center city business establishments are generally Republican, helping to finance campaigns and providing cadres of young lawyers and accountants as party workers. Most big city newspapers have Republican ties, sometimes giving sympathetic treatment to favored candidates in their news columns as well as on editorial pages. In a few cities, like Cincinnati and Philadelphia, Republicans maintain fairly formidable machines of their own, responsive to the hard goods of politics. All of these help swell the vote for Republican candidates in statewide elections, and their spokesmen appear at the governor's office after a victorious campaign to claim attention for the urban problems which most concern them.

Generally, however, Republican state candidates in recent years have sought to reach outside areas of normal party strength to gather additional urban support. Methods have varied. In Ohio, James Rhodes, who missed carrying Cleveland by only 16,000 votes in his successful race for reelection as governor in 1966, has relied on a sort of Chamber-of-Commerce booster approach, urging city voters to follow his leadership into a promised land of economic prosperity for all. In California, Ronald Reagan has appealed to the indignation felt by many city dwellers against unruly demonstrators on the state's college campuses. In states like Pennsylvania, Massachusetts, and Illinois, Republican candidates have tried to make common cause with municipal reform movements against entrenched Democratic city machines. But in most populous states, the primary means employed by Republicans to build their urban constituencies has been to campaign on platforms that promise more state aid to cities, and later, if elected, actually to devote a good deal of effort to meeting city needs.

It has for many years been a paradoxical rule-of-thumb in New York politics that Republican governors work harder for the city, and Democratic governors do more for the upstate—each leaning over backwards to gain support outside his natural constituency. In keeping with this tradition, state aid to New York City quadrupled from 1959 to 1969 under Nelson Rockefeller's administration, and the state pioneered with programs in housing, mass transportation, and economic development of the ghettoes. Rockefeller won his political reward in 1966: running for his third term, he carried three of New York City's five boroughs, and lost the city by only 70,000 votes.

Republican governors of other urban states have been similarly responsive to city needs. In Pennsylvania, William Scranton established the nation's first state department of community affairs in 1966, and secured enactment of a school subsidy program which includes population density and relative poverty among the factors determining the size of payments to districts. Raymond Shafer, Scranton's Republican successor, has inclined even more heavily toward the cities. In Michigan, George Romney won approval for the income tax and began the state's first housing program. In Illinois, Republican Richard Ogilvie, who became governor in 1969 after eight years of Democratic rule, pushed through the income tax, established a program of sharing state revenues with cities, and set up a department of local government during his first six months in office. California, where Reagan installed an avowedly conservative administration in 1967, appears to offer a variant case. Even here, however, the conservative governor found it necessary to sponsor the largest single tax increase ever enacted by any state, and generally expanded rather than curtailed the state's broad range of social programs. Also, Reagan's running mate, Lieutenant Governor Robert Finch, before leaving the state to join the Nixon cabinet in 1969, sought to establish a liberal image essentially similar to those projected by Rockefeller, Scranton, and Romney.

THE REPUBLICAN ADVANTAGE

In the urban states, Republican governors, beside having a special practical motive for appealing to the cities, are generally better situated than Democratic chief executives to win legislative approval for progressive programs. When Democrats control the governorship and both houses of the legislature, the Republican minority is likely to form an intransigent bloc of conservative opposition. Rivalries between the governor and Democratic legislative leaders can then produce stalemates in state government. In Massachusetts, Democratic governors have frequently received rough treatment from legislatures overwhelmingly controlled by members of their own party. Similarly, in California, the second term of Governor Pat Brown devolved into a legislatively unproductive power struggle between Brown and Speaker Unruh, which helped pave the way for the election of Reagan in 1966. When, as is now much more often the case outside the South and lower New England, Republicans control at least one legislative house, Democratic governors face almost certain frustration. Governor Richard Hughes of New Jersey, the only liberal Democrat among the chief executives of the top ten states in 1969, was regularly balked by the legislature after the Republicans won heavy majorities in both houses in 1967. Besides turning down various tax proposals made by Hughes to raise funds to aid the cities, the legislature rewrote the governor's urban education bill to favor the suburbs rather than the core cities.

Republican governors, on the other hand, can often win normally conservative Republican legislators to the support of progressive measures. The success of Ogilvie's legislative program, for instance, was largely due to the support he obtained from W. Russell Arrington, the conservative president pro tem of the Illinois senate. Ogilvie had maintained a close personal relationship with Arrington from the time he entered Cook County politics in the early sixties. Similarly, Romney and Scranton got Republican legislatures to approve city oriented measures which had been rejected when offered by their Democratic predecessors. When conservative defections reduce their own ranks, progressive Republican governors can often find the votes they need among liberal Democrats, who are necessarily committed to legislation helping the cities. Both Romney and Ogilvie needed Democratic votes to win passage of their income taxes. Likewise, Republican governors confronted with Democratic legislatures can, despite a certain amount of skirmishing for credit, usually maintain good legislative records. Scranton did about equally well with a Democratic controlled house of representatives during the last two years of his administration as he had with a Republican house in the first two. Rockefeller, too, got pretty much what he wanted out of Democratic controlled assemblies from 1965 to 1969. In 1966, after seven tries, Republican Governor John Volpe of Massachusetts won approval for a sales tax to finance increased aid to schools and local governments from a legislature more than two-to-one Democratic.

The distance that a governor can lead his party depends to a large extent on personal relationships, and of course varies according to circumstance. Particularly after the party has enjoyed power for a prolonged period, the conservatism of Republican legislators may begin to assert itself against the wishes of a progressive governor. In Pennsylvania, Raymond Shafer's liberalism brought him under growing attack from outstate and suburban Republican legislators. When Shafer proposed a state personal income tax in 1969, his fellow Republicans in the state house of representatives voted unanimously to oppose his request. The same year in Wisconsin, Republicans in the legislature revolted against the leadership of Governor Warren Knowles, and made drastic cuts in the three-term governor's ambitious urban aid program.

Still, a determined Republican governor, even after many years in office, retains powerful sanctions which can be imposed against party legislators. When Rockefeller's proposal for a state Urban Development Corporation bogged down in the legislature in 1968, he called the holdouts, one by one, into his office. Within a few hours, the necessary majority was rounded up. "That man has an extraordinary understanding of power," says Edward Logue, who became the Urban Development Corporation's first director. "He didn't promise them this or that. He said, 'I'll cut you off—nothing!' "

CITY-BASED EXECUTIVES

But cannot the cities do better than dependence on the good will of governors who, whatever their progressive leanings, remain in the end most beholden for their elections to the suburban-out-state coalition? Cannot city leaders themselves rise to the mastery of states? Although it has long been a political axiom that the mayor's office is a dead-end job, the truth is that city political figures during the late forties and fifties enjoyed a period of rising success. In 1948 Mayor Hubert Humphrey of Minneapolis and former Alderman Paul Douglas of Chicago were both elected, against heavy odds, to the United States Senate. In the decade that followed, former Mayor Joseph Clark of Philadelphia joined them in the Senate, and former Mayor Theodore McKeldin of Baltimore, Mayor David Lawrence of Pittsburgh, and former Mayor Michael DiSalle of Toledo became governors of, respectively, Maryland, Pennsylvania, and Ohio. After 1960, however, the trend went the other way. Former Mayor Dilworth of Philadelphia lost the governorship of Pennsylvania to Scranton in 1962. In the same year, DiSalle was defeated for reelection by Rhodes, who, though he had once been mayor of Columbus, had operated at the state level of Ohio politics since the early fifties. In 1966, Mayor Samuel Yorty of Los Angeles and former Mayor George Christopher of San Francisco lost their respective party primaries for governor of California, while Mayor John Collins of Boston and Mayor Jerome Cavanaugh of Detroit were losing the Democratic primaries for United States senator in Massachusetts and Michigan. The series was perhaps rounded off when Douglas was ousted from the Senate by Charles Percy (of suburban Cook County) in 1966, followed by the defeat of Clark for reelection by Congressman Richard Schweiker (of suburban Montgomery County in Pennsylvania) in 1968. Also in 1968, the public career of former Mayor Humphrey, who had risen the highest, was at least temporarily cut off by a product of southern California's quintessence of suburbia.

Still, the wheel of politics continues to turn, and in all probability during the coming decade it will produce some state administrations whose chief electoral bases are in the cities. Although they form a minority of the population in all states, the Democratic blocs in large urban centers retain powerful allies beyond the city limits. Foremost among these is organized labor, which can produce a sizable minority vote in the outstate regions. Many mining or industrial small towns are, in fact, normally Democratic. In the suburbs, independent liberals of the kind that rallied to the causes of Eugene McCarthy and Robert Kennedy in 1968 will give substantial support to attractive Democratic candidates. Other sources of Democratic strength outside the cities (not including for the moment the states of the South and Southwest where the outstate is still overwhelmingly Democratic) survive for one or another historic reason. The outstate of northern California is traditionally Democratic, partly in reaction to the Republicanism of southern California. In Maryland, Eastern Shore Democrats, who trace their party loyalty to the Civil War and the doctrine of white supremacy, co-exist uneasily with the Democratic legions of Baltimore. Similarly, regions of copperhead strength during the Civil War in Illinois, Indiana, Kentucky, Ohio, and Pennsylvania still lean Democratic. Taken together, these forces combined with normal Democratic majorities from the cities make the Democratic party a respectable contender for power in every urban state. Given the disenchantment which is bound to set in with Republican state regimes long in power, Democrats are sure to recover control of some executive offices during the seventies. (Republican possession of the White House also will probably help the Democrats in state elections. The Republicans, who did well in the states during the forties, began to lose governorships soon after Dwight Eisenhower became president in 1953. By 1959, only two of the top ten states had Republican governors. Soon after the Democrats regained the presidency in 1961, the Republicans returned to power in most of the urban states. Other factors were involved in these shifts, but there does seem to be some tendency for voters to favor at the state level the party that is out of power in Washington.) Although some accommodation will have to be made with the more conservative views of their outstate collaborators, Democratic city politicians, whether of the machine or reform variety, will then once again enjoy the advantages which go with easy access to the governor's office, clearance of executive appointments, and influence over preparation of the state's operating and capital budgets.

Over the long run, however, the outlook for durable Democratic control of most state governments in the North and West is not favorable. The mathematics of population are working against a city-based party. The political effectiveness of the unions is in decline. The support of outstate Democrats is wavering. The emergence of black administrations in city halls may further divide the Democratic party. The Democrats seem likely to fall to the status occupied by the Republicans in the fifties—able to win elections when the public grows bored or outraged with the rival party, but lacking the basic strength to develop consistent majorities. During the seventies, therefore, the cities will probably continue to hold no more than a second mortgage on the attention of most urban state governors.

THE CHANGING SOUTH

In the states of the South and Southwest, finally, most of the outstate remains traditionally Democratic, and Democrats have until recently held virtual one-party control of state governments. Of these 14 states (including West Virginia, Oklahoma, and New Mexico, as well as the states of the old Confederacy), ten had more than 50 percent of their populations living outstate in 1960. In these, both legislatures and gubernatorial races are usually dominated by rural counties, and the cities must make do with whatever concessions they can gain by throwing their strength into the scales in contests between outstate factions. Even in the four Southern states with non-outstate majorities, political organizations based on outstate counties have normally held the upper hand. In Louisiana, this was accomplished for many years by the Longs and their political heirs, who exploited outstate hostility toward New Orleans, while collaborating with the machine faction known as the "old regulars" in the city. In Virginia, the Byrd organization, based on rural county courthouses, kept the state's six metropolitan areas politically weak and divided. More loosely organized alliances of rural and business interests have usually maintained control of Texas and Florida.

In the last three of these states, the growing strength of the cities has coincided with the recent emergence of the Republican party. Contrary to the situation in the North, southern Republicans have been more effective in the cities than outstate (except for traditional outstate Republican strongholds, like the mountain regions of Virginia, North Carolina, and Tennessee, and the "German counties" of central Texas). Continued Democratic dominance of the outstate counties is due in part to the tenacity of courthouse political organizations and the power of tradition, in part to the influence of the race issue, and in part to the persistence of rural poverty. Republican incursions in the cities, on the other hand, result from growth of an urban middleclass as a product of industrialization, and the tendency of many members of this class, which in the North would by now be mainly suburban, to continue to live within city limits. (Historically, the first effect of industrialization on politics has often been business dominance. The pre-Civil War Whig party, controlled by bankers and businessmen, had its principal strength in northern cities. Midwestern cities, industrialized after the Civil War, remained largely Republican until the New Deal.) The Republican party is now the most vigorous element in many Southern cities. At first, this has seemed to isolate the cities further from the political mainstream; but as the Republicans begin to win state elections, it may enhance the influence of the cities—or at least of their ruling business establishments.

At the same time, an urban liberal Democratic party has begun to develop in Southern cities like Houston and Norfolk. In time, more typical distribution of geographic strength between the parties may occur, with the important exception that rural blacks, as they gain political strength, will presumably remain loyal to the Democrats. Whether through Republican administrations in which city business leaders have a major voice, or through renewed Democratic control based on an alliance between urban liberals and rural blacks, the long-range prospect for increased city influence in state governments may be brighter in some parts of the South than in most of the urban North. For the next decade, however, the dominant mood of the South will probably remain conservative.

A New Politics?

But at the end, one must ask, does not this analysis overlook new and decisive forces at work in American politics? Is there not a "new politics" which will soon sweep away all these petty quarrels pitting rural against urban interests, suburbs against cities, whites against blacks? Will not the new politics distribute the resources of the states—which are much richer than old fogey reactionaries have ever been willing to admit—on the basis of need rather than of political power? Or, as the more toughminded suggest, is not power itself shifting: a new generation rising which will turn the guns, literal as well as figurative, of popular democracy against suburbs, conservatives, and temporizing politicians?

If by "new politics" is meant the radical demonstrators who have recently been provoking the authorities in cities and on college campuses, their chief effect on state and local politics so far has been to provide conservatives, including a good many sleazy operators whose conservatism is only incidental, with easy targets at which to aim their campaigns. Conservative forces would probably be increasing their influence within both national parties at this point in history anyhow, but their strength has certainly been augmented by middle class reaction to the demonstrators, both white and black. (The general unpopularity of the Vietnam war and the fall of the Johnson administration in 1968 gave the radicals a misleading impression of strength. The demonstrators, particularly those who were willing to "clean up for Gene," did contribute *something* to these developments, but both, to the extent that their causes had any ideological coloration, sprang as much from conservative as from radical impulses. As Korea helped usher in the benign conservatism of Eisenhower, so the ultimate result of Vietnam in 1968 was, after all, the election of Richard Nixon.) Many radicals welcome this movement to the right on the ground that it will "polarize" American politics, preparing the way for their eventual triumph. The election of Reagan as governor of California in 1966 was greeted with almost as much satisfaction by student radicals at Berkeley as by right-wing millionaires in Los Angeles. The fact that such polarization would lead inevitably to a prolonged period of repression seems either not to have occurred to the new radicals, or to be regarded as the necessary prelude to some international Armageddon leading to the final overthrow of established authority in the United States.

If, on the other hand, "new politics" means the gradual increase of enlightenment among the electorate, this seems at least possible. The rising level of education (at least more people are staying in school longer) does seem to produce *some* increase in liberalism, in the sense of a more generous, more tolerant, more open-minded attitude toward politics. In addition, current disenchantment with the efficacy of bureaucracy, both corporate and governmental, not only provides a tie between old right and new left, but also creates a humanistic counterforce against the coercive elements which are simultaneously gathering strength in society. This kind of new liberalism *may* provide a political climate—in the states as elsewhere—favorable to the cities.

It would be illusory, however, to believe that general benevolence will persuade the three-quarters of the population who live outside cities to do much more than help stave off disaster for the one-quarter who occupy the major metropolitan centers. (And even within this context, of course, many thousands of individual personal disasters will be permitted to continue.) To achieve any genuine reconstruction of the cities, it will be necessary, as Edward Faltermayer, my colleague at *Fortune* has suggested, to include the needs of the cities in some *total program* for the reconstruction of our entire society. In this way, the interest as well as the moral sympathy of the suburban and outstate majority could be touched. Creation of such a program, and development of the political enthusiasm that would be needed to put it into effect, are of course unlikely, but they are not impossible. If they should appear, at least some of the political inhibitions that now prevent the states from doing more to help their cities would no doubt become irrelevant.[2]

[2] Some of the material in this chapter was gathered for an earlier article titled "The States Hold the Keys to the Cities" which appeared in the June 1969 issue of *Fortune* magazine.

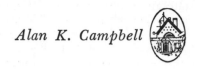

Alan K. Campbell

8

Breakthrough or Stalemate?
State Politics

States: The Whipping Boys Again

If governments are to serve their citizens effectively, they must be responsive to changing conditions. Federal and local governments have undergone many reforms in attempting to adjust to the increasing metropolitanization of the nation. State governments have not kept pace. In fact, the states have enjoyed public favor only during the early years of the nation's history when they provided leadership for the revolution and became the building blocks of the nation. Since those early days, the states have undergone periodic reexamination and have always been found wanting. The result has been continuous demands for reform, demands that, if met at all, were met only partially.

Early demands for reform arose because of the undemocratic characteristics of most state governments, many of which were controlled by oligarchic cliques. Some reforms were made during the Jacksonian period of democracy when the voting franchise was broadened and legislative power enhanced. Later, however, as legislative power was more and more abused, demands for restrictions on the power of states became prevalent—in New York State, for example, there was an insistence that the legislature be denied the power to give away the state to the New York Central Railroad. Restrictions on state power growing out of such abuses were often given constitutional sanction.

Moving into the twentieth century, states, along with their cities, became the targets of the muckrakers. Boss dominance, big business influence, and general corruption were documented and described for state after state and city after city. Building on these exposés, students of government and other reformers designed an extensive set of proposals for institutional change. These included the primary, the initiative, the referendum, civil service requirements, and hierarchical administrative systems which would pinpoint responsibility. Success in the adoption of these reforms varied from state to state, but every state felt their impact.

Depression and war caused the federal government to become increasingly involved in domestic affairs and although the power of the states did not actually decline, their relative position did. It is true that in some parts of the country state governments provided support for rear-guard action against New Deal social measures, but in others these social measures were welcomed; in all cases, however, the states were responders to federal initiative rather than self-starters.

The search for a means to move states into a more meaningful role in the governmental system and an analysis of their weaknesses led to an effort to pinpoint the causes of their inadequacies. Rural domination of state legislatures and administrative inadequacies in the executive branch were most frequently cited as the chief causes.

The first of these causes, rural domination, was thought to be the reason for state government's mistreatment of their cities, and reapportionment was prescribed as the cure. Home rule for cities, an acceptable substitute, was also sought, since it seemed doubtful that legislators would abandon a power allocation which served their interest.

ADMINISTRATIVE REORGANIZATION

Even more attractive than reapportionment or home rule, however, was reorganization of the executive branch because the political obstacles here were less formidable. Further, the federal government provided an example of how to proceed.

Following World War II there was a widespread move to increase the efficiency and responsiveness of the federal government. Building on the administrative reorganization reforms of the New Deal, the post-war period saw the appointment of two Hoover Commissions whose assignment was to investigate and make recommendations for changes in the national government's administrative and executive branches. Following this example, a majority of the states underwent reorganization studies, too. All such investigations resulted in recommendations for cleaning up the administrative structures of state governments. In general, this meant the clear delineation of responsibility among administrative officials, an increase in the power of the chief executive, abandonment of many elective offices and commissions, and reductions in the number of executive departments—all actions consistent with the traditional wisdom believed necessary to make government more responsive.

LEGISLATIVE REFORM

Attention shifted, somewhat, in the 1950s from the executive branch to the legislative. More and more, people became convinced that state performance would not improve until legislatures became more responsive. To achieve this, demands grew for increased pay, annual sessions, better staffing, a rational committee structure and, above all else, reapportionment. "To restore the people's confidence in state government, the revision of legislative apportionment in most states is imperative," the Eighth American Assembly argued in 1955.

This emphasis on legislatures continues and was reaffirmed by the Twenty-ninth American Assembly in 1966. Alexander Heard, who wrote the final article in the volume produced for that Assembly, *State Legislatures in American Politics,* listed 12 legislative reforms which included recommendations about length of sessions, terms of office, compensation, employees, number of committees, modern equipment, adequate finance, and better facilities. Although some states have introduced a few such reforms, it is not known what difference in the effectiveness of state government would ensue from wholesale adoption of the recommendations—probably much less than hoped.

What is known is that the most important of all reforms, reapportionment, has not had the impact anticipated. It was hoped that, apart from providing simple democratic fairness, it would cause the states to turn their attention to the problems of their cities. Unfortunately, reapportionment came a generation too late for that, and it has been the suburbs which have gained from it. Although Wallace Sayre's earlier proposition that the states are governed by the rural areas at the expense of the cities for the sake of the suburbs has to be somewhat altered, state favoritism has not, in fact, changed.

Federalism: Old and New

As students and reformers tried many routes to improving state government, they discovered that relations between governmental levels were as important as effectiveness within each level. This brought about a national revival of interest in federalism, and newly concerned scholars soon recognized that older doctrines concerning the nature of American federalism were no longer valid. John E. Bebout points this out:

> When I first started teaching political science, which was more than 50 years ago, I thought I knew something about federalism, but any political scientist who lectures to his students today in terms in which I lectured then should be fired. Maybe I should have been fired anyway, but nobody knew much better in those days. We still talked about dual federalism and thought in terms of a national government with rather strictly limited specific powers.

Anyone who knows John Bebout knows that he should not have been fired, but he is quite right, and typically so, when he argues that dual federalism hardly represented reality even when it was taught, and certainly does not now. Since "dual federalism" does not describe reality, efforts are constantly being made to find new phrases which do. The first tried was "cooperative federalism" which emphasizes the involvement of all parts of the governmental system—federal, state, and local—in nearly all domestic functions. It became clear in the 1960s, however, that the system required more than cooperation to make it work, so other phrases were tried. President Johnson opted for "creative," while Bebout prefers "partnership." But whatever the phrase, they are only slogans. They do not describe a system that anyone understands, nor do they delineate with any precision the roles of the various institutions and agencies which compose the system.

President Nixon emphasized, during his 1968 presidential campaign, his belief in the viability of the states, and he has attempted to give his campaign promise about strengthening the states credence by calling for a "new" federalism. Thus far such newness as he has suggested is confined to his recommendations for revenue sharing, and for giving to the states responsibility for manpower training. Since the funds provided through revenue sharing would carry few, if any, federal requirements, it is indeed a new approach. In view of the state performance described in this volume, serious questions might be raised about whether "newness" is a sufficient justification for such a change. The manpower training transfer is similar to the attempts made in the Eisenhower administration to find functions which might be assigned to the states. Success at that time was minimal.

Actually, the "dual federalism" concept is still the way many people view the system, and this is demonstrated by their continuing effort to respond to new patterns of inter-governmental relations by trying to determine which functions should be assigned to which level of government. Assignment of functions, however, is not the issue, but rather the assignment of power and responsibility relative to functions. Power over matters of policy, administration, and financing are distributed in an almost unlimited number of combinations among the levels of government, and among functions.

The essays in this volume accept this distinction and concentrate on describing and analyzing how the states are exercising their power, and the limitations, self-imposed or otherwise, on this exercise. The emphasis is on these limitations, and how they affect the ability and willingness of states to respond to urban problems.

Most analyses of state government have not taken this approach. They have emphasized, instead, structural and procedural arrangements, judging these by various principles of government—are they democratic, are they efficient, are they economical, or, rather, do they promote these ends? The central issue of this volume is different. Although many of the traditional questions are raised here, they are raised in the context of the relevance of state government—its internal structure, financing, and policies—to issues of substantive urban policy.

The States and Metropolitanism

An assembly on the state and its cities was held in Illinois in 1966. The report on that assembly says,

> It might have been expected that assembly participants would want initially to discuss some of the problems and needs of the cities. A logical second step would be to explore ways in which the state might act to meet these needs. However, it was clear that participants did not want to talk about substantive problems, such as housing or education, but rather about intergovernmental structure and finance. This may have been based on any one of three assumptions: (1) that solutions to substantive problems are sufficiently well understood to require no additional general discussion; (2) that substantive problems of urban life are not direct responsibilities of state government; or (3) that professionally trained people do have solutions and the duty of the state is to give them the freedom and the authority to do what needs to be done.[1]

[1] James H. Andrews, ed., *The State and Its Cities*, report and background papers, Assembly on the State and Its Cities, *University of Illinois Bulletin*, Vol. 64, No. 108 (April 18, 1967), pp. 2 and 3.

Although not as much is known about the solutions to urban problems as is suggested by this summary, its views are correct in at least two ways. First, more is known about urban problems than has been acted upon by all levels of government, most notably by state governments. Second, there is a close relationship between solving urban problems and the structure, finance, and politics of state government.

Students of state government who have concerned themselves with this relationship have cited home rule and reapportionment as the most likely means for improving the relationship. As has been amply demonstrated by Frank Grad, in his essay in this volume, the home rule panacea has been found wanting for good and sufficient reason, and, as James Reichley has shown, reapportionment favors suburban over city interests.

Other reasons often cited for the failure or lack of state action include constitutional restrictions on states' powers, the inadequacy of local government organization, and fiscal restraints, both constitutional and political. As is demonstrated by Grad, Grant, and Bahl, these are genuine restraints, and, unless removed, states will not be able to respond with either alacrity or boldness, or with sufficient resources to meet their urban challenges.

REMOVING THE OBSTACLES TO STATE ACTION

But what would happen if all these obstacles—constitutional, legal, fiscal, and organizational—were removed? Would states then respond?

It has been argued that what the states are doing is exactly what the majority of the people want them to do. Most politicians contend that such is the case. They explain that the people back home want lower taxes and less government. They will admit, however, that these demands for lower taxes and less government are often accompanied by equally insistent demands for more and better specific services—education, highways, welfare, health, etc.

The social scientist, like the politician, also is likely to argue that things are as they are because that is the way the underlying forces make them. The new post-World War II scientific thrust of the social sciences has removed, particularly from political science, its reform orientation. The quality of social science research, as a result, has improved, but findings based on such research take on an inevitability characteristic.

Since social science tools are, at best, only precise enough to explain why things are as they are, they often miss important shifts or movements in underlying forces. Their predictive ability is small. For example, the racial situation immediately after World War II was well described and explained by social scientists, but the racial revolution was not predicted—nor was the changing role of young people in society, nor the change in the nature of warfare, nor the massive deterioration in the urban environment. Some social scientists found hints of all these changes, others suggested the range of alternatives, but none made future projections with any amount of precision.

The articles in this volume reflect this characteristic of social science research—no significant signs of a breakthrough in state urban action are uncovered. The question is whether this lack reflects reality, or whether it is simply a product of the weakness of the social scientist's research tools.

BREAKTHROUGH OR STALEMATE

The evidence is strong that the findings actually do reflect reality. If change is to come through political action, the evidence does not suggest that the forces pushing for such action are strong enough to accomplish it. Perhaps a stalemate has been reached in American politics; perhaps the democratic system is simply not able to respond to a situation in which there is a majority unwilling to take those actions which a minority insists are necessary. Democratic theory requires that minorities be allowed to make their wishes known through free speech, right of assembly and of petition, and a free press, but it does not require that policies be adopted to meet their demands.

What do minorities do in this situation? Joseph Featherstone, in a *New Republic* article, suggests that "They have two perennial weapons of the underdog: the appeal to the universal values—equality, justice—America says it lives by, and the threat of disruption. The first has produced some gains, but is not likely to carry them very much farther, and the second is wearing dangerously thin."

Another alternative which has worked to some extent in American politics is for minorities to join together, thereby creating a majority with a diversified program meeting at least some of the demands of each of the participating minority groups. Such a coalition in American politics seems highly unlikely at the moment. The minority groups simply do not have enough common interests to agree on a common program. "It is somehow difficult to imagine that a working political coalition of civil rights groups, college students, clergymen, and the poor can replace the familiar triad of organized farmers, organized labor, and small businessmen." [2]

Some have argued that strong and well-articulated political leadership could provide the answer. If society could be made aware of the problems it faces and their consequences, the voters, it is suggested, would respond by supporting the kind of action needed. However, no social scientist—be he sociologist, psychologist, or political scientist—has been able to predict, or even provide, the bases for understanding what produces such leadership and under what conditions it is effective. Nevertheless, it seems unlikely that such leadership could come from any source in the American political system other than "the bully good pulpit" which Theodore Roosevelt believed the president's office to be. Certainly no governor has been able to use his office in that way in recent times.

Leadership from the private sector is perhaps a meaningful alternative and, to some extent, is being tested by John Gardner and his Urban Coalition. Whether the Coalition can do more than provide some legitimacy for the demands which are being made on the system is still not clear. There is very little evidence to date, however, that the Coalition possesses the necessary political muscle to accomplish the changes it champions.

Needed: A New Program

If neither minority rights nor political leadership offer a way out of the current stalemate, perhaps a new all-inclusive program does. James Reichley, in the conclusion of his essay, suggests this route:

> To achieve any genuine reconstruction of the cities, it will be necessary, as Edward Faltermayer, my colleague at *Fortune,* has suggested, to include the needs of the cities in some *total program* for the reconstruction of our entire society. In this way, the interest as well as the moral sympathy of the suburban and outstate majority could be touched. Creation of such a program, and development of political enthusiasm that would be needed to put it into effect, are of course unlikely, but they are not impossible. If they should appear, at least some of the political inhibitions that now prevent the states from doing more to help their cities would no doubt become irrelevant.

[2] Alan K. Campbell and Jesse Burkhead, "Public Policy for Urban America," Part IV in *Issues in Urban Economics,* edited by Harvey S. Perloff and Lowdon Wingo, Jr. (published for Resources for the Future, Inc., by The Johns Hopkins Press, Baltimore.)

Putting together such a program is extremely complex, however. The needs of these various groups, as they see them, are often competitive rather than complementary. Certainly many whites, some of whom find George Wallace attractive, feel that too much already is being done for those in poverty. The attitudes characterizing this mood were well illustrated at a construction workers' rally in Pittsburgh in 1969. This rally occurred when construction projects in that city were closed down by Negroes who demanded more jobs and admission to construction workers' unions. In a counter-demonstration, picket signs and bumper-stickers carried such slogans as "I Fight Poverty by Work," "We Build the City—Not Burn It Down," "We Are the Majority."

Other dramatic illustrations of the division in contemporary American society are represented by school difficulties in New York City, Black Panther activities in San Francisco and Oakland, and, perhaps most relevant of all, election returns in cities like Los Angeles, Minneapolis, Denver, and New York.

With these kinds of antagonism dominating the American political scene it seems doubtful, at best, that a program capable of binding the groups together in common political action could be developed. No political party to date has found the right formula. Further, if the strategy suggested for the Republican Party by Kevin P. Phillips[3] is followed, that party will not even try. Needless to say, there are others in the Republican Party who do not accept this strategy and who are trying hard, as are some members of the other party, to find the right program mix.

Certainly there are common interests. The deterioration of the urban environment contains dangers and problems for all citizens, not just the poor, but the cityite and the suburbanite alike, and even the farmer who is dependent on metropolitan areas for both markets and services. With this substantial common interest it would seem a program mix could be developed which would serve all.

The mix would include, at a minimum, education and health services, environmental pollution control, adequate housing and jobs for all. The problem is not finding areas of common concern, but rather in finding solutions which would satisfy all concerned. All solutions require resources, however, and the allocation of such resources among functions and among areas often produces political quarrels and deep societal divisions.

[3] Kevin P. Phillips, *The Emerging Republican Majority* (New Rochelle, N.Y.: Arlington House, 1969).

There is, for example, no easy way to convince the suburban homeowner that he should pay more taxes to improve education in city ghettos. Similarly, the middle-income taxpayer does not look with favor upon providing government-supported health insurance so that his low-income fellow citizens may obtain health services. Thus, finding areas of common interest is not sufficient. And the present system in which power resides with the majority makes it highly unlikely that a permanent minority, if such exists, could ever acquire sufficient influence to overcome majority resistance to their demands.

RIGHTS AND PARTICIPATION FOR MINORITIES

Basically, the issue is whether coalition politics has ceased working. Can the minorities combine effectively enough to win some policy victories? Professor Gans argues that they cannot, that if the minorities are to be protected and provided a fair share of public goods, the system must be altered.[4]

Gans suggests a variety of such changes. These include adding new constitutional economic and social rights to present political and social rights. In addition, he calls for greater opportunities for participating in the political process. To accomplish such participation, he suggests that clients of the social services be given a place on their governing boards, that some version of proportional representation be adopted, a two-step process in voting in legislative assemblies requiring any provision which receives 25 percent of the vote to be reconsidered until a compromise is obtained and final passage accomplished, that political boundaries be altered to provide minorities with jurisdictions in which they possess political power, that geographic representation be changed to economic and social representation, and, finally, that groups within communities, dissatisfied with their schools or other public services, be given the opportunity to opt out and to establish their own facilities through grants given for this purpose.

However, Professor Eugene Lewis argues that Gans' proposals are unnecessary, that pluralism still characterizes the system, and that current minorities can move into the system. He says:

> What Professor Gans wants for the poor and the black is a seat at the table. Given our pluralistic, amorphic, confusing political system, such a thing is possible without any kind of majority. How did we get an Agriculture Department? A Labor Department? A NASA? Determined

[4] Herbert Gans, "We Won't End the Urban Crisis Until We End Majority Rule," *The New York Times Magazine*, August 3, 1969, p. 12.

minorities pushed aside some of the other chairs at the table of public policy formation and pulled one up themselves. Disapproving majority opinions seldom slowed this process in the past. Money helps, but numbers are just as good. Before it got as obese as the rest of us, the labor movement was lean but populous. I think the poor and the black *are* elbowing their way to the table and pushing their bureaucratic advocates aside.[5]

Lewis may be right in the long run, but, as he says, "I don't know if the incremental, pluralistic public policy-making style of American politics will respond quickly or thoroughly enough to solve problems."

The evidence is strong that it is not responding. The dissatisfaction of blacks and the young is apparent to all, and the large following attracted by George Wallace shows that dissatisfaction is by no means restricted to these groups.

Actually, to some degree, these dissatisfactions are a product of the very reforms introduced at other times to solve other problems. These reforms, designed to correct political and economic ills of an earlier age, now appear to be at the root of some of the dissatisfaction which permeates society.

REFORM AND PARTICIPATION

In order to pinpoint responsibility, to improve the quality of public services, and to introduce more democracy—a democracy of majority rule—into the system, earlier reforms accepted a set of doctrines which have had considerable influence on the character of contemporary American government.

The separation of policy-making from administration, the removal of politics from the administrative process, the establishment of a merit system for employment in the public service, the professionalization of that service, a hierarchical system of administrative organization, and increased centralization are the doctrines which came to characterize good government theory, and in varying degree have been adopted.

In practice these doctrines have tended to remove government from direct citizen involvement, particularly the direct involvement of the less affluent. The separation of policy and administration has made it almost impossible for those receiving public services—education, health, welfare—to have any influence on the kind, the quality, or the quantity of service. And establishing blue ribbon citi-

[5] Eugene Lewis, letter to the editor, *The New York Times Magazine,* August 22, 1969.

zens advisory boards has not notably influenced the ability of the poor to influence those services which are directly relevant to their daily lives.

Equally, professionalism has made it difficult to effectively criticize administrators. In many instances professionalism has simply become a collection of credentials rather than a guarantee of improved performance. And lastly, centralization has moved these services further and further away from the final recipient.

This is not to suggest that the earlier reform doctrines were improper for their time and place, nor unrelated to the evils they were designed to correct. But it is also a mistake to assume that new times with new problems do not offer a legitimate basis for evaluating whether these earlier doctrines are effective today. Just as it may be necessary to centralize before it is possible to decentralize, it may be necessary to reform earlier reforms if they are to apply to contemporary conditions.

COMBINING OLD REFORMS WITH THE NEW

Separation of policy and administration, professionalism, and hierarchical control must be reassessed. Protection of minority rights, responsiveness, and, above all else, a system which protects the self-respect of all who are recipients of government services—be that service welfare, crop subsidy, or a government guaranteed FHA mortgage—must be introduced in their place.

Dissatisfaction with many of these earlier doctrines is responsible in part for the new demands for community control. Many citizens would rather not trust the management of services to general government, and have turned to community control as a device which will provide them with some influence on the quality of services delivered to them and to their children. On the other hand, others have vigorously opposed the decentralization drive because it is inconsistent with earlier doctrines that favored centralization and professionalism, and, in fact, the arguments against decentralization still contain much merit. It is true that America's conservatism has tended to be bound up with its small communities. It is true that most of the social progress in this country has been led by the federal government and not by state and local governments. And it is also true that small unit government can be very inefficient.

As one critic of community control has pointed out,

> . . . the larger the political subdivision the more likely will its disadvantaged minority blocs, ethnic as well as economic, receive a fair shake. When racial standpatters barricaded themselves behind states'

rights, liberals successfully relied on more inclusive, more progressive federal powers. Where municipalities have refused to better themselves in order to meet the needs of topsy-growing megalopolises, liberals have championed more inclusive, more progressive metropolitan government. In the past two years, however, compassionate liberals . . . have U-turned. They, it is, who are pushing 'decentralization' in education and 'community control' of sociopolitical institutions.[6]

The arguments about community control and decentralization tend to assume they are mutually exclusive. They are not. Although students of American federalism have for generations tried to divide the functions of government among the levels in a clear-cut and precise fashion, such a division is impossible.

It is not functions which are assigned to parts of the governmental system, but rather power. It is quite possible to design a system where local communities are given substantial influence in the administration of functions, even though those functions must, for technological and economic reasons, be performed on an area-wide basis. The transportation system must be planned area-wide, but that does not mean that local communities cannot have some influence on the placement of a highway relative to where it passes through their area. Perhaps what is needed is a modern restatement of checks and balances—checks provided for the small community whether they be on educators, highway engineers, or welfare administrators, and balances provided by the technological and social advantages of larger-scale government.

The desire for community involvement, the need for citizens to have a participating role in the system, goes far beyond disadvantaged blacks and discontented young people. Underlying, in part, the movement to suburbia by the white-middle-class was a search for community. As Joseph Featherstone suggests,

> In moving out to the suburbs many people were choosing, among other things, to sacrifice certain amenities of city life for a setting in which they had some leverage on government and access to the authorities—or, at the very least, choices about such matters as the educational environment in which their children were to grow up.[7]

Perhaps turning back to an emphasis on place of residence—the family, the home, the community—is a genuine need in newly afflu-

[6] Nathan Perlmutter, "We Don't Help Blacks by Hurting Whites," *The New York Times Magazine*, October 6, 1968, p. 31.

[7] Joseph Featherstone, "Anti-City, A Crisis of Authority," *The New Republic*, Volume 161, Nos. 8–9, August 23 and 30, 1969.

ent America. Perhaps the mass society characterized by uniformity, ugliness, and technological wizardry is getting to people.

At present there is no research, no internally coherent theory, no clear constituency demand which supports the kinds of change suggested here. Rather, there is a mood. It is a mood of despondency and discontent.

A Role for State Governments

Of all the governmental units in the American system none is in a better position to explore the underlying causes of this mood than state government. Daniel Elazar is quite right when he argues that state governments are "the keystones of the American governmental arch." They are particularly responsible for the kinds of problems created by the contemporary urban crisis. States may experiment with local government structure. They may provide the fiscal resources necessary to operate a system of community participation. They may provide the necessary administrative innovations which will make it possible for those who receive government service to take part in the administrative process.

None of these changes may be termed either liberal or conservative. They are, in fact, something new, something only vaguely felt by the dissatisfied citizen.

There are 50 states. Certainly one, two, or three of them might begin moving in these new directions. One of the advantages always claimed for the American federal system is that the states provide laboratories for experimentation. There have been brief periods in history when some states, most notably Wisconsin and New York, have played that role. Perhaps now is another time for the employment of that kind of state power.

The substantive problems of metropolitanism are known and at least partial solutions are available. The need is for a system which will embrace those solutions. Before this occurs, new life and vigor must be injected into state government.

Selected Bibliography

Advisory Commission on Intergovernmental Relations, *Urban America and the Federal System* (Washington: G.P.O., 1969).

————, *Fiscal Balance in the American Federal System*, 2 Vols. (Washington: G.P.O., 1967).

————, *Governmental Structure, Organization, and Planning in Metropolitan Areas* (Washington: G.P.O., 1961).

————, *Metropolitan Social and Economic Disparities: Implications for Intergovernmental Relations in Central Cities and Suburbs* (1965).

————, *State and Local Taxes: Significant Features* (1968).

————, *State Constitutional and Statutory Restrictions on Local Taxing Powers* (1962).

————, *State Constitutional and Statutory Restrictions on Local Government Debt* (1961).

Anderson, William, *The Nation and the States: Rivals or Partners?* (Minneapolis: University of Minnesota Press, 1955).

Bahl, Roy W., "The Determinants of State and Local Government Expenditures: A Review," in *Functional Federalism: Grants-in-Aid and PPB Systems* by Selma Mushkin and John Cotton (State-Local Finances Project, George Washington University, November 1968).

————, *Metropolitan City Expenditures: A Comparative Analysis* (Lexington: The University Press of Kentucky, 1969).

Beckman, Norman, "How Metropolitan Are Federal and State Policies?" *Public Administration Review*, 26 (June 1966).

Brazer, Harvey E., *City Expenditures in the United States*, Occasional Paper #66 (New York: National Bureau of Economic Research, Inc., 1959).

————, "Some Fiscal Implications of Metropolitanism," in Guthrie S. Birkhead, ed., *Metropolitan Issues: Social, Governmental, Fiscal* (Syracuse: Maxwell Graduate School, Syracuse University, 1962). Background papers for the Third Annual Faculty Seminar on Metropolitan Research, August, 1961.

Campbell, Alan K., "Metropolitan Organization, Politics, and Taxation," in *Municipal Income Taxes, Proceedings of the Academy of Political Science,* Vol. XXVII, No. 4 (1968).

————, "States at Crossroads," *National Civic Review,* 55 (November 1966).

———— and Seymour Sacks, *Metropolitan America: Fiscal Patterns and Governmental Systems* (New York: The Free Press, 1967).

Cleaveland, F. N., and Associates, *Congress and Urban Problems* (Washington, D.C., Brookings, 1969).

Committee for Economic Development, *Fiscal Issues in the Future of Federalism,* Supplementary Paper 23 (New York, 1968).

Connery, Robert H., and Richard H. Leach, "Southern Metropolis: Challenge to Government," *Journal of Politics,* 26 (February 1964).

Davies, David, "Financing Urban Functions and Services," *Law and Contemporary Problems,* XXX (Winter, 1965).

Dye, Thomas R., "Urban Political Integration: Conditions Associated with Annexation in American Cities," *Midwest Journal of Politics,* 8 (November 1964).

Elazar, Daniel J., *American Federalism: A View from the States* (New York: Thomas Y. Crowell, 1966).

Forrester, Jay W., *Urban Dynamics* (Cambridge: The M.I.T. Press, 1969).

Grad, Frank P., "The State Constitution: Its Function and Form for Our Time," *Virginia Law Review,* LIV, No. 5 (1968).

Grant, Daniel R., and H. C. Nixon, *State and Local Government in America,* Second Edition (Boston: Allyn and Bacon, Inc., 1968).

Graves, W. Brooke, *American Governmental Relations* (New York: Scribner, 1964).

————, "Creative Federalism's Challenge to the States" (unpublished paper prepared for the Committee for Economic Development, July 5, 1966).

Greene, Lee S., Malcolm E. Jewell and Daniel R. Grant, *The States and the Metropolis* (University, Ala.: University of Alabama Press, 1968).

Grodzins, Morton, *The American System* (Chicago: Rand McNally, 1969). Ed. by Daniel T. Elazar.

Jacob, Herbert, and Kenneth N. Vines, eds., *Politics in the American States* (Boston: Little, Brown and Company, 1965).

Jewell, Malcolm, *The State Legislature* (New York: Random House, 1962).

Lockard, Duane, *New England State Politics* (Princeton: Princeton University Press, 1959).

——, *The Politics of State and Local Government* (New York: The Macmillan Co., 1963).

Martin, Roscoe C., *The Cities and the Federal System* (New York: Atherton Press, 1965).

Meyerson, Martin, and Edward C. Banfield, *Boston: The Job Ahead* (Cambridge: Harvard University Press, 1966).

Myers, Wil S., "Measures of Making the State and Local Revenue System More Productive and Equitable" (paper presented at National Tax Association Meetings, San Francisco, 1968).

National Commission on Urban Problems, *Building the American City* (1968).

National Municipal League, *Model State Constitution*, 6th Ed., revised (1968).

——, *Salient Issues of Constitutional Revision*, John P. Wheeler, ed. (1961).

Reichley, A. James, "The States Hold the Keys to the Cities," *Fortune Magazine* (June 1969).

——, *States in Crisis* (Chapel Hill: University of North Carolina Press, 1964).

Research and Policy Committee of the Committee for Economic Development, *Modernizing Local Government* (Committee for Economic Development, New York, 1966).

Sacks, Seymour, and William F. Hellmuth, Jr., *Financing Government in a Metropolitan Area* (New York: The Free Press, 1961).

Sanford, Terry, *Storm Over the States* (New York: McGraw-Hill Book Co., 1967).

Sayre, Wallace S., "New York City and the State," in *Modernizing State Government: The New York Constitutional Convention of 1967, Proceedings of the Academy of Political Science*, XXVIII, No. 3 (January 1967).

Shannon, John, "Tax Relief for the Poor," *Proceedings of the Sixtieth Annual Conference of the National Tax Association* (Atlanta, Ga., 1967).

Wise, Harold F., "More Than Planning," *National Civic Review*, 55 (May 1966).

Ylvisaker, Paul N., "The Growing Role of State Government in Local Affairs," *State Government* (Summer, 1968).

Index

The American Assembly
COLUMBIA UNIVERSITY

About the American Assembly

The American Assembly was established by Dwight D. Eisenhower at Columbia University in 1950. It holds nonpartisan meetings and publishes authoritative books to illuminate issues of United States policy.

An affiliate of Columbia, with offices in the Graduate School of Business, the Assembly is a national, educational institution incorporated in the State of New York.

The Assembly seeks to provide information, stimulate discussion, and evoke independent conclusions in matters of vital public interest.

AMERICAN ASSEMBLY SESSIONS

At least two national programs are initiated each year. Authorities are retained to write background papers presenting essential data and defining the main issues in each subject.

About 60 men and women representing a broad range of experience, competence, and American leadership meet for several days to discuss the Assembly topic and consider alternatives for national policy.

All Assemblies follow the same procedure. The background papers are sent to participants in advance of the Assembly. The Assembly meets in small groups for four or five lengthy periods. All groups use the same agenda. At the close of these informal sessions participants adopt in plenary session a final report of findings and recommendations.

Regional, state, and local Assemblies are held following the national session at Arden House. Assemblies have also been held in England, Switzerland, Malaysia, Canada, the Caribbean, South America, Central America, the Philippines, and Japan. Over one hundred institutions have co-sponsored one or more Assemblies.

ARDEN HOUSE

Home of the American Assembly and scene of the national sessions is Arden House, which was given to Columbia University in 1950 by W. Averell Harriman. E. Roland Harriman joined his brother in contributing toward adaptation of the property for conference purposes. The buildings and surrounding land, known as the Harriman Campus of Columbia University, are 50 miles north of New York City.

Arden House is a distinguished conference center. It is self-supporting and operates throughout the year for use by organizations with educational objectives.

AMERICAN ASSEMBLY BOOKS

The background papers for each Assembly program are published in cloth and paperbound editions for use by individuals, libraries, businesses, public agencies, non-governmental organizations, educational institutions, discussion and service groups. In this way the deliberations of Assembly sessions are continued and extended.

The subjects of Assembly programs to date are:

1951——United States–Western Europe Relationships
1952——Inflation
1953——Economic Security for Americans
1954——The United States' Stake in the United Nations
——The Federal Government Service
1955——United States Agriculture
——The Forty-Eight States
1956——The Representation of the United States Abroad
——The United States and the Far East
1957——International Stability and Progress
——Atoms for Power
1958——The United States and Africa
——United States Monetary Policy
1959——Wages, Prices, Profits, and Productivity
——The United States and Latin America
1960——The Federal Government and Higher Education
——The Secretary of State
——Goals for Americans
1961——Arms Control: Issues for the Public
——Outer Space: Prospects for Man and Society
1962——Automation and Technological Change
——Cultural Affairs and Foreign Relations
1963——The Population Dilemma
——The United States and the Middle East
1964——The United States and Canada
——The Congress and America's Future
1965——The Courts, the Public, and the Law Explosion
——The United States and Japan
1966——State Legislatures in American Politics
——A World of Nuclear Powers?
——The United States and the Philippines
——Challenges to Collective Bargaining
1967——The United States and Eastern Europe
——Ombudsmen for American Government?
1968——Uses of the Seas
——Law in a Changing America
——Overcoming World Hunger
1969——Black Economic Development
——The States and the Urban Crisis
1970——The Health of Americans